THE *Gourmet* LIBRARY

Gourmet's MENUS FOR CONTEMPORARY LIVING

Gourmet's
MENUS FOR CONTEMPORARY LIVING

Text by EVIE RIGHTER

With wine suggestions by GERALD ASHER

Recipes and preparation of food for photography by
ZANNE E. ZAKROFF, E. KEMP MILES, BONNIE P. KEELER,
SARA MOULTON, GEORGIA C. DOWNARD, ELIZABETH B. SMITH

Photographs styled by
NANCY PURDUM *and* MARJORIE H. WEBB

Photographed at Gourmet's studios by
LUIS LEMUS *and* ROMULO YANES

ALFRED A. KNOPF *New York* 1985

Library of Congress Cataloging in Publication Data
Righter, Evie.
Gourmet's menus for contemporary living.
Includes index.
1. Cookery. 2. Menus. 3. Wine and wine making.
I. Gourmet. II. Title. III. Title: Menus for contemporary living.
TX715.R584   1985   641.5   85-40120
ISBN 0-394-54589-3

Manufactured in Belgium
First Edition

Contents

Illustrations

Gourmet's
MENUS FOR
CONTEMPORARY
LIVING

Chapter One

Breakfasts, Brunches, Lunches

⤫

BREAKFASTS

There are many reasons to get up in the morning and among the best of them is the anticipation of breakfast. But not just any breakfast—a *good* breakfast—one with wonderful, varied flavors, one to relax and linger over, one that actually starts a day the right way.

The breakfast menus that follow provide that special type of inspiration and impetus. They are anything but boring fare. One centers around a casserole made savory with sausage and cheese. Another features Chocolate Waffles with Cinnamon Honey Butter. Another, Orange Yogurt Pancakes with Strawberries. Soft-boiled eggs may not be unique, but when served with a yeasty Maple Pecan Wreath, as they are in our first breakfast menu, they are delicious.

None of the preparations for these breakfasts are trying or complicated either. Nor should they put any undue burden on the cook. The dough for Maple Pecan Wreath, for example, can be prepared in advance and refrigerated. The waffle iron can be taken to the table, with the waffles made right there. Create an event and make the pancakes ensemble in two skillets.

Breakfast as a meal too often gets short shrift. Had on the run, on the way to the train station or the school bus, it seldom seems to get its just rewards. Don't let that happen to these menus. Think of them not just as weekend menus, but special menus, superb ways of starting any day.

EGGS FOR BREAKFAST

Maple Pecan Wreath
Soft-Boiled Eggs
Mulled Apple Cider
Cocoa

SUGGESTIONS

To reduce the possibility of eggs cracking when either soft- or hard-boiled, prick them at the large end only with a straight pin. This will reduce the air pressure in the eggs as they expand in the hot water. Another general rule: the smaller the egg, the stronger the shell. And always try to start with eggs at room temperature. Their cooking time is more easily calculable, and there are fewer chances of their cracking upon impact with the hot water. Eggs for soft-boiling can also be started in *cold* water, as shown in the recipe on page 6.

   Cocoa is good, but cocoa with a dollop of whipped cream is even better!

The dough for Maple Pecan Wreath can be made 24 hours in advance and kept, covered, in the refrigerator. In fact, the wreath can be assembled well in advance and frozen. Simply thaw it in the refrigerator the evening before. The next morning, allow about 2 hours in all to let the dough stand, bake, and cool.

Maple Pecan Wreath

Makes one 12-inch wreath

For the dough

1 package active dry yeast
   (For suggestions on baking with yeast, see A Bread Box, pages 22–23.)
¼ cup granulated sugar
¾ cup lukewarm water
2¾ to 3¼ cups all-purpose flour
¾ teaspoon salt
½ stick (¼ cup) unsalted butter, softened
1 large egg, beaten lightly

For the filling

2 tablespoons unsalted butter, melted and cooled
2 tablespoons maple syrup
¾ cup chopped pecans
⅓ cup firmly packed light brown sugar

egg wash: 1 egg beaten with 2 tablespoons water

Maple Pecan Wreath and Mulled Apple Cider

Make the dough: In a small bowl proof the yeast with a pinch of the granulated sugar in the lukewarm water for 15 minutes, or until foamy.

In a large bowl combine 1 cup of the flour, the remaining granulated sugar, and the salt, then beat in the yeast mixture and the butter. Continue to beat, scraping down the sides of the bowl occasionally, for 2 minutes. Beat in the egg and ¼ cup of the flour, and beat for 2 minutes. Add enough of the remaining flour, a little at a time, to form a soft dough. Turn the dough out onto a floured surface and knead for 10 minutes, or until smooth and elastic. If the dough appears satiny and almost shiny, you have kneaded enough. Then put the dough in a lightly floured bowl and let it rest, covered with plastic wrap and a towel, in a warm place for 15 minutes.

Make the filling: While the dough is resting, in a small bowl combine well all the filling ingredients.

To assemble and bake the wreath: Punch down the dough, roll it into a 16-by-8-inch rectangle on a floured surface, and sprinkle the filling over it. Starting with a long side roll up the dough jelly-roll fashion, pinch the seam to seal the roll, and form the roll into a ring. Arrange the ring, seam side down, on a buttered baking sheet, pinch the ends together securely, and with scissors cut two-thirds of the way into the ring at 1-inch intervals. Turn each cut section on its side so that the filling is visible, brush the dough with some of the egg wash, and chill, covered loosely with plastic wrap, for 2 hours or overnight.

Let the chilled ring stand, uncovered, at room temperature for 10 minutes, brush it lightly with the remaining egg wash, and bake it in the upper third of a preheated 375° F. oven for 20 to 25 minutes, or until golden brown. (Some of the filling may melt onto the baking sheet.) Let the wreath cool on a rack for 15 minutes.

Soft-Boiled Eggs

Serves 4   8 large eggs at room temperature
               (see Suggestions)

In a large saucepan cover the eggs with cold water. Bring the water to a simmer over moderate heat, stirring occasionally, and simmer the eggs for 2 to 3 minutes, or until cooked to the desired degree of softness. Drain the eggs and put them briefly in cold water to stop their cooking. Serve immediately in their shells in egg cups or shelled in small bowls, with salt and freshly ground pepper to taste.

Mulled Apple Cider

Serves 4   6 cups apple cider   6 whole allspice
              3 tablespoons light brown sugar   8 cloves
              five 3-inch cinnamon sticks   ¼ teaspoon freshly grated nutmeg

In a large saucepan bring the cider, sugar, 1 of the cinnamon sticks, the allspice, cloves, and nutmeg to a boil and simmer, stirring occasionally, for 10 minutes. Let cool and chill, covered, overnight.

In a saucepan reheat the cider over moderately low heat, strain it into heated mugs, and garnish each mug with 1 of the remaining cinnamon sticks.

Cocoa

Serves 4   ¼ cup water   a pinch of salt
              5 tablespoons unsweetened cocoa powder 2 cups milk
              ⅓ cup sugar   2 cups half-and-half

In a saucepan bring the water, cocoa powder, sugar, and salt to a boil and simmer, whisking to dissolve any lumps, for 2 minutes. Add the milk and half-and-half in a stream, stirring, and bring the cocoa just to the boiling point. Serve in heated mugs.

A SAVORY START

*Sautéed Apples, Oranges, and Pear with
Orange Marmalade
Sausage and Cheese Strata
Toasted Rye Bread
Café au Lait*

SUGGESTIONS

Bananas would be a good addition to the fruit starter. So would golden raisins and a sprinkling of walnuts and wheat germ.

For a different taste entirely, replace the orange marmalade in the fruit course with ginger marmalade. It will be fiery and fun.

Try combining Monterey jack and Cheddar for a variation on the strata. Sharp Cheddar is preferred.

For a Southwestern touch, layer a few well-chopped *jalapeño* peppers into the strata.

∽

Remember that the strata must stand at room temperature a full 45 minutes before baking. In its last 15 minutes of baking time, prepare the fruit. When you've finished it at table, the strata will be cool enough to serve.

Sautéed Apples, Oranges, and Pear with Orange Marmalade

2 Golden Delicious apples, peeled and
  cut into eighths
1 Anjou pear, peeled and cut into eighths
3 tablespoons fresh lemon juice

3 tablespoons unsalted butter
¼ cup bitter orange marmalade
3 navel oranges, peeled and sectioned,
  with membranes removed

Serves 4

In a bowl toss the apples and pear with the lemon juice.

In a large skillet cook the fruit mixture in 2 tablespoons of the butter over moderately high heat, turning the fruit gently, until the apples are tender, and with a slotted spoon transfer the mixture to a bowl.

Add the remaining butter and the marmalade to the skillet and cook over moderate heat, stirring, until melted. Pour the sauce over the fruit, add the oranges, and toss gently.

Sausage and Cheese Strata

Serves 4

½ pound sausage meat
8 slices homemade-type white bread, crusts removed and the bread cut into ½-inch cubes
¾ pound Monterey jack cheese, grated
4 large eggs, beaten lightly
1½ cups milk

½ teaspoon salt
1 teaspoon Dijon-style mustard
a pinch of cayenne
½ teaspoon Worcestershire sauce
3 tablespoons unsalted butter, melted and cooled

In a skillet brown the sausage over moderately high heat, breaking it up with a fork, and with a slotted spoon transfer it to paper towels to drain.

Brush a 1-quart soufflé dish with some of the fat remaining in the skillet, arrange one-third of the bread cubes in the bottom of the dish, and sprinkle them with one-third of the cheese. Top the cheese with all the sausage, top the sausage with half the remaining bread, and sprinkle half the remaining cheese over the bread. Top the strata with the remaining bread and press the layers together slightly.

In a bowl whisk together the eggs, milk, salt, mustard, cayenne, and Worcestershire sauce, pour the mixture over the strata, and sprinkle the top with the remaining cheese. Drizzle the top with the melted butter and chill, covered, for at least 1 hour or overnight.

Remove the strata from the refrigerator and let it stand at room temperature for 45 minutes. Put the dish in a baking pan and add enough hot water to the pan to reach halfway up the sides of the dish. Bake the strata in a preheated 350° F. oven for 1 hour to 1¼ hours, or until golden brown and set.

Café au Lait

Serves 4

1½ cups milk
1½ cups hot strong freshly brewed coffee

sugar to taste

In a saucepan heat the milk over moderate heat until bubbles form around the edges and pour it into a heated pitcher. Pour the milk and coffee into heated mugs; add sugar to taste.

Sautéed Apples, Oranges, and Pear with Orange Marmalade;
Sausage and Cheese Strata; and Café au Lait

A PANCAKE BREAKFAST

Minted Grapefruit Juice
Orange Yogurt Pancakes with Strawberries
Corkscrew Bacon
Cinnamon Coffee

SUGGESTIONS

Herbal tea would be a gentle accompaniment to this springlike breakfast.

∽

The juice, the pancake batter, and the bacon can all be made in advance, but let the batter stand for no more than 1 hour, as the baking soda will begin to lose its punch.

   If need be, you can even prepare the pancakes in advance. Brush with melted butter and keep warm in a preheated 200° F. oven.

Minted Grapefruit Juice

Serves 4

½ cup water
¼ cup sugar
¼ cup minced fresh mint leaves

3½ cups fresh grapefruit juice, strained
mint sprigs for garnish

In a saucepan combine the water, sugar, and minced mint leaves. Bring the water to a boil, stirring to dissolve the sugar, and simmer the syrup for 5 minutes. Remove the pan from the heat and let the mint steep, covered, for 20 minutes.

   Strain the mint syrup into a pitcher and add the grapefruit juice. Stir to combine, then chill, covered, for at least 1 hour or overnight. Divide the juice among chilled 8-ounce glasses and garnish each glass with a mint sprig.

Orange Yogurt Pancakes with Strawberries, Corkscrew Bacon, and Minted Grapefruit Juice

Orange Yogurt Pancakes
with Strawberries

Serves 4

1 cup hulled and sliced strawberries
2 teaspoons sugar

For the batter
1 naval orange
3 large sugar cubes
⅓ cup fresh orange juice
1 cup plain yogurt
1 large egg
2 tablespoons unsalted butter, melted and
   cooled, plus additional melted butter
   for brushing the griddle and pancakes
1 cup all-purpose flour
1 teaspoon baking soda
½ teaspoon double-acting baking powder
¼ teaspoon salt

blanched julienne strips of orange rind
   for garnish (optional)
maple syrup

In a bowl toss the strawberries gently with the sugar and let stand for 30 minutes.

Make the batter: Rub the skin of the orange with the sugar cubes until the cubes are a deep orange color. In a bowl dissolve the sugar cubes in the orange juice, crushing them with the back of a spoon and stirring. Add ¾ cup of the yogurt, the egg, and 2 tablespoons of the melted butter, and beat the mixture until combined well.

In a bowl sift together the flour, baking soda, baking powder, and salt. Add the yogurt mixture and stir the batter until combined well. NOTE: The batter will be thick.

To make pancakes: Heat a heavy griddle or skillet over moderately high heat until hot and brush it generously with some of the additional melted butter. Spoon tablespoons of the batter onto the griddle, spreading the batter with the back of a spoon, to form 3-inch rounds, and cook the pancakes for 1 to 2 minutes, or until the undersides are golden brown and the tops are bubbly. Turn the pancakes and cook for 1 minute more, or until the undersides are golden.

Divide the pancakes among plates and garnish each stack with a dollop of the remaining yogurt and some of the berries. Sprinkle the blanched orange rind over the berries, if desired, and serve the pancakes with Corkscrew Bacon (recipe follows) and maple syrup, warmed.

Corkscrew Bacon

8 slices of bacon

Serves 4

Twist the bacon slices into spirals, arrange them in rows on the rack of a broiler pan, and thread skewers through the ends of the bacon strips so that the spirals will not untwist while cooking. Bake in a preheated 375° F. oven for 20 minutes, or until crisp.

Cinnamon Coffee

4 cups hot strong freshly brewed coffee
½ teaspoon cinnamon

1 to 2 tablespoons sugar, or to taste
milk or heavy cream to taste

Serves 4

In a coffeepot combine the coffee, cinnamon, and sugar. Divide the coffee among cups and add milk or cream.

TO MAKE CRÈME FRAÎCHE

Crème fraîche is a thickened cream with a slightly acidic, nutty flavor that is used in France, its place of origin, in a myriad of wonderful ways—to make sauces, to thin soups, to garnish both hot and cold preparations. While there are commercial brands of *crème fraîche* on the market, usually in specialty-foods stores, it is expensive and not all that easy to find. It is easy to make, however, and a very good facsimile can be done at home.

In a jar combine 1 cup heavy cream and 1 tablespoon buttermilk, and shake, tightly covered, for at least 1 minute. Then let the mixture stand, uncovered, at room temperature for at least 8 hours, or until thick. Store *crème fraîche*, covered, in the refrigerator, where it will keep from 4 to 6 weeks. Makes about 1 cup.

Use *crème fraîche* as you would sour cream—as a garnish—on fresh or broiled fruit. Or stir it into cold soups. Or serve it as a dip on fresh vegetables.

A WAFFLE BREAKFAST

Winter Fruit Compote
Chocolate Waffles with Cinnamon Honey Butter
Spiced Coffee

SUGGESTIONS

Make up extra waffles and freeze them. They make a good, last-minute dessert when topped with ice cream and a homemade chocolate sauce (pages 80 and 238).

Cinnamon Honey Butter freezes well, covered airtight, and for thawing should simply be removed to the refrigerator the evening before serving. Remember to let it stand at room temperature for 30 minutes to come to full flavor.

℘

Winter Fruit Compote can be readied as much as 2 days ahead and kept, covered and chilled, in a glass bowl in the refrigerator. Like many fruit mélanges, it improves in flavor with such standing.

Prepare the waffle batter in advance, up to the point of folding in the beaten egg whites. Then take the batter and waffle iron to the table. It's fun and will turn that interminable wait for the next hot waffle into a shared adventure.

Winter Fruit Compote

Serves 2

½ cup apple juice
a 3-inch cinnamon stick
2 cloves
¼ cup fresh orange juice
1 Granny Smith apple, cut into ½-inch pieces

½ cup seedless green grapes, halved
2 navel oranges, peeled and sectioned, with membranes removed
2 kiwis, peeled and cut into 2-inch pieces

In a small saucepan bring the apple juice to a boil with the cinnamon stick and cloves and simmer for 10 minutes. Let cool, then add the orange juice, and strain into a bowl.

Stir in gently all the fruit and chill the compote, covered, until ready to serve.

Winter Fruit Compote and Chocolate Waffles
with Cinnamon Honey Butter

Chocolate Waffles with Cinnamon Honey Butter

Makes six 4-inch waffles

For the butter
1 stick (½ cup) unsalted butter, softened
½ teaspoon cinnamon
1 tablespoon honey

For the waffles
⅔ cup all-purpose flour
½ teaspoon double-acting baking powder
½ teaspoon plus pinch of salt

1½ tablespoons unsweetened cocoa powder
⅓ cup sugar
¼ cup sour cream
3 tablespoons unsalted butter, melted and cooled
2 large egg yolks
2 large egg whites at room temperature
a pinch of cream of tartar

Make the butter: In a small bowl cream the butter, beat in the cinnamon and honey, and let stand at room temperature for 30 minutes.

Make the waffles: Sift together the flour, baking powder, ½ teaspoon salt, cocoa powder, and sugar into a bowl.

In a small bowl combine the sour cream, melted butter, and egg yolks.

In another bowl beat the egg whites with the cream of tartar and the pinch of salt until they hold stiff peaks.

Add the sour-cream mixture to the flour mixture and stir until combined. Fold in the egg whites gently but thoroughly. Using a ¼-cup measure for each waffle, pour the batter into a preheated non-stick waffle iron and cook the waffles according to the manufacturer's directions. As the waffles are done, remove them from the iron and keep them warm in a single layer on a baking sheet in a low oven. Serve the waffles with the cinnamon honey butter.

Spiced Coffee

Serves 3 or 4

2 cups water
1 tablespoon dark brown sugar
two 3-inch cinnamon sticks
two 2½-inch strips of orange rind

¼ teaspoon ground allspice
3 cups very hot strong freshly brewed coffee

In a saucepan combine the water, sugar, cinnamon sticks, orange rind, and allspice. Bring the mixture just to the boiling point over moderate heat, then remove the pan from the heat. Let the mixture stand for 5 minutes and strain it into a coffeepot containing the coffee.

BRUNCHES

Brunch. Not exactly breakfast or lunch, but a great excuse to invite people over at midday in the hope that they will linger to dusk.

Our brunch menus have a breakfast feel to them, but with a decided fillip added to each. An omelet is accompanied by potatoes Anna and homemade raisin toast. Creamed spinach fills an egg *roulade* that is then deliciously gratinéed to bubbly brown-golden. Poached eggs are served as a salad, with *niçoise* olives and potatoes and beans and creamy mayonnaise. The fillips are fancy and meant to be fun and many can be accomplished well in advance.

A brunch should be relaxed and inviting, and whether it is served with the Sunday paper on the table, as part of the menu, or as an interlude between the end of one tennis match and the start of the next, it is to be lively and interesting—an informal occasion to gather for good company and equally good food. The food in these menus won't disappoint.

FRENCH FLAIR IN AN EGG BRUNCH

Cranberry Juice Cocktail
Poached Eggs Niçoise
Rye Rolls
Assorted Seasonal Fruit
Chocolate-Dipped Oatmeal Lace Cookies

Cranberry Juice Cocktail

½ cup dry white wine
¼ cup cranberry juice, or to taste

a twist of lemon

Makes 1 drink

Pour the wine into a tumbler filled with ice cubes and add the cranberry juice. Stir and garnish with the lemon twist.

SUGGESTIONS ON POACHING EGGS

The fresher and colder the eggs, the better they hold their shape while poaching.

Vinegar helps set the whites. Don't forget to add it to the skillet.

The edges of the finished eggs will probably be ragged. Trim with scissors before arranging on the plates. If you are new to poaching eggs, start by cooking them one at a time. Practice will enable you to poach several at once. The trick is not to overcook them. The whites should be opaque and firm, the yolks still runny.

To serve poached eggs hot, reheat them for 1 to 2 minutes in hot, not boiling, water.

To alter the feeling of this brunch quite dramatically, serve Apple Tarts (page 253) for dessert. More formal and refined.

Poached Eggs Niçoise

Serves 6

For the potato salad
1½ pounds new potatoes
¼ cup dry white wine
¼ cup chicken stock (page 154) or canned chicken broth
1¼ cups Mustard Vinaigrette (recipe follows)
3 tablespoons minced scallion

1 pound green beans
1 head of Boston lettuce
1 cup Quick Mayonnaise (page 20)

1 tablespoon tomato paste
6 large very fresh eggs
2 tablespoons distilled white vinegar
3 tomatoes
salt
olive oil

For garnish
anchovy fillets, rinsed and patted dry
minced fresh parsley leaves
1 cup imported French black olives, such as *niçoise* olives

Make the potato salad: Steam the potatoes in a vegetable steamer set over boiling water, covered, adding more boiling water if necessary, for 25 to 30 minutes, or until just tender. Let the potatoes cool until they can be handled, peel them, and cut them into ½-inch-thick slices.

Depending upon how quick you are in the kitchen, reserve a full morning and part of the afternoon to accomplish the following agenda.

THE DAY BEFORE:

Mix and dress the potato salad.

Boil and trim the beans, wash the lettuce, prepare the tomatoes, and reserve all, wrapped and chilled.

Make the mayonnaise.

Poach the eggs and store in a bowl of water in the refrigerator.

Bake the cookies and store them in an airtight tin at room temperature.

Prepare rye dough and let it rise in the refrigerator overnight.

THE DAY OF:

Roughly 2 hours in advance of serving brunch, punch down the dough, roll it into a log, and cut it into pieces. Proceed with the recipe for baking the rolls.

Plate the salad. Remember that the salad will be at its most full *provençale* flavor if served at room temperature.

In a large bowl combine the potatoes while still warm with the wine and stock or broth, toss the mixture gently, and let it stand, covered, for 20 minutes.

While the potatoes stand, make the Mustard Vinaigrette and reserve.

Pour off any unabsorbed liquid from the potato salad, add to it ½ cup of the vinaigrette and the scallion, and pour the mixture over the potatoes. Toss gently and let stand, covered, for 30 minutes.

In a saucepan of boiling salted water cook the beans for 5 to 6 minutes, or until just tender. Drain, and submerge immediately in a bowl of ice water for 2 minutes. Drain, pat the beans dry, and trim. Wrap the beans in paper towels and chill until ready to use.

Separate the leaves from the head of lettuce, rinse, and pat dry. Wrap the lettuce in paper towels and/or place in a plastic bag and chill until ready to use.

Make Quick Mayonnaise and into 1 cup of it whisk the tomato paste. Reserve the remaining mayonnaise, chilled, for another use. Chill the tomato-flavored mayonnaise, covered.

To poach the eggs and assemble the salad: Fill a wide non-aluminum skillet, 3 inches deep, three-quarters full of water, add the vinegar, and bring the water to a rolling boil. Break 1 egg into each of 3 ramekins, slide each egg into the boiling water directly over a boiling area, and reduce the heat to a simmer. Immediately push the egg whites over the yolks with a slotted spoon, gently moving the eggs, and simmer for 3 minutes. Transfer the eggs with the slotted spoon to a pan of cold water. Poach the remaining 3 eggs in the same manner.

Halve the tomatoes horizontally and with a small spoon remove the seeds and juice without squeezing the tomatoes. Sprinkle the tomatoes with salt and let drain on a rack for 15 minutes. Meanwhile, bring the eggs to room temperature by reheating them in a bowl of hot, *not* boiling, water for 1 to 2 minutes.

Arrange the lettuce decoratively on a large platter, put the tomatoes, cut sides up, around the rim of the platter, and top each tomato with 1 to 2 tablespoons of the tomato-flavored mayonnaise. Put 1 of the poached eggs, patted dry, on each tomato half, brush the eggs lightly with olive oil, and garnish the top of each egg with 1 anchovy. Arrange the potato salad in the center of the platter and sprinkle with the minced parsley.

In a bowl toss the beans with ½ cup of the vinaigrette and arrange them in bunches decoratively on the platter with the olives.

Serve the remaining tomato-flavored mayonnaise and vinaigrette separately.

Mustard Vinaigrette

Makes about 1¼ cups

1 large egg
¼ cup tarragon vinegar
2 teaspoons Dijon-style mustard
1 teaspoon salt

white pepper to taste
¾ cup olive oil at room temperature
2 garlic cloves, minced (optional)

In a bowl set in a larger bowl of warm water combine the egg, vinegar, mustard, salt, and white pepper to taste and beat the mixture until it is light and foamy and lukewarm. Remove the bowl from the water, add the olive oil in a stream, whisking, and whisk the dressing until it is smooth. Stir in the garlic, if desired, and add salt and white pepper to taste.

Quick Mayonnaise

Makes about 1 cup

1 large egg at room temperature
5 teaspoons fresh lemon juice
1 teaspoon Dijon-style mustard
¼ teaspoon salt

¼ teaspoon white pepper
1 cup olive oil, peanut oil, or a
   combination of both

In a food processor fitted with the metal blade or in a blender with the motor on high, blend the egg, lemon juice, mustard, salt, and white pepper. Add the oil in a slow, steady stream, and blend the mayonnaise until it is just emulsified. Thin the mayonnaise with heavy cream or water, if desired.

Rye Rolls

Makes 12 rolls

2 packages active dry yeast
    (For suggestions on baking with yeast,
    see A Bread Box, pages 22–23.)
1½ cups milk
1 tablespoon dark brown sugar
2 tablespoons unsulfured molasses
1 tablespoon salt

1 teaspoon fennel seeds (optional)
3 cups all-purpose flour
1 cup rye flour
cornmeal for sprinkling on the
    baking sheet
egg wash: 1 egg beaten lightly with
    a pinch of salt

In a large bowl proof the yeast in ½ cup lukewarm milk with the brown sugar for 15 minutes, or until foamy.

A BREAD BOX

Everyone recognizes the incomparable aroma of bread baking. It is simultaneously acrid and sweet, identifiable by the singular smell of yeast, bringing with it memories of all the attendant pleasures—the measuring, the kneading, the resting, the rising—that the making of bread involves. It is hearth and home. It requires patience and practice. But once a breadmaker, always a breadmaker.

Some tips on baking with yeast follow, as well as information on baking powder and baking soda, leavening agents used most frequently in the making of cakes, cookies, and quick breads—so called because they are just that.

Yeast is a fungus and is the catalyst that makes dough rise. It first must be made active by dissolving in warm water, usually with a little sugar. Then, incorporated into dry ingredients, yeast feeds on the starch in the flour and in so doing produces carbon dioxide. It is the carbon dioxide that makes the cells in the dough expand and grow.

Yeast comes in three basic forms: active dry yeast, compressed fresh yeast, and a quick-rise variety. Far and away the most readily available and easiest to use successfully is active dry yeast—dry granules, which are sold in ¼-ounce packages, yielding 2¼ teaspoons, in supermarkets near the refrigerator case. Store in a cool dry place or in the refrigerator.

To proof—to be made active, active dry yeast must be dissolved in lukewarm water. The temperature of the water is very important because too-hot water will kill the yeast, while too-cool water will activate it, but less quickly. The temperature of the water ideally should range between 105° F. and 115° F. To gauge the water

In a bowl combine the remaining 1 cup milk, the molasses, salt, and fennel seeds, if desired, and add the mixture to the yeast mixture. With a wooden spatula stir in the all-purpose and rye flours and combine the mixture to form a soft, sticky dough. Knead the dough on a floured surface, incorporating more all-purpose flour if the dough is too sticky, for 8 to 10 minutes, or until smooth. (The dough should remain slightly sticky.) Form the dough into a ball, put it in an oiled bowl, and turn it to coat it with the oil. Let the dough rise in a warm place, covered loosely, for 1½ hours, or until it is double in bulk.

Sprinkle a baking sheet lightly with cornmeal. Punch down the dough, roll it into a 20-inch log, and cut it crosswise into 12 pieces. Form each piece into a smooth ball, arrange the balls on the baking sheet, and let them rise in a warm place, covered loosely, for 1 hour, or until almost double in bulk. Brush the rolls with the egg wash and bake them in a preheated 400° F. oven for 15 minutes, or until they sound hollow when the bottoms are tapped. Let the rolls cool to room temperature on a rack and serve them with softened unsalted butter.

---

temperature, sprinkle a little warm water on your wrist, and judge it as you would test the temperature of milk in a baby's bottle.

Once the dissolved yeast mixture is stirred into the dry ingredients a mass of dough forms, which is rough and uneven in texture. It will require kneading—a specific type of handling—which develops the gluten, a protein, in the flour, which, in turn, expands to form a web that allows the dough to rise.

To knead: Choose a table or counter approximately hip or waist high on which to knead the dough. Dust the table lightly with flour and turn the dough out onto its surface. Extending both arms out in front of you, push the dough away from you with the heels of both hands, then fold it in half and give it a quarter turn. Continue this pushing, folding, and turning, creating your own rhythm, until the outside of the dough is smooth and satiny and the texture is springy and elastic. Depending upon the temperature of your kitchen and of your hands, this first kneading should take about 10 to 15 minutes.

Once the dough is smooth and elastic, it will need *to rise*. Place it in a greased, oiled or buttered, bowl, turn it to coat it with the fat, and cover the bowl tightly with plastic wrap. It is a good idea to put the bowl in a warm place, but not absolutely necessary—it will just take longer to rise. Allow 1 to 1½ hours for the dough to double in bulk.

To test for rising, press 2 fingers into the dough. If the indentations remain, the dough is ready to be taken to the next stage, meaning ready to be punched down.

To punch down, deflate the dough by jabbing it all over several times with your fists. Then compress the dough into a ball and knead it gently for a minute or two. The dough is now ready for shaping, and/or for a second rising.

For specific shaping and baking instructions, see the individual recipes.

Chocolate-Dipped Oatmeal Lace Cookies

Makes about 30 cookies

1 large egg, beaten lightly
¼ cup firmly packed light brown sugar
¼ cup granulated sugar
1 cup old-fashioned rolled oats
¼ teaspoon salt

¼ teaspoon almond extract
1 tablespoon unsalted butter, melted
  and cooled
4 ounces semisweet chocolate,
  chopped coarse

In a bowl with an electric mixer beat the egg with the brown sugar and the granulated sugar until the mixture is thick and pale. Add the oats, salt, almond extract, and butter and stir until combined well. Drop the batter by rounded teaspoons 3 inches apart onto baking sheets lined with buttered foil, and flatten each mound with the back of a fork dipped in water. Bake the cookies in the middle of a preheated 325° F. oven for 7 minutes, or until golden around the edges. Let the cookies cool on the baking sheets and peel them off the foil gently.

In the top of a double boiler set over barely simmering water melt the chocolate, dip an edge of each cookie in it, and put the cookies on racks while the chocolate hardens.

Chocolate-Dipped Oatmeal Lace Cookies and Molasses Cashew Cookies

A SPRING BRUNCH

Spinach Roulade
Dilled Ham Toasts
Asparagus, Radish, and Scallion Salad
Caramelized Bananas with Vanilla
Custard Ice Cream

ᔕ

Young, fruity California Gamay, or a recent
vintage of Beaujolais-Villages

SUGGESTIONS

If you like the taste of salty and sweet, spread the ham purée, with the dill either omitted entirely or reduced to a hint, on homemade date-nut bread.

Cooked asparagus spears, cut into pieces, then wrapped in slices of baked ham that have been lightly touched with mustard mayonnaise, make a good spring hors d'oeuvre. The same combination layered on a slice of dark bread also makes a very tempting open-faced sandwich.

Caramelized bananas, without the liqueur, make a sweet but very satisfying fruit course for breakfast.

ᔕ

Make the spinach filling for the *roulade* as well as the ham purée ahead and keep it, covered and chilled, in the refrigerator.

Have all the components of the salad cooked, minced, and sliced, respectively; make the dressing, and you are ½ minute away from serving the salad.

Of course, if you are making the homemade Vanilla Custard Ice Cream, do that ahead. Remember to let it soften for serving.

For best results, brown the *roulade* and heat the bananas at the last minute.

Spinach Roulade

Serves 4 to 6

6 large egg yolks
1 stick (½ cup) unsalted butter, melted
  and cooled
2 tablespoons fresh lemon juice
3 tablespoons minced fresh parsley leaves
½ teaspoon salt
¼ teaspoon white pepper
6 large egg whites at room temperature
a pinch of cream of tartar

For the filling
1 onion, minced
1 garlic clove, minced
2 tablespoons unsalted butter
a 10-ounce package frozen chopped
  spinach, thawed and squeezed dry
2 ounces cream cheese, cut into bits
1 tablespoon fresh lemon juice
½ cup sour cream
1 teaspoon Dijon-style mustard
⅓ cup minced fresh parsley leaves
salt and pepper

1 tablespoon freshly grated Parmesan
1 tablespoon fine fresh bread crumbs

In a large bowl with an electric mixer beat the egg yolks until thick and pale, beat in the butter, lemon juice, parsley, ½ teaspoon salt, and white pepper, and beat the mixture until combined.

In another bowl beat the egg whites with the cream of tartar and a pinch of salt until they hold soft peaks and fold them into the yolk mixture.

Line a buttered 15½-by-10½-by-1-inch jelly-roll pan with wax paper and butter and flour the paper. Spoon the mixture into the pan, spreading it evenly, and bake it in a preheated 350° F. oven for 15 to 20 minutes, or until puffed and golden brown. Invert the egg sponge onto a baking sheet lined with wax paper and peel off the wax paper on the top.

Make the filling: In a saucepan cook the onion and garlic in the butter over moderately low heat, stirring, until the onion is softened. Add the spinach, and cook the mixture, stirring occasionally, for 4 to 5 minutes, or until the excess moisture has evaporated. Stir in the cream cheese and cook the mixture, stirring, until the cheese is melted. Stir in the lemon juice, sour cream, mustard, parsley, and salt and pepper, and purée the mixture in a food processor fitted with the metal blade or in a blender.

Spread the purée evenly over the egg sponge, leaving a 1-inch border on all sides. Beginning with a long side, roll up the egg sponge jelly-roll fashion, peeling away the wax paper as you roll. Trim the ends and transfer the *roulade,* seam side down, to a flameproof platter. Sprinkle the *roulade* with the Parmesan and bread crumbs, brown the topping under a preheated broiler about 4 inches from the heat for 2 to 3 minutes, and cut the *roulade* into 1-inch slices.

Dilled Ham Toasts and Asparagus, Radish, and Scallion Salad

Dilled Ham Toasts

Makes 8 toasts

¼ pound thinly sliced baked ham
½ stick (¼ cup) unsalted butter, softened
1 teaspoon snipped fresh dill

4 slices of homemade-type white bread,
   toasted, crusts removed, and the
   slices halved diagonally
dill sprigs for garnish

In a food processor fitted with the metal blade purée the ham, reserving 1 slice for garnish. Add the butter and snipped dill, and blend the mixture until it is a smooth paste. Spread the mixture on the toast triangles and garnish the toasts with the reserved ham slice, cut into small triangles, and the dill sprigs.

Asparagus, Radish, and Scallion Salad

Serves 4

1 pound asparagus, trimmed and cut
   diagonally into 1-inch pieces
1 large egg yolk
1 tablespoon white-wine vinegar
½ teaspoon Dijon-style mustard

salt and pepper
¼ cup olive oil
6 radishes, minced
3 scallions, sliced thin
lettuce leaves for lining the plates

In a kettle of boiling salted water cook the asparagus for 4 to 5 minutes, or until just tender, drain, and refresh under cold water. Pat the asparagus dry.

   In a large bowl whisk together the egg yolk, vinegar, mustard, and salt and pepper to taste, add the oil in a stream, whisking, and whisk the dressing until emulsified. Add the asparagus, the radishes, and the scallions, and toss the mixture with the dressing. Divide the salad among chilled salad plates lined with the lettuce.

Vanilla Custard Ice Cream

*Makes about
1 quart*

an 8-inch vanilla bean, cut into bits
¾ cup sugar
4 large egg yolks

½ cup milk
2 cups heavy cream
⅛ teaspoon salt

In a blender or food processor fitted with the metal blade grind fine the vanilla bean, add the sugar, and pulverize the mixture.

In a metal bowl with an electric mixer beat the egg yolks with the milk and the vanilla sugar. Set the bowl over a pan of simmering water and beat the mixture for 7 to 10 minutes, or until thickened and double in volume. Set the bowl in a bowl of ice and cold water and beat the mixture until cold. Beat in the cream and salt and beat until thickened and almost double in volume. Freeze the mixture in an ice-cream freezer according to the manufacturer's instructions.

Caramelized Bananas with Vanilla Custard Ice Cream

2 tablespoons unsalted butter	3 bananas, cut into ¼-inch slices	*Serves 4*
¼ cup firmly packed dark brown sugar	2 tablespoons orange-flavored liqueur	
2 tablespoons fresh orange juice	1 quart Vanilla Custard Ice Cream	
1 tablespoon fresh lemon juice	(preceding recipe)	

In a large skillet melt the butter over moderate heat, stir in the sugar, orange and lemon juice, and cook the mixture, stirring, until the sugar is dissolved. Add the bananas and liqueur and cook the mixture, stirring gently, until the bananas are hot and coated with the syrup. Scoop the ice cream into small bowls and spoon the banana mixture over it.

A BOUNTIFUL BRUNCH

Watercress, Sour Cream, and Crouton Omelets
Grilled Canadian Bacon
Potatoes Anna
Raisin Toast
Iced Ice Coffee

SUGGESTIONS

Make not only your own croutons with leftover homemade-type bread but your own bread crumbs as well. For crumbs just spin any extra bread, torn into pieces, in the food processor fitted with the metal blade. Store in a container in the refrigerator or freeze them. Store croutons, on the other hand, in a cool dry place.

Potatoes Anna are nothing more than sliced potatoes baked in butter, and for such a simple preparation, they are indeed superb. Who Anna was is still a question, but she was immortalized early in the twentieth century by M. Dugléré, chef of the Café Anglais in Paris.

Long white potatoes are all-purpose potatoes and can be identified by their thin, almost transparent light-colored skin. Use them for frying and boiling, too.

Canadian bacon, from the eye of a loin of pork, is cured and hot-smoked. As such, it is fully cooked but needs finishing—a quick grilling or frying.

∽

Do the potatoes first so they are all done and ready to go when you start the omelets.

Speaking of timing, assuming you have all the ingredients for the omelets prepared, cooking time per omelet, including heating the butter, should be no more than 1½ minutes. And, if you are practiced, it should probably hover somewhere nearer 1 minute.

Best to bake raisin bread 1 day ahead. Then it is just a matter of toasting it up. Freeze what is left in a freezer bag or well sealed in plastic wrap. Or, better yet, consider making bread pudding. With your own homemade raisin bread, you are well on your way to a sensational treat.

Watercress, Sour Cream, and Crouton Omelets

Serves 2

For the croutons

3 slices of homemade-type white bread, crusts removed, and the slices cut into ⅓-inch dice

2 tablespoons unsalted butter

For the omelets

⅓ cup watercress leaves, chopped coarse

½ cup sour cream, or to taste

4 large eggs

2 tablespoons cold water

salt

1 tablespoon unsalted butter

Make the croutons: In a small skillet sauté the bread cubes in the 2 tablespoons butter over moderately high heat, stirring, until golden

Make the omelets: In a small bowl combine the watercress and sour cream.

In another bowl beat the eggs lightly with the cold water and salt to taste.

In a non-stick skillet or 7½-inch omelet pan heat 1½ teaspoons of the butter over moderately high heat until the foam begins to subside. Add half the egg mixture and cook, undisturbed, for 5 seconds. Now, with the back of a fork, stir the uncooked egg, shaking the pan at the same time and letting any uncooked egg run underneath, until the omelet is barely set. Sprinkle ¼ cup of the croutons over the center of the omelet and with a spatula loosen the edges, shaking the pan. Fold the top third of the omelet over the croutons, then fold the bottom third over the middle, and tilting the pan away from you, slide the omelet to the lower edge of the pan. Invert the omelet onto a heated plate and keep it warm.

Make the second omelet with the remaining butter, egg mixture, and ¼ cup of the croutons in the same way.

Garnish each omelet with half of the watercress mixture and half the remaining croutons, and serve immediately with Grilled Canadian Bacon (recipe follows).

Grilled Canadian Bacon

Serves 2

1½ teaspoons unsalted butter, softened

6 ounces Canadian bacon, cut into ⅛-inch slices

Heat a well-seasoned ridged grill pan or skillet over moderately high heat until very hot, brush it with the butter, and on it grill the bacon slices for 2 minutes on each side.

Potatoes Anna

Serves 4 to 6

2 pounds long white potatoes,
   scrubbed and peeled

1 stick (½ cup) unsalted butter,
   melted and cooled
salt and pepper

Cut the potatoes crosswise into ⅛-inch slices with a mandoline or similar slicing device, and pat them dry. Coat the bottom of a 9-inch non-stick cake pan or non-stick ovenproof skillet with 2 tablespoons of the butter and in it arrange an overlapping layer of potato slices. Drizzle the potatoes with 1 tablespoon of the remaining butter, and sprinkle them with salt and pepper. Layer the remaining potato slices and butter, sprinkling each layer with salt and pepper. Cook the potatoes, covered tightly with a double layer of buttered foil and weighted with a heavy saucepan, over moderate heat for 5 minutes from the time the butter sizzles. Remove the saucepan only and bake the potatoes in a preheated 450° F. oven for 30 minutes. Weight the potatoes again with the saucepan and bake them for 20 to 30 minutes more, or until they are tender and the top is golden. Invert a serving dish over the cake pan and invert the potatoes onto it.

Raisin Bread

*Makes
2 loaves*

1½ cups raisins
1 tablespoon minced orange rind
1 tablespoon minced lemon rind
2 packages active dry yeast
   (For suggestions on baking with yeast,
   see A Bread Box, pages 22–23.)
1½ cups milk
¼ cup plus 1 teaspoon firmly packed
   dark brown sugar
1 stick (½ cup) unsalted butter, melted
   and cooled, plus additional melted
   butter for brushing the dough

2 large eggs
1 tablespoon salt
¼ teaspoon ground mace
¼ teaspoon ground ginger
¼ teaspoon cinnamon
5 cups all-purpose flour plus additional
   flour as needed
egg wash: 1 egg beaten with a pinch
   of salt

In a heatproof bowl let the raisins soak in boiling water to cover for 30 minutes, or until plumped and softened, and drain them. Add the orange and lemon rinds and mix well.

In a large bowl proof the yeast in ½ cup lukewarm milk with the 1 teaspoon dark brown sugar for 15 minutes, or until foamy. Add the remaining 1 cup milk, the butter, eggs, remaining ¼ cup dark brown sugar, salt, mace, ginger, and cinnamon. With a wooden spatula stir in the flour, 1 cup at a time. Combine the dough well, adding more flour if necessary to make a soft and sticky dough. Knead the dough on a floured surface, incorporating more flour if it is too sticky, for 8 to 10 minutes, or until smooth. Form the dough

Watercress, Sour Cream, and Crouton Omelets and Grilled Canadian Bacon

into a ball, put it in a bowl coated with vegetable oil, and turn it to coat it with the oil. Let the dough rise in a warm place, covered loosely, for 1½ hours, or until it is double in bulk. Punch down the dough and let it rise, covered loosely, for 30 minutes more.

Halve the dough, roll each half into a 16-by-8-inch rectangle, and brush each rectangle with the additional melted butter. Divide the raisin filling between the rectangles, and beginning with a short side roll each rectangle, enclosing the raisin mixture, into a loaf. Fit the loaves, seam side down, into buttered loaf pans, 8½ by 4½ by 2⅝ inches, and let them rise in a warm place, covered loosely, for 1 hour, or until they have risen 1 inch above the tops of the pans. Brush the loaves with the egg wash and bake them in a preheated 400° F. oven for 30 minutes, or until they sound hollow when the bottoms are tapped. Turn the loaves out on the rack and let them cool completely.

Iced Ice Coffee

4 cups strong freshly brewed coffee, chilled

sugar to taste
milk or heavy cream to taste

Serves 2

Fill an ice-cube tray with the dividers in place with some of the coffee, reserving the rest, and freeze until solid. Put 3 of the coffee cubes into each of 4 chilled 10-ounce glasses and pour in the remaining coffee. Stir in sugar and/or milk or cream to taste.

LUNCHES WITH PANACHE

We all know what a ho-hum lunch is and have had many too many of them in our times. A lunch with panache is the exact opposite. It suggests the unexpected. There is a surprise in store. Something amusing and pleasing is bound to occur.

For example: How can you balk at the prospect of our first menu, starring *Croque-Monsieur*—that glorious Gallic combination of ham and cheese grilled on buttery toast? Who would argue with another of our menus—three different kinds of pizza? Or with hosting a pizza party where to have any lunch at all you actually have to make the pies yourselves. Our menu for Danish Open-Faced Sandwiches combines delicacies such as Avocado Purée and shrimp on the bread, and ends with something even more original—Almond Cornets with Strawberry Meringue. By any standards, that's not just lunch.

These menus are also not complicated. In fact, all we're suggesting you serve up is an easy good time.

SUGGESTIONS

It's not often, we'd wager, that *Croque-Monsieur*—that basic combination of ham and cheese on bread, but with a flourish—are called fast food. But they are that, and then some. They also happen to be perfectly delicious.

If your *batterie de cuisine* does not include a *croque-monsieur* toasting iron, make the sandwiches in a skillet. The presentation won't be as pretty, but the flavor will be every bit as good.

As a general rule, when it is clarified, butter loses about one-fourth of its original volume.

By the way, it is important to use clarified butter when grilling the sandwiches because clarified butter will not burn.

Granita is the Italian word for an ice, to which no milk, cream, or egg white is added. Because it is stirred while freezing, it has an icy, grainy texture and is extremely refreshing and light. It is not to be confused with sherbet, to which either milk or cream is usually added and whose texture is smooth by comparison to that of a granita.

∽

Start the granita 3 hours ahead. Remember that you will have to let it soften slightly, for about 5 minutes, before serving.

With a food processor the preparation for this lunch should take all of about 10 minutes. In it grate the cheese for the sandwiches and all the vegetables for the salad. You can also make the dressing for the salad in the processor for that matter.

FAST FOOD FOR LUNCH

Croque-Monsieur
Carrot, Turnip, and Red Cabbage Salad
Minted Orange Tea Granita

Chilled Red Valdepeñas

Croque-Monsieur

Serves 4

1½ cups finely grated Gruyère, or other
    full-flavored Swiss cheese
3 tablespoons sour cream
1½ tablespoons Dijon-style mustard
1½ tablespoons kirsch

8 slices of homemade-style white bread
Clarified Butter (see box, page 37)
8 thin slices of cooked ham
cornichons (French sour gherkins) and
    cocktail onions for garnish

In a bowl combine well the Gruyère, sour cream, mustard, and kirsch.

Brush the bread slices lightly with some of the clarified butter, then spread each slice with 2 tablespoons of the cheese mixture, leaving a ¼-inch border. Top the cheese mixture with 1 slice of the ham. Make 4 sandwiches, pressing the slices together firmly, remove the crusts, and brush the sandwiches, including the edges, generously with more of the clarified butter. Grill the sandwiches on a preheated moderately hot griddle for 3 minutes, or until the bottoms are golden brown. Turn them, and weight them with a 1-pound weight or heavy plate. Grill the sandwiches for 3 minutes more, or until the bottoms are golden brown. (Or grill the sandwiches, 2 at a time, in a *croque-monsieur* toasting iron over moderately high heat for 3 minutes, or until golden brown. Turn the iron and grill the sandwiches for 3 minutes more, until golden.) Transfer the hot sandwiches to a platter, garnish the platter with the *cornichons* and small onions, and serve at once.

Carrot, Turnip, and Red Cabbage Salad and Croque-Monsieur

Carrot, Turnip, and Red Cabbage Salad

Serves 4

1 cup Lemon Dressing (recipe follows)
2 cups grated carrot
1 cup peeled and grated white turnip
  (do not use rutabaga)

1 cup cored and grated red cabbage
spinach leaves, washed, patted dry,
  stemmed, and sliced thin

Make the Lemon Dressing and reserve in a serving bowl.

On a platter arrange in alternate rows the carrot, turnip, and cabbage. Garnish the salad with the spinach leaves and serve with the dressing on the side.

Lemon Dressing

3 tablespoons fresh lemon juice
1 tablespoon Dijon-style mustard
1 large egg yolk

¼ teaspoon salt
white pepper to taste
¾ cup olive oil

*Makes about
1 cup*

In a bowl combine the lemon juice, mustard, egg yolk, salt, and white pepper. Add the olive oil in a stream, beating, and beat the dressing until emulsified.

Minted Orange Tea Granita

Serves 4

1 large orange
¾ cup large sugar cubes
2 cups water
1 tablespoon minced fresh mint leaves
  or 1 teaspoon dried

2 tablespoons black tea
½ cup fresh orange juice, strained
3 tablespoons fresh lemon juice, strained
fresh mint leaves for garnish

Rub the skin of the orange with the sugar cubes until the cubes are orange-colored and all the pigment on the orange has been rubbed away.

In a saucepan combine the water, sugar cubes, and minced mint leaves. Bring the water to a boil, stirring until the sugar is dissolved, and simmer the syrup for 5 minutes. Stir in the black tea, let the mixture steep, covered, for 20 minutes, and strain into a bowl. Add both the orange juice and lemon juice and pour the mixture into a freezer tray.

Freeze the mixture until firm but not frozen hard. Then break the mixture up into large granules with a fork and freeze it again in the tray for 3 hours more, or until firm.

Before serving, let the granita stand at room temperature for about 5 minutes, or until it is just soft enough to scoop. Divide the ice among dessert dishes and garnish each serving with some mint leaves.

CLARIFIED BUTTER

In a heavy saucepan melt 2 sticks (1 cup) unsalted butter, cut into 1-inch pieces, over low heat. Remove from the heat, let stand for 3 minutes, and skim the froth from the surface. Strain the butter through a sieve lined with a double thickness of rinsed and squeezed cheesecloth, leaving the milky solids in the bottom of the pan. Pour the clarified butter into a jar or crock and store it, covered, in the refrigerator. This way the butter will keep indefinitely. Makes about ¾ cup.

A LIGHT LUNCH TO LINGER OVER

Danish Open-Faced Sandwiches
Beet, Celery, and Apple Salad with Horseradish Cream
Almond Cornets with Strawberry Meringue

Iced Lager

SUGGESTIONS

To devein shrimp: First shell the shrimp. Then, with the tip of a sharp knife, make a slit down the back of each shrimp and pluck out the thin dark intestinal vein.

To cook shrimp: Bring a saucepan of water to a rolling boil. Add the shrimp and boil them for 1 minute, or until pink and just firm to the touch. Drain immediately, rinse under cold water, and pat dry.

Using a pastry bag takes practice, practice, and more practice to develop the right amount of pressure on the bag and the correct ways of using the bag with the various decorative tips. If you are still learning and uneasy about your mastery, simply bring the cornets and the strawberry meringue to the table and let people spoon the meringue into the horns.

Make Curry Butter in advance and reserve at room temperature for easy spreading.

Have all the remaining components for the sandwiches readied in the refrigerator. It will then just be a matter of assembling them.

Almond cornets, by virtue of their delicacy, cannot be filled in advance. Fill *just* before serving. The cornets, however, can be made in advance, up to 2 days. Store in an airtight container.

Danish Open-Faced Sandwiches and Almond Cornets
with Strawberry Meringue

Danish Open-Faced Sandwiches

Serves 4

16 shelled and deveined whole shrimp,
   cooked (see Suggestions)
½ pound cooked turkey breast
4 hard-boiled large eggs
   (see page 41)
6 red radishes

1 large seedless cucumber
Curry Butter (recipe follows)
Avocado Purée (page 40)
4 slices of Danish dark rye or
   pumpernickel bread
sprigs of dill for garnish

Let the shrimp cool completely. Slice the turkey breast, eggs, radishes, and cucumber thin and set aside.

Make Curry Butter and let stand at room temperature.

About 30 minutes to 1 hour before serving the sandwiches, make Avocado Purée.

To serve, spread the bread with a layer of the butter. Arrange some of the turkey, eggs, vegetables, and shrimp decoratively on top. Then fill a pastry bag fitted with the star tip with the Avocado Purée and pipe the purée onto each sandwich. Garnish the sandwiches with the dill sprigs, transfer to a platter, and serve immediately. Serve the remaining Avocado Purée separately.

Curry Butter

*Makes a little
less than
½ cup*

¾ stick (6 tablespoons) unsalted butter,
   softened

2 teaspoons curry powder

In a small bowl cream together the butter and curry powder. Chill the mixture, covered, for 30 minutes, or until firm but of a spreading consistency.

Avocado Purée

*Makes about
1 cup,
depending
on size of
avocado*

about 2 teaspoons onion juice
   made by pressing chopped onion
   in a garlic press
1 very ripe avocado, chopped coarse

4 ounces cream cheese, softened
1 tablespoon sour cream
2 teaspoons fresh lemon juice
Tabasco to taste

In a bowl mash together all the ingredients until smooth. Cover the purée with a lightly oiled round of wax paper and chill it for no more than 1 hour.

Beet, Celery, and Apple Salad with Horseradish Cream

Serves 4

4 or 5 large beets, scrubbed and trimmed, leaving ½ inch of the tops attached
1 cup sour cream
2 tablespoons heavy cream
2 tablespoons fresh lemon juice
2 tablespoons minced onion
2 tablespoons well-drained bottled horseradish, or to taste
1 teaspoon salt
2 cups peeled and diced apple
1 cup diced celery
minced scallion top for garnish

In a large saucepan cover the beets with cold water, bring the water to a boil, and simmer the beets, covered, for about 45 minutes, or until tender. Drain the beets, peel them, and dice them.

In a large non-metallic bowl combine the sour cream, heavy cream, lemon juice, onion, horseradish, and salt. Add the apple, the beets, and the celery, toss the salad well, and garnish the top of it with the scallion.

NOTES ON BOILED EGGS

The cooking time for the perfect soft-boiled egg has been disputed for eons, with the answer lying somewhere between 2 minutes and the outer limits of personal preference. Not so the hard-boiled egg. Strange as it may sound, a hard-boiled egg may be *over*-boiled into oblivion. To avoid the pitfalls:

Bring a pan of water to a rolling boil, then lower the heat to a gentle simmer.

Pierce the egg at the large end with a straight pin to prevent the shell from cracking when submerged into the water. Lower the egg carefully into the water and simmer gently for 12 to 15 minutes, depending on the size of the egg and its temperature when added to the water.

When done, drain and plunge the egg immediately into a bowl of cold water. This stops further cooking and impedes the formation of a dark line around the yolk—a sure sign of an overcooked egg.

A thoroughly cooled egg is much easier to slice.

Almond Cornets with Strawberry Meringue

Makes
4 cornets

¼ cup granulated sugar

2 tablespoons unsalted butter, softened

⅓ cup finely chopped blanched almonds, toasted

1 large egg white, beaten lightly

2 tablespoons all-purpose flour

½ teaspoon almond extract

For the strawberry meringue

2 large egg whites

a pinch of cream of tartar

a pinch of salt

½ cup superfine granulated sugar

6 strawberries, hulled

1 teaspoon kirsch

1 teaspoon fresh lemon juice

whole strawberries for garnish

In a bowl cream together the granulated sugar and the butter until the mixture is light. Stir in the almonds and the egg white. Fold in the flour and the almond extract until the batter is just barely combined.

Trace four 5-inch rounds at least 3 inches apart on a well-buttered baking sheet. Drop 2 tablespoons of the batter into the center of each round and spread it evenly with the back of a wet spoon to the edge of the rounds. Bake the rounds in a preheated 425° F. oven for 4 minutes, or until the edges are golden brown. Remove the baking sheet from the oven and with a metal spatula invert 1 round onto the counter. (To keep the rounds from hardening and cooling, return the sheet to the oven and leave the door open.) Form the hot round quickly into a cornet by overlapping 2 edges of it to make a cone shape, and stand the cone in a tall glass to cool completely and harden. Continue to make cornets in the same manner. Or form cornets by rolling each round around a 4½-inch cornet mold (available at specialty kitchenware stores), let cool on the counter for 1 minute, then remove the mold. Transfer to a rack and let cool completely. See Suggestions for storing the cornets.

Make the meringue: In a large, clean metal bowl beat the egg whites with the cream of tartar and the salt until they hold soft peaks. Beat in the superfine sugar, 1½ teaspoons at a time, and beat the meringue for 5 minutes, or until it holds very stiff peaks and is shiny. In a food mill fitted with the coarse blade purée the strawberries, transfer the purée to a glass bowl, and stir in the kirsch and lemon juice. Fold the purée into the meringue gently but thoroughly.

Just before serving, fill a pastry bag fitted with a star tip with the meringue and pipe the meringue into each cornet. Transfer the cornets to a platter and garnish the platter with the remaining berries. Serve immediately.

PIZZAS

Eggplant, Mushroom, and Tomato Pizza
Shrimp and Feta Pizza
Pepperoni, Green Pepper, and Olive Pizza
Two-Bean Salad with Red Onion
Coffee Sherbet with Mocha Sauce

Beer or red and white carafe wines

SUGGESTIONS

This is a clever party menu. Just ready some of the basics ahead of time, then let your guests loose in the kitchen to make the pizzas. To make it even easier you can also make the pizza dough in a food processor fitted with the plastic blade.

Proof the yeast as directed in the recipe and add it to the work bowl.

Add the remaining ½ cup lukewarm water, the flours, and oil, then process the mixture until a ball of dough forms. Knead the dough by letting it spin in the processor for 15 seconds. If the dough is still too sticky, process in 1 tablespoon of all-purpose flour a little at a time until it forms a smooth and soft dough.

Remove the dough from the bowl, put it in a well-oiled bowl, turning it to coat it with the oil, and let the dough rise. Proceed with the recipe.

Making dough in the processor should take a matter of minutes.

Make the Coffee Sherbet and Mocha Sauce ahead of time.

The basics to have on hand when your guests arrive: the dough, Tomato Pizza Sauce, and the eggplant topping—the last two can be prepared one full day in advance. Keep covered and chilled. If you are doing the Shrimp and Feta and/or Pepperoni, Green Pepper, and Olive fillings, they are put together at the last minute, but the Tomato Pizza Sauce must be ready.

Pizza dough is more flexible than you think. You can hasten along the rising of the dough by placing the bowl in an oven warmed by a pilot light with a pan of boiling water in the bottom of the oven. Ideally, you should leave the dough there until it is double in bulk. However, if you want to proceed with the recipe before that point, by all means do so. You'll be pleased to discover that the crust when baked is only slightly chewier and cakier.

Whole-Wheat Pizza Dough

Makes enough dough for three 8-inch pizzas

1 package active dry yeast
(For suggestions on baking with yeast, see A Bread Box, pages 22–23.)
¾ cup lukewarm water
a pinch of sugar

1 cup all-purpose flour
¾ cup whole-wheat flour
¾ teaspoon salt
2 tablespoons olive oil

In a bowl proof the yeast in ¼ cup of the water with the sugar for 15 minutes, or until foamy.

In a large bowl combine the flours and salt, stir in the remaining ½ cup water, the oil, and the yeast mixture, and combine the mixture until it forms a rough dough. Knead the dough on a floured surface for 10 minutes, or until smooth and satiny. Or make in the food processor; see Suggestions. Put the dough in a well-oiled bowl, turn it to coat it with the oil, and let it rise, covered with plastic wrap, in a warm place for 1 to 1½ hours, or until double in bulk.

Meanwhile prepare the Tomato Pizza Sauce (recipe follows) and whatever fillings you are using.

Punch down the dough and divide it into thirds. Fill and bake according to the instructions in the pizza recipe you are using.

Tomato Pizza Sauce

Makes about 2¾ cups

a 2-pound-3-ounce can Italian plum tomatoes
⅓ cup olive oil
a 6-ounce can tomato paste
1 large onion, halved

1 bay leaf
1 teaspoon sugar
1 teaspoon salt
¾ teaspoon dried orégano, or to taste
additional salt and pepper

Purée the tomatoes with their juice through the fine disk of a food mill into a heavy saucepan. Stir in the remaining ingredients, bring the sauce to a boil over moderately high heat, stirring, and cook the sauce at a bare simmer over low heat, stirring occasionally, for 1 hour. Discard the onion and bay leaf, and add salt and pepper to taste.

Eggplant, Mushroom, and Tomato Pizza

Whole-Wheat Pizza Dough (page 44)
a 1-pound eggplant
1 cup chopped onion
1 large garlic clove, mashed to a paste
6 tablespoons olive oil
salt and pepper to taste
¼ pound mushrooms, sliced

1 tablespoon cornmeal
1⅓ cups grated mozzarella
⅔ cup Tomato Pizza Sauce
   (preceding recipe)
2 tomatoes, peeled and cut into
   ⅓-inch slices
dried orégano to taste

*Makes one
8-inch pizza*

Prepare whole-wheat pizza dough through the point of dividing it into thirds. The remaining dough can be kept in a bowl, covered with plastic wrap and chilled, for anywhere from 2 to 24 hours.

In a shallow baking pan bake the eggplant in a preheated 375° F. oven for 1 hour. Let the eggplant cool until it can be handled, peel it, and put the flesh in a bowl. In a small skillet cook the onion and garlic in 2 tablespoons of the oil over moderately low heat, stirring, for 5 minutes, or until softened. Stir the mixture into the eggplant, and add salt and pepper to taste. In the skillet cook the mushrooms in 2 tablespoons of the remaining oil over moderate heat, stirring, for 5 minutes and remove the skillet from the heat and let the mixture cool.

Knead one-third of the pizza dough lightly on a floured surface and pat it into a 4-inch round. Being careful not to tear the dough, stretch it evenly and gently into a 7-inch round, and with a rolling pin roll it into a 9-inch round. Sprinkle a baking sheet with the cornmeal, transfer the round to the sheet, and make a rim around the edge, forming an 8-inch round. Sprinkle the round evenly with ⅔ cup of the mozzarella and pour the ⅔ cup pizza sauce over the cheese. Spread the eggplant mixture evenly over the sauce and top it with the mushrooms, the tomato slices, the remaining ⅔ cup mozzarella, and the orégano. Drizzle the remaining 2 tablespoons oil over the top and bake the pizza on the lowest shelf of an electric oven or on the floor of a gas oven preheated to 400° F. for 15 to 20 minutes, or until the crust is golden.

Shrimp and Feta Pizza

Makes one 8-inch pizza

Whole-Wheat Pizza Dough (page 44)
1 tablespoon cornmeal
¾ cup grated mozzarella
¾ cup Tomato Pizza Sauce (page 44)
6 ounces shrimp, shelled, deveined, and halved lengthwise

3 ounces feta, drained if necessary and crumbled
fresh rosemary sprigs or crumbled dried rosemary to taste
3 tablespoons olive oil

Prepare whole-wheat pizza dough through the point of dividing it into thirds. The remaining dough can be kept in a bowl, covered with plastic wrap and chilled, for up to 24 hours.

Knead one-third of the pizza dough lightly on a floured surface and pat it into a 4-inch round. Being careful not to tear the dough, stretch it evenly and gently into a 7-inch round, and with a rolling pin roll it into a 9-inch round. Sprinkle a baking sheet with the cornmeal, transfer the round to the sheet, and make a rim around the edge, forming an 8-inch round. Sprinkle the dough evenly with the mozzarella, pour the pizza sauce over the cheese, and arrange the shrimp on top. Sprinkle the pizza with the feta and rosemary, drizzle it with the oil, and bake it on the lowest shelf of an electric oven or on the floor of a gas oven preheated to 500° F. for 15 to 20 minutes, or until the crust is golden.

Pepperoni, Green Pepper, and Olive Pizza

Makes one 8-inch pizza

Whole-Wheat Pizza Dough (page 44)
1 tablespoon cornmeal
1 green bell pepper, sliced thin
¼ cup olive oil

1¼ cups grated mozzarella
¾ cup Tomato Pizza Sauce (page 44)
3 ounces pepperoni, sliced thin
3 large pitted black olives, halved

Prepare whole-wheat pizza dough through the point of dividing it into thirds. The remaining dough can be kept in a bowl, covered with plastic wrap and chilled, for up to 24 hours.

Knead one-third of the pizza dough lightly on a floured surface and pat it into a 4-inch round. Being careful not to tear the dough, stretch it evenly and gently into a 7-inch round, and with a rolling pin roll it into a 9-inch round. Sprinkle a baking sheet with the cornmeal, transfer the round to the sheet, and make a rim around the edge, forming an 8-inch pizza.

In a large skillet cook the bell pepper in 2 tablespoons of the oil over moderate heat for 3 minutes, or until softened, and remove the skillet from the heat.

Sprinkle the dough with ¾ cup of the mozzarella and pour the pizza sauce over the cheese. Arrange the pepperoni on the sauce and arrange the bell pepper and olives on it. Sprinkle the remaining ½ cup mozzarella over the peppers, drizzle the pizza with the remaining 2 tablespoons oil, and bake it on the lowest shelf of an electric oven or on the floor of a gas oven preheated to 500° F. for 15 minutes.

Two-Bean Salad with Red Onion

½ pound navy beans, picked over
   and rinsed
salt to taste
2 teaspoons Dijon-style mustard
3 tablespoons balsamic vinegar* or
   3 tablespoons red-wine vinegar

½ cup olive oil
½ pound green beans, trimmed
⅔ cup chopped red onion

*Italian aged vinegar, available at specialty-foods
  stores and some supermarkets.

Serves 3 or 4

In a large saucepan combine the beans and triple their volume of cold water, bring the water to a boil, and cook the beans, uncovered, over moderate heat for 2 minutes. Remove the pan from the heat and let the beans soak for 1 hour. Drain them, add enough water to cover them by 3 inches, and bring the water to a boil. Cook the beans over moderate heat for 30 minutes, or until just tender, and let them cool in the liquid for 10 minutes. Add salt to taste and let them cool in the liquid until just warm.

Two-Bean Salad with Red Onion

In a small bowl combine the mustard, vinegar, and salt to taste, add the olive oil in a stream, whisking, and whisk the dressing until emulsified.

Drain the navy beans. In a bowl toss them with half the dressing, and let them marinate for at least 1 hour, or overnight.

In a saucepan of boiling salted water cook the green beans for 7 minutes, or until tender but still *al dente*. Drain them in a colander, and refresh them under running cold water. Pat the green beans dry and in a bowl toss them with the remaining dressing.

Arrange the green beans in the center of a shallow serving dish, arrange the navy beans on each side, and sprinkle the salad with the onion.

Coffee Sherbet with Mocha Sauce

Makes about 1 quart

¾ cup sugar
3 cups hot strong freshly brewed coffee
¾ teaspoon cinnamon

2 teaspoons vanilla
Mocha Sauce (recipe follows)

In a bowl dissolve the sugar in the coffee and stir in the cinnamon. Let cool for 10 minutes, add the vanilla, and chill for at least 2 hours. Freeze the mixture in an ice-cream freezer according to the manufacturer's instructions.

While the sherbet is freezing, make Mocha Sauce.

To serve, scoop the sherbet into bowls and top with the sauce.

Mocha Sauce

Makes about 1 cup

⅔ cup heavy cream
2 tablespoons unsweetened cocoa powder
½ cup sugar

1 tablespoon unsalted butter
2 tablespoons coffee-flavored liqueur

In a heavy saucepan combine all the ingredients except the liqueur, bring the mixture to a boil, whisking, and boil it for 3 minutes. Let the sauce cool for 10 minutes, stir in the liqueur, and chill the sauce, covered, for at least 1 hour.

COLD LUNCHES

Whether the weather is already warm or just heating up, our cold lunches will comfort you. The menus are clever, pleasing combinations that include crabmeat-stuffed avocado halves, a stunning salad of ham and hard-boiled eggs and asparagus in shimmering aspic, an Oriental Noodle and Chicken Salad that just begs to be composed, it is so delicious, and a kasha loaf, studded with cashews and made lovely wrapped in cabbage leaves. As varied as these dishes are, though, they all share one thing in common: all can be prepared in advance and be held either at room temperature or in the refrigerator until the moment of serving. And remember the desserts that accompany them are only our suggestions. Depending upon your schedule, the temperature, and your inclinations, vary them at your will.

Postscript: Even though these menus are to be served either chilled or at room temperature, they are not exclusively hot-weather fare. It would be a shame to limit such pleasures to only one season of the year.

A LUNCH FOR A BALMY DAY

Crabmeat and Avocado Louis
Cheese Puff Rings
Orange Walnut Turkish Tart

One of California's richer Chardonnays

Crabmeat and Avocado Louis

Serves 4

For the sauce
1 cup Quick Mayonnaise (page 20)
⅓ cup bottled chili sauce
1 tablespoon grated onion
1 tablespoon drained horseradish
cayenne to taste
salt
½ cup well-chilled heavy cream

1 pound cooked crabmeat, thawed if frozen, picked over, and flaked
2 avocados, halved, peeled, pitted, and rubbed with the juice of 1 lemon
1 tablespoon snipped fresh chives
½ pound Belgian endive, separated into leaves
1 hard-boiled large egg, quartered
whole chives for garnish

Make the sauce: In a bowl combine the mayonnaise, chili sauce, onion, horseradish, cayenne, and salt to taste. In a bowl beat the cream until it holds soft peaks and fold it into the mayonnaise mixture. Chill the sauce, covered, for at least 1 hour or up to 4 hours.

In a bowl toss the crabmeat with ½ cup of the sauce and mound the mixture in the avocado halves. Sprinkle the filling with the snipped chives, arrange the avocados on a platter with the endive, egg wedges, and whole chives, and drizzle the egg wedges with some of the sauce. Serve the remaining sauce separately.

SUGGESTIONS

A hard, flavorless avocado can ruin a lovely salad. So be sure to lay in avocados—we recommend California ones, which are rough-textured and *dark* in color when ripe (as opposed to the smooth-skinned, bright green ones also available)—enough in advance to allow them to ripen. A good method: Put the avocados in a brown paper bag. If upon cutting into them they are still unripe, don't try to salvage anything by serving them. You'll be doing the crab a disservice. Simply arrange the endive nouvelle-style, in a spokelike pattern, on the plate and mound the salad on top.

The price of crab per pound can be high. If it seems too hefty a price to pay, reduce the amount called for in the recipe and add chopped celery, minced water chestnuts, or julienne strips of cucumber to the mixture. Or garnish the plate with marinated artichoke hearts.

Cheese Puff Rings, otherwise known as *gougères* in French, are made with a *pâte à choux* batter, the same batter from which cream puffs are made—a very useful technique to master.

ꜱ

Prepare the crab salad fully in advance and reserve in the refrigerator.

You can begin making Cheese Puff Rings about 2½ hours in advance of serving the salad.

You will need 30 minutes, more or less, for making the dough and preparing the baking sheet.

You will need 45 minutes for baking the puffs. Once made, the puffs can be kept in the oven up to 1 hour.

Prior to baking the puffs, however, bake the *phyllo* tart shell. In that way you will also have partially preheated the oven for baking the Cheese Puff Rings.

Cheese Puff Rings

Makes 2 rings,
serving 4 to 6

1 cup water
1 stick (½ cup) unsalted butter,
    cut into bits
¼ teaspoon salt
1 cup all-purpose flour

4 or 5 large eggs
1 cup minced Gruyère
egg wash: 1 egg beaten with
    1 tablespoon milk

In a saucepan bring to a boil the water, butter, and salt over high heat, reduce the heat to low, and add the flour all at once. Beat the mixture with a wooden spoon for 2 to 3 minutes, or until the dough leaves the sides of the pan and forms a ball. Transfer the dough to the bowl of an electric mixer, and with the mixer at high speed beat in 4 of the eggs, 1 at a time, beating well after each addition. The dough should be thick enough to just hold soft peaks. If it is too stiff, break the remaining egg into a bowl, beat it lightly, and add enough of it to thin the dough to the right consistency. Beat in the Gruyère, reserving 2 tablespoons for the topping.

On a buttered and floured baking sheet outline 2 circles, each 5¾ inches in diameter, at least 3 inches apart. Drop spoonfuls of the dough in a ring inside each circle, dividing the dough evenly between the 2 circles and mounding it slightly, and using a buttered spatula shape the rings evenly. Brush the rings with the egg wash, sprinkle them with the reserved 2 tablespoons Gruyère, and bake them in a preheated 425° F. oven for 10 minutes. Reduce the heat to 375° F. and bake the rings for 10 minutes more. Reduce the heat to 350° F. and bake the rings for 20 to 25 minutes more, or until they are golden brown and puffed. Turn off the oven and let the puffs stand in the oven for at least 15 minutes or up to 1 hour. Serve the cheese puffs warm.

Orange Walnut Turkish Tart

Makes one
8-inch tart

1¼ cups coarsely ground walnuts
⅓ cup fine dry bread crumbs
1 cup sweet orange marmalade
2 tablespoons orange-flavored liqueur
¾ stick (6 tablespoons) unsalted butter,
    melted and cooled

10 sheets of *phyllo,* stacked between
    2 sheets of wax paper and covered
    with a dampened dish towel
1 tablespoon confectioners' sugar
an 11-ounce can mandarin oranges,
    drained well

In a small bowl combine the walnuts and bread crumbs.

In a small saucepan melt ¾ cup of the marmalade with the liqueur and 2 tablespoons of the butter over moderately low heat, stirring, and keep the mixture warm over low heat.

Trim the *phyllo* sheets into 13½-inch squares and keep them stacked between the wax paper and dish towel while assembling the dessert.

Brush an 8-inch pie tin with some of the remaining butter, fit 1 sheet of the *phyllo* into the tin, pressing it flat against the sides and bottom with a brush dipped in the butter and letting the edges extend above the tin. (Do not butter the extending edges of the *phyllo*.) Layer 3 more sheets of the *phyllo* in the pan, brushing each sheet, but not its edges, lightly with the butter.

Sprinkle one-third of the walnut mixture over the bottom, drizzle it with one-third of the marmalade mixture, and add 2 more *phyllo* sheets, brushing each sheet lightly with butter. Make 2 more layers in the same manner, brush the top of the tart with butter, and bake the tart in the lower third of a preheated 375° F. oven for 30 to 35 minutes, or until the *phyllo* is golden brown. If the *phyllo* edges brown too quickly, cover them gently with foil. Let the tart cool in the pan on a rack for 10 minutes, center an empty coffee can gently in the tart shell, and invert the tart shell onto the coffee can. Invert the shell carefully onto a serving platter.

Sift the confectioners' sugar around the edges of the tart, arrange the oranges in concentric circles in the center, and brush them with the remaining ¼ cup of marmalade, heated and strained.

Orange Walnut Turkish Tart

A DAZZLING ASPIC SALAD

Ham, Eggs, and Asparagus in Aspic
Mustard Mayonnaise
Mango and Papaya Whip

ᔆ

Light Moselle wine of Kabinett quality

SUGGESTIONS

You will see that the recipe for clarifying the broth or stock called for in the aspic for this salad differs slightly from the one in A Stock File (page 154). The reason for this is simple: the more ingredients used in the stock mixture, the fuller the flavor.

You will also see that we have called for canned chicken broth as a first choice for making the aspic. Homemade chicken stock is, of course, also recommended, but because we cannot know the amount of gelatin in any given homemade stock, we can only guess at the amount that will need to be added. Begin with 1 table-spoon and adjust if need be.

To cook asparagus: Tie the spears, trimmed of the tough ends and their stalks, peeled (if desired), into a bunch with a piece of string. In a saucepan bring enough water to cover the bunch to a boil with salt to taste, add the asparagus, and simmer until firm-tender. Drain immediately and plunge into cold water to set the color.

ᔆ

Provided you have the stock already made and clarified and the ham cooked and diced, you will need about 5 hours to bring the salad, in all its shimmering loveliness, to final presentation.

It's best not to prepare whipped cream combinations, like the whip, too far in advance. The cream, even when covered, has the tendency to take on the other flavors in the refrigerator and its texture does change—it separates. If that occurs, simply whip it again into peaks. Four hours should be the maximum time to let it stand.

Ham, Eggs, and Asparagus in Aspic

For the ham mixture
2 cups diced cooked ham
1½ tablespoons minced shallot
2 tablespoons minced fresh parsley leaves
1 tablespoon tarragon vinegar
1 tablespoon dry white wine
1 small garlic clove, minced

For the aspic
4 cups canned chicken broth
   (see Suggestions) or chicken
   stock (page 154)
1 cup water
the crushed shells of 4 large eggs
4 large egg whites, beaten lightly
1 stalk of celery, chopped fine
1 leek including the green top, washed
   well and chopped fine
2 tomatoes, chopped
½ carrot, chopped fine

Tie together in a cheesecloth bag
6 parsley stems
½ teaspoon dried thyme
½ teaspoon dried tarragon
½ bay leaf
2 cloves

salt
2 envelopes unflavored gelatin
3 tablespoons Sercial Madeira

5 hard-boiled large eggs, halved
   lengthwise (see page 41)
1 hard-boiled large egg, cut lengthwise
   into 5 wedges (see page 41)
10 cooked asparagus spears
   (see Suggestions, opposite)
dill sprigs for garnish
Mustard Mayonnaise (recipe follows)

Serves 4

Make the ham mixture: In a bowl combine all the ingredients for the ham mixture and chill, covered, for at least 1 hour or overnight.

Make the aspic: In a large saucepan combine the broth or stock, water, egg shells, egg whites, celery, leek, tomatoes, carrot, cheesecloth bag, and salt and bring the liquid to a boil, stirring constantly. As the liquid comes to a boil, a crust will form on the surface of the mixture. Simmer the mixture, undisturbed, for 30 minutes. While the mixture is simmering, in a small bowl sprinkle the gelatin over the Madeira and let soften. Ladle the mixture through a fine sieve lined with a double thickness of rinsed and squeezed cheesecloth into a bowl.

In a large bowl measure 4 cups of the hot clarified broth, reserving any remaining for another use, add the gelatin mixture, and stir it until it is dissolved. Let the aspic cool and chill it until it is thickened but still liquid.

To assemble the salad: Rinse a shallow 12-inch round glass serving dish with cold water, but do not dry it, and chill until cold. Into the serving dish ladle enough of the aspic to measure ¼ inch, rotate the dish to coat it evenly with the aspic, and chill it until the aspic is just set. Drain the ham mixture and arrange it in an even layer on the aspic in the dish. Ladle enough of the remaining liquid aspic over the ham to measure ¼ inch and chill until the aspic is just set. Arrange the hard-boiled egg halves and wedges and asparagus decoratively on the

aspic, ladle enough of the remaining liquid aspic over the dish to cover the asparagus by ¼ inch, and chill until the aspic is set. Dip the dill sprigs into the remaining liquid aspic, arrange them decoratively on the eggs and in the center of the dish, and chill until the garnish is set. Finally, ladle enough of the remaining liquid aspic over the dish to measure ¼ inch and chill the dish for 3 hours, or until the aspic is completely set.

Pour the remaining liquid aspic into a rinsed but not dried jelly-roll pan and chill until set. Transfer the chilled aspic with a spatula to a sheet of moistened wax paper and with a rinsed large knife chop it. Garnish the dish with the chopped aspic and serve it with the Mustard Mayonnaise.

Mustard Mayonnaise

¾ cup Quick Mayonnaise (page 20)
2 tablespoons fresh lemon juice
1½ tablespoons Dijon-style mustard

⅓ cup well-chilled heavy cream beaten
  until it just holds soft peaks
salt

Makes about
1½ cups

In a serving bowl combine the mayonnaise, lemon juice, and mustard, fold in the whipped cream, and add salt to taste.

Mango and Papaya Whip

1 very ripe large mango, peeled
  and chopped
1 very ripe large papaya, peeled
  and chopped

3 tablespoons fresh lime juice,
  or to taste
2 tablespoons sugar, or to taste
1 cup well-chilled heavy cream

Serves 4 to 6

In a food processor fitted with the metal blade purée the mango and the papaya until smooth, transfer the purée to a bowl, and stir in the lime juice and sugar to taste.

In a chilled bowl beat the cream until it holds soft peaks, fold it into the purée, and chill the fruit whip, covered, for at least 1 hour.

Ham, Eggs, and Asparagus in Aspic

A CHINESE SALAD LUNCH

Oriental Noodle and Chicken Salad
Creamy Peanut Sauce
Coconut Curd with Litchis and Mandarin Oranges

California Chenin Blanc

SUGGESTIONS

If time is a real factor, substitute either smoked turkey or smoked chicken breast for the poached chicken in the salad.

Fresh Oriental noodles are available in various widths: try the thin thin ones. They freeze very well, by the way, and can be plunged frozen into boiling water.

Be warned: Hot pepper oil is very *hot* and grows even hotter as it stands. Unless you have a particularly ironlike palate, 2 teaspoons should be the maximum amount used.

The litchis and mandarin oranges called for in the dessert serve primarily as garnishes. Buy the size cans most readily available—usually an 11-ounce—and decorate the curd with the fruits according to your preference.

Assemble the salad in stages, if you like. Cook the noodles, toss them in the oil, and while they are cooling poach the chicken. Then, prepare the vegetables and reserve in plastic bags in the refrigerator. All that remains at that point is the sauce, and even it can be whirred up in advance. Just don't add the cream until you're ready to serve the salad.

The coconut curd will need a minimum of 3 hours to set.

Oriental Noodle and Chicken Salad with Creamy Peanut Sauce

Oriental Noodle and Chicken Salad

Serves 4 to 6

1 pound skinless, boneless chicken breast
2 cups chicken stock (page 154) or
   canned chicken broth
1 small onion, quartered
½ celery stalk, sliced thick
1 bay leaf
6 parsley stems
6 peppercorns
3 quarts water
2 tablespoons peanut oil
10 ounces thin Chinese egg noodles*
   or *spaghettini*

2 teaspoons Oriental sesame oil*
1 cup bean sprouts
1 cup thinly sliced carrot
1 cup thinly sliced cucumber
1 cup thinly sliced scallion
a 15-ounce can baby corn,* drained
   and rinsed
Creamy Peanut Sauce (recipe follows)

*Available at Oriental markets and some
supermarkets.

In a saucepan combine the chicken, stock or broth, onion, celery, bay leaf, parsley, and peppercorns. Bring the stock to a simmer, and poach the chicken over moderately low heat for 5 minutes. Let the chicken cool in the stock, then shred it. Strain the stock into another saucepan and reduce it over moderately high heat to about ⅓ cup. Reserve the reduction for making the sauce.

In a kettle bring the water to a boil with 1 tablespoon of the peanut oil, add the noodles, and cook them until they are just *al dente*. Drain them in a colander, rinse them under running cold water, and drain them well. On a platter toss the noodles with the remaining peanut oil and the sesame oil and chicken.

In a saucepan of boiling water blanch the bean sprouts for 10 seconds, drain them, then refresh them under running cold water. Garnish the platter with the sprouts, carrot, cucumber, scallion, and corn. Serve the salad with the Creamy Peanut Sauce.

Creamy Peanut Sauce

Makes about 2 cups

½ cup smooth peanut butter
⅓ cup reserved chicken stock
   from poaching the chicken
   (preceding recipe), or ⅓ cup
   canned chicken broth
¼ cup soy sauce
4 tablespoons Oriental sesame oil*
2 tablespoons minced garlic

2 tablespoons peeled and minced
   gingerroot
2 tablespoons sugar
2 tablespoons red-wine vinegar
2 teaspoons hot pepper oil,* or to taste
¼ cup heavy cream

*Available at Oriental markets and some
supermarkets.

In a food processor fitted with the metal blade or in a blender blend all the ingredients, except the heavy cream, until smooth. With the motor running, add the cream in a stream and blend the sauce until smooth. Serve the sauce in a sauceboat or serving bowl.

Coconut Curd with Litchis and Mandarin Oranges

2 envelopes unflavored gelatin
¼ cup cold water
2 cups milk
1 cup heavy cream
⅓ cup sugar
a 3½-ounce can sweetened grated
   coconut, plus additional coconut
   for garnish

½ teaspoon vanilla
1 can litchis,* drained
   (see Suggestions)
1 can mandarin oranges, drained
   (see Suggestions)

*Available at Oriental markets.

Serves 4

In a small bowl sprinkle the gelatin over the cold water and let it soften for 15 minutes. Set the bowl over a pan of hot water and stir the mixture until the gelatin is dissolved.

In a saucepan combine the milk, heavy cream, and sugar, and bring the mixture to a boil, stirring. Add the grated coconut and bring to a boil. Stir in the gelatin mixture and the vanilla, pour the mixture into a bowl, and let it cool, stirring occasionally. Pour the mixture into a 9-inch square cake pan that has been rinsed with cold water but not dried, and chill it, covered, for 3 hours, or until set.

Run a thin knife around the edge of the pan, dip the pan in hot water for 30 seconds, and invert a plate over it. Invert the curd onto the plate, and with a sharp knife cut it into diamonds. Garnish each serving with some of the litchis, oranges, and additional coconut.

A VEGETARIAN LUNCH

Miso-Flavored Soup
Kasha Nut Loaf with Yogurt Sauce
Pineapple and Kiwi Compote

White Crozes-Hermitage, a dry California Chenin Blanc,
or other white wine of bold style but discreet flavor

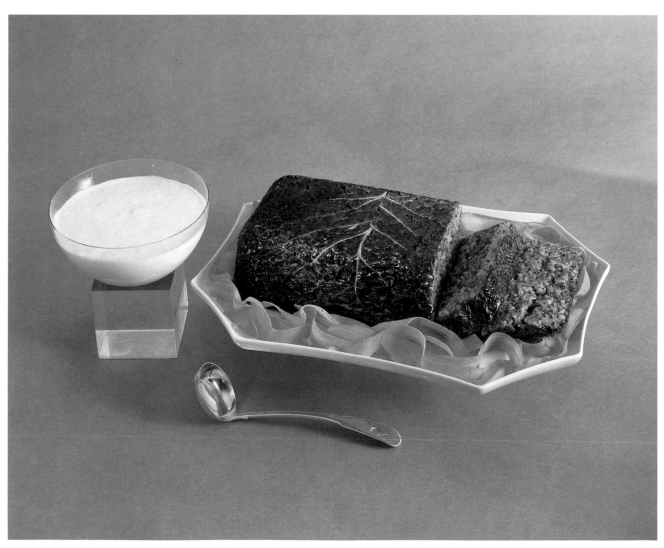

Kasha Nut Loaf with Yogurt Sauce

SUGGESTIONS

Some of the ingredients called for in this menu may not be familiar to you nor will they be available in the markets you frequent on a daily basis. Look for them in your nearest Oriental market and/or health-food store. Some pointers follow for when you get there:

Both *konbu* and *miso* are most readily obtainable in Japanese markets. *Konbu* is a seaweed that is processed into powder or sheets and is sold in packets. It is used primarily for flavoring. *Miso,* a paste derived from fermenting soybeans and rice, has a very distinct taste and, as a consequence, is used to flavor soups, dressings, and marinades. For the soup here you need dark *miso;* it is sold in jars or pouches, usually near the soy sauces.

Look for bean curd in the vegetable section of your Oriental market or your supermarket, and store it at home fully submerged in water in the refrigerator. (If exposed to the air, it develops an unpleasant crust.) And change the water daily.

Bean curd, because of its texture, is difficult to dice. The following method of cutting it should insure even pieces. With a cleaver or a large knife slice the bean-curd square horizontally into three ½-inch layers. Holding the square with your free hand so that it does not slip apart, then cut the square vertically at ½-inch intervals. Still holding the square as firmly together as possible, now cut it vertically at ½-inch intervals at right angles to the cuts you just made. You should now have bean curd in even dices.

Kasha, toasted buckwheat groats, is available at your supermarket or health-food store in boxes and comes ground coarse, medium, and fine. It is frequently used as a stuffing.

Unsalted unroasted cashews and *tahini,* sesame-seed paste, are also sold at health-food stores. If you buy *raw* cashews, roast them yourself in a preheated 350° F. oven until golden. Store *tahini,* once opened, in the refrigerator.

℘

Kasha Nut Loaf can be served either hot or cold. We're assuming you're serving it cold, so prepare it the day before and chill overnight. Slice with a very sharp knife.

Yogurt Sauce and the Pineapple and Kiwi Compote can both be prepared the morning of the day they are to be served. *Miso*-Flavored Soup can be readied in advance up to the point of adding the *miso.* Do that at the last minute.

Miso-Flavored Soup

Serves 4

4½ cups cold water
a 4-inch square of *konbu* (see
   Suggestions), wiped with a damp cloth
4 mushrooms, sliced thin
a 3-inch square of bean curd, rinsed and
   cut into ½-inch dice (see Suggestions)

¼ cup dark *miso* (see Suggestions)
1 tablespoon imported soy sauce
1 tablespoon Sercial Madeira,
   or dry Sherry or Port
salt
minced green scallion for garnish

In a saucepan combine the cold water and *konbu* and bring the water to just below a boil. Remove the pan from the heat and let stand for 10 minutes. Discard the *konbu,* add the mushroom slices and bean curd, and cook the mixture at a bare simmer for 5 minutes.

While the soup is simmering, put the *miso* in a small sieve, then submerge the sieve partially in the soup base, and with the back of a spoon force the *miso* through the sieve into the soup. It is important not to let the liquid come to a boil or the flavor of the broth will turn bitter. Add the soy sauce, Madeira, and salt to taste, and keep the soup at a bare simmer for 2 minutes. Divide the soup among heated bowls and garnish each bowl with some of the minced scallion.

Kasha Nut Loaf

Serves 4

1 cup coarse kasha (see Suggestions)
2 cups thinly sliced mushrooms
½ stick (¼ cup) unsalted butter
1 cup minced onion
½ cup minced celery
1 carrot, grated coarse
2 garlic cloves, minced
salt and pepper
6 large savoy cabbage leaves

1½ cups ground unsalted roasted cashews
3 large eggs, beaten lightly
¼ cup minced fresh parsley leaves
½ teaspoon dried thyme
½ teaspoon dried sage
½ teaspoon dried rosemary
carrot shavings for garnish
Yogurt Sauce (recipe follows)

Cook the kasha according to the package instructions and transfer it to a bowl.

In a heavy skillet cook the mushrooms in 2 tablespoons of the butter over moderately high heat, stirring, for 3 to 5 minutes, or until most of the liquid is evaporated, and add them to the kasha. Melt the remaining 2 tablespoons butter in the skillet over moderate heat, add the onion, celery, grated carrot, garlic, and salt and pepper to taste, and cook the vegetables, stirring, until the onion is softened. Add the vegetable mixture to the kasha, toss until well combined, and let the mixture cool.

In a large saucepan of boiling salted water blanch the cabbage leaves for 3 to 5 minutes, or until pliable. Drain in a colander, refresh the leaves under cold water, and pat them dry. Line a well-buttered loaf pan, 8½ by 4½ by 2½ inches, with as many of the leaves as are needed, smooth side down, to cover the bottom and sides, leaving enough overhang to fold over and cover the top of the loaf.

Add to the kasha mixture the cashews, eggs, parsley, the dried herbs, all ground in a spice grinder, and salt and pepper to taste, and combine the mixture well.

Spoon the mixture into the prepared loaf pan, rap the pan sharply on the counter to expel any air bubbles, and smooth the top. Fold the overhanging leaves over the mixture, and cover the top of the pan with a double layer of buttered foil. Put the loaf pan in a baking pan, pour enough hot water into the baking pan to reach halfway up the sides of the loaf pan, and bake the loaf in a preheated 350° F. oven for 1 hour, or until a skewer inserted in the center comes out clean. Let the loaf stand on a rack for 10 minutes. Run a thin knife around the inside of the loaf pan, invert a platter over the pan, and invert the loaf onto the platter. Blot up any liquid with paper towels. Garnish the platter with the carrot shavings and serve the loaf with Yogurt Sauce.

Yogurt Sauce

2 cups plain yogurt
3 tablespoons fresh lemon juice
1 tablespoon Dijon-style mustard

¼ teaspoon minced garlic (optional)
white pepper to taste
2 tablespoons *tahini* (see Suggestions)

Makes about 2¼ cups

In a glass bowl combine well all the ingredients.

Pineapple and Kiwi Compote

1 pineapple, peeled, cored, and cut
  into 1-inch cubes
4 kiwis, peeled and cut into 6 wedges

¼ cup fresh lemon juice
2 tablespoons sugar, or to taste

Serves 4

In a serving bowl combine all the ingredients, adding sugar to taste, and chill the compote, covered, for at least 1 hour.

CLASSY LUNCHES

For a classy lunch, an occasion is required—pretty linen, perhaps, a flower or two—some wonderful reason to serve something as special as halibut with Pernod hollandaise and Rhubarb Raspberry Tart.

There are other menus in this book that could easily be included in this selection. The menus that follow seemed to warrant such singular attention. When you taste them, you will know why.

A SEATED SPRING LUNCH

Halibut Steaks with
Broccoli Fennel Purée and Pernod Hollandaise
Romaine and Bibb Salad
Rhubarb Raspberry Tart

Macon-Villages or a light, crisp style of California Chardonnay

---

SUGGESTIONS

One of the best ways of keeping hollandaise warm is in a Thermos.

If your hollandaise separates while adding the butter, reconstruct it thus:

Remove the separated sauce from the pan.

In a clean pan put 2 teaspoons warm water. Put the pan over low heat and very gradually, drop by drop, start whisking the split sauce into the water. When you have incorporated about a third of the separated mixture, begin whisking in the remaining hollandaise in a stream.

If, on the other hand, your egg-yolk mixture looks lumpy, you have already overcooked it, and you will have to begin again.

You will see in the halibut recipe that in three instances—to store the hollandaise, to oven-poach the fish, and to cook the fennel—the ingredients are covered with a buttered sheet of wax paper, a device to prevent a skin from forming or to retain

Halibut Steaks with Broccoli Fennel Purée and Pernod Hollandaise

moisture while the ingredients cook. Simply cut the paper to fit the pan, butter the paper, and place it *flush* on the surface of the respective ingredients.

$\wp$

There are a certain number of steps involved in the preparation of this menu. To make it go smoothly and easily,

THE DAY BEFORE:

Prepare the *court bouillon*.

Make the tart shell and reserve at room temperature.

Cook the broccoli and fennel and purée. Reserve, covered, in the refrigerator.

THE DAY OF:

Finish the tart and store at room temperature.

Wash the lettuces and compose the salad an hour before serving.

Prepare the hollandaise and oven-poach the fish, both of which can be accomplished in half an hour's total cooking time.

Halibut Steaks with Broccoli Fennel Purée and Pernod Hollandaise

Serves 4

For the court bouillon (makes 9 cups)
⅔ cup chopped onion
⅔ cup chopped carrot
⅔ cup chopped celery
½ stick (¼ cup) unsalted butter
8 cups water
1 cup dry white wine

For the hollandaise
about 3 tablespoons Pernod
2 tablespoons dry white wine
1 tablespoon cold water
1 large egg yolk, beaten lightly
1 stick (½ cup) unsalted butter, cut
   into 8 pieces, at room temperature

2 teaspoons fresh lemon juice
salt to taste
cayenne and white pepper to taste
1 pound fennel bulb, chopped
⅔ stick (6 tablespoons) unsalted butter
1 pound broccoli, trimmed, separated
   into flowerets, and stalks peeled
   and sliced

four ½-inch halibut steaks, each weighing
   about 6 to 8 ounces

Make the court bouillon: In a large saucepan sauté the onion, carrot, and celery in the butter for 5 minutes. Add the water and wine and simmer the mixture for 20 minutes.

Make the hollandaise: In a small heavy saucepan combine 2 tablespoons of the Pernod and the wine and reduce the liquid over high heat to about 1 tablespoon. Remove the pan from the heat and add the cold water. Add the egg yolk and whisk the mixture until thick. Return the pan to the burner, and over low heat whisk in the butter, 1 piece at a time, lifting the pan occasionally to cool the mixture and making certain that each piece of butter is incorporated before adding the next. Whisk the sauce until it is thickened and add the lemon juice and 2 teaspoons of the remaining Pernod, or to taste, and salt, cayenne, and white pepper to taste. (The sauce will be thin enough to pour.) Keep the hollandaise warm, covered with a buttered round of wax paper, in a shallow pan of warm water.

In a saucepan cook the fennel slowly in 4 tablespoons of the butter, covered with a buttered round of wax paper and the lid, over moderately low heat for 10 minutes, or until just tender. Cook the mixture, uncovered, over moderate heat for 3 to 5 minutes, or until the excess liquid is evaporated. Keep the fennel warm, covered.

In a saucepan of boiling salted water cook the broccoli for 8 to 10 minutes, or until tender, and drain it.

In a food processor fitted with the steel blade or in a food mill chop the broccoli and fennel together in batches until it forms a coarse purée, transfer it to a bowl, and beat in the remaining 2 tablespoons butter, softened, and salt and pepper to taste. Keep the purée warm.

Arrange the halibut steaks in one layer in a lightly buttered large flameproof baking dish. Add enough *court bouillon* to just cover the steaks, bring the liquid to a boil, and oven-poach the fish, covered with a buttered sheet of wax paper, in a preheated 350° F. oven for 3 to 5 minutes, or until it just flakes when tested with a fork. Remove the skin and bones at the end of each steak.

Spread the purée decoratively on a platter, arrange the halibut steaks over the purée, and pour some of the hollandaise over the steaks. Serve the remaining hollandaise separately.

Romaine and Bibb Salad

Serves 4

1 garlic clove, halved
2 scallions, including the green tops,
   sliced thin
2 tablespoons minced fresh parsley leaves
1½ tablespoons wine vinegar
¼ teaspoon dried thyme
¼ teaspoon dried or 1 teaspoon chopped
   fresh basil

salt and pepper to taste
3 tablespoons olive oil
1 head Bibb lettuce, separated into leaves,
   rinsed, and patted dry
6 romaine leaves, rinsed, patted dry, and
   torn crosswise into 1-inch pieces

Rub a salad bowl with the cut sides of the garlic, and in it combine the scallions, parsley, vinegar, thyme, basil, and salt and pepper. Add the olive oil and stir to combine. Add the Bibb and romaine and toss the salad gently to coat the greens with the dressing.

Rhubarb Raspberry Tart

Serves 4 to 6

For the shell
1 recipe basic pastry
   (For suggestions on pastry making,
   see A Pastry Primer, page 202.)
raw rice for weighting the shell
1 large egg white, beaten lightly

For the glaze
3 tablespoons orange marmalade
2 tablespoons water

For the filling
3 clementines or small tangerines
1 pound rhubarb, trimmed and chopped,
   or 1 pound frozen rhubarb, thawed
a 10-ounce package frozen raspberries,
   thawed, drained, and forced through a
   sieve to remove the seeds
⅓ cup sugar
2½ tablespoons quick-cooking tapioca

Make the shell: On a floured surface roll the dough into a rectangle ⅛ inch thick, fit it into a 14-by-4½-inch rectangular flan form set on a baking sheet or a 9-inch tart pan with a removable fluted rim, and crimp the edge decoratively. Prick the bottom of the shell with a fork and chill the shell for 1 hour. Line the shell with wax paper, fill the paper with the raw rice, and bake in the lower third of a preheated 425° F. oven for 10 minutes. Remove the rice and paper carefully and brush the bottom of the shell with the beaten egg white. Bake the shell for 10 to 15 minutes more, or until it is golden, and let it cool on a rack. Remove the flan form carefully.

Make the filling: Grate enough rind from the clementines or tangerines to measure 2 teaspoons. Peel the clementines, cut the sections from the membranes, and reserve the fruit.

In a lightly buttered casserole combine all the filling ingredients, except clementines, as well as the grated rind, and bake the mixture, covered, in a preheated 400° F. oven for 20 to 25 minutes, or until the rhubarb is just tender. Let the filling cool slightly.

Spread the filling in the shell and bake the tart in the preheated oven for 20 minutes, or until it is puffed and just begins to bubble. Transfer the tart to a rack and let it cool completely.

To glaze and assemble the tart: In a small saucepan combine the marmalade and the water, bring the mixture to a boil, stirring, and simmer it for 1 minute. Strain the glaze through a fine sieve into a small bowl and keep it warm.

Arrange the clementines in decorative diagonal strips over the tart, and with a small pastry brush glaze the tart. Transfer the tart carefully with 2 spatulas to a serving plate and serve it at room temperature.

Rhubarb Raspberry Tart

A VARIETY OF VEGETABLES FOR LUNCH

Vegetable Sauté with Millet
Avocado, Spinach, and Red Leaf Lettuce Salad
Bananas Broiled with Brown Sugar
and Honey

ℰ

California White Zinfandel

SUGGESTIONS

Millet is a cereal grain and can most readily be found in natural-food or health-food stores. We use it in this menu as we would white rice, brown rice, or couscous.

Put the reserved broccoli stalks to good use by boiling them until tender, draining, then puréeing in a food processor. Add some butter and a little heavy cream and you've a lovely vegetable dish or garnish.

You can render broiled bananas perfectly irresistible with a generous dollop or two of Devon cream or *crème fraîche*. See page 13 for making your own *crème fraîche*.

ℰ

Have the greens for the salad washed and in the refrigerator. Similarly prepare the Yogurt Sauce and reserve.

Cook the vegetables for the sauté in advance and chill, well wrapped. Then it is just a matter of cooking the millet and, while it steams dry, sautéing the vegetables and making the sauce. Attention should be paid to sautéing the vegetables. You don't want to overcook them.

The trick to the sauce for the vegetables is not to overheat it. It's more prudent to make it at the last minute.

Bake, peel, and put the bananas in the gratin dish in advance. You will need only 5 minutes or so to finish them.

Vegetable Sauté with Millet

½ pound broccoli, separated into
    3-inch flowerets, reserving the stalks
    for another use (see Suggestions)
¼ pound Brussels sprouts, trimmed
8 cups water
2 cups millet
salt
½ cup olive oil
½ pound button mushrooms
½ pound baby carrots
pepper to taste
1 tablespoon minced garlic
1 cup dry white wine
⅓ cup white-wine vinegar

Tie together in a cheesecloth bag
1 tablespoon dried thyme
1 tablespoon dried basil
1½ teaspoons dried orégano
2 bay leaves
12 parsley stems

½ pound small white onions, blanched
    and peeled
3 cups water
3 tablespoons tomato paste
1 red bell pepper, cut into 1-inch pieces
½ stick (¼ cup) unsalted butter

Serves 4

In a large saucepan of boiling salted water cook the broccoli for 3 minutes, transfer it with a slotted spoon to a colander, and refresh it under running cold water. Pat the broccoli dry and put it on a plate. In the boiling water cook the Brussels sprouts for 6 minutes, drain them, and refresh them under running cold water. Put the sprouts on the plate with the broccoli, cover the vegetables with dampened paper towels and plastic wrap, and chill them until ready to use.

In a large saucepan combine the 8 cups water, millet, and 2 teaspoons salt. Bring the water to a boil, and cook the mixture over moderately high heat for 10 to 12 minutes, or until the millet grains just crack. Drain the millet in a large colander, rinse it under running cold water, and put the colander over a pan of boiling water. Steam the millet, covered, for 10 to 12 minutes, or until fluffy and dry. Remove the pan from the heat, add salt to taste, and let the millet stand, partially covered, until ready to use.

In a heavy 10-inch skillet, at least 2½ inches deep, heat the olive oil over moderately high heat until it is very hot. Add the mushrooms, carrots, and salt and pepper to taste and sauté the vegetables, tossing them, for 1 minute. Add the garlic and sauté the mixture, tossing it, for 30 seconds more. Add the wine, vinegar, and cheesecloth bag, and reduce the liquid over high heat to ¾ cup. Add the onions, the 3 cups water, the tomato paste, and salt and pepper to taste. Bring the liquid to a boil, and boil the mixture for 8 minutes, or until the onions are tender. Add the red pepper and cook for 3 minutes. Add the broccoli and sprouts and cook the mixture for 3 minutes more, or until the vegetables are heated through. Add salt and pepper to taste and transfer the sauté with a slotted spoon to a platter and keep it warm, covered.

Reduce the cooking liquid in the skillet over moderately high heat until it is thickened slightly. Swirl in the butter, 1 tablespoon at a time, making certain that each piece is incorporated before adding the next, and cook the mixture until the butter is just incorporated.

The butter must not get hot enough to liquefy. (Should the butter liquefy, meaning rise to the surface, transfer the sauce to a blender and blend to recombine. Add any remaining butter to the blender, then carefully, over low heat, warm the sauce.) Strain the sauce into a bowl, pressing hard on the cheesecloth bag, and spoon it over the vegetables or serve it separately. Transfer the millet to a heated serving bowl and serve it with the vegetables.

Avocado, Spinach, and Red Leaf Lettuce Salad

Serves 4

2¼ cups Yogurt Sauce (page 65)
1 avocado, peeled and cut into ⅓-inch cubes
2 tablespoons fresh lemon juice
½ pound spinach leaves, washed well and patted or spun dry

½ pound red leaf lettuce, rinsed and patted or spun dry
1 small red onion, sliced thin
minced fresh parsley leaves

Have Yogurt Sauce ready in a serving bowl.

In a small bowl toss the avocado with the lemon juice.

Tear the spinach and lettuce into bite-size pieces and divide the greens among chilled plates. Arrange the avocado and the onion over the greens, sprinkle the salads with the parsley, and serve with the sauce.

Bananas Broiled with Brown Sugar and Honey

Serves 4

4 ripe but firm unpeeled bananas
4 teaspoons fresh lemon juice
4 teaspoons honey

4 teaspoons light brown sugar
a total of 6 teaspoons unsalted butter, cut into bits

Bake the bananas on a baking sheet in a preheated 350° F. oven for 10 minutes, or until the skins turn black. Cut off the ends of each banana and peel them, leaving a narrow strip on the underside of each to help retain its shape. Put the bananas in a gratin dish, sprinkle each with 1 teaspoon each of the lemon juice, honey, and brown sugar, and 1½ teaspoons of the butter. Put the dish under a preheated broiler about 6 inches from the heat for 3 to 5 minutes, or until the bananas are golden brown.

Chapter Two

Options Al Fresco

ↄ

GRILLS AND SALADS

We're firm believers in making the most of the fair-weather months. The living, as an old song suggests, should be easy. The food should be light. The most serious thinking should take place around the fire and center around the exact time per pound for beef on the grill!

With that said, and whether you are cooking out or simply taking cool food onto the terrace or porch, do make the living easy for yourself. Prepare all you can ahead of time. In menus such as Intimations of India (page 87) or A Cool Light Lunch Italian Style (page 91) that means the *entire* meal. What could be more conducive to a good time other than, perhaps, the pure congeniality that comes from grilling a beautiful cut of beef, such as the fillet on page 78 or the London Broil on page 103, that is then served, respectively, with such imaginative pleasures as grilled onions and Smoked Mozzarella and Sun-Dried Tomato Salad.

A STYLISH SUMMER GRILL

Bacon-Wrapped Scallops
Grilled Beef Fillet with Blue Cheese Sauce
Buttered Sugar Snap Peas
Grilled Red Onions
Escarole, Orange, and Walnut Salad
Snowballs with Hot Chocolate Sauce

California Barbera

SUGGESTIONS

You will be hard-pressed not to dazzle your family or guests with this superlative menu. From start to finish the ingredients called for are superb. As a menu, they make one of those simple classic collections. Furthermore, you have the night air and stars working for you. Here is a cookout to remember.

You want the timing of this menu right. To make it easy, try the following:

Make the snowballs and freeze them. Prepare the Chocolate Sauce in advance as well and keep in a covered glass jar in the refrigerator. Before serving, put the jar, uncovered, into a pan of hot water, and let the sauce soften in the water bath.

After marinating the scallops, wrap them in the bacon, skewer, then reserve in the refrigerator, well covered, until ready to grill.

Make Blue Cheese Sauce well in advance, refrigerate, but serve at room temperature.

A MINI-SCHEDULE:

At least 2 hours in advance of grilling, start marinating the onions.

About 1 hour in advance of grilling, start the fire. Begin the fillet, and when it is done (and standing) put the onions and scallops on the grill. Then prepare the salad and peas. By the time the scallops and onions are done, about 15 minutes later, all the components of the main course will also be complete.

Grilled Red Onions, Buttered Sugar Snap Peas, and
Grilled Beef Fillet with Blue Cheese Sauce

Bacon-Wrapped Scallops

Serves 6 as an hors d'oeuvre

For bourbon marinade
  (makes about 1 cup)
¼ cup bourbon
¼ cup soy sauce
¼ cup firmly packed light brown sugar
¼ cup minced scallion
¼ cup Dijon-style mustard

1 teaspoon salt
a dash Worcestershire sauce
pepper to taste

15 large sea scallops, halved
10 slices of very lean bacon, cut
  crosswise into thirds

Make bourbon marinade: In a bowl combine well all the marinade ingredients, stirring to dissolve the sugar. Add the scallops and let them marinate, tossing them occasionally, for 1 hour.

Wrap a piece of bacon around each scallop half and thread the scallops onto three 13-inch metal skewers, leaving ¼ inch between scallops. Grill the scallops over a bed of glowing coals about 3 inches from the heat, turning them twice, for 10 to 15 minutes, or until the bacon is crisp. Slide the scallops off the skewers onto a heated platter and serve.

Grilled Beef Fillet

Serves 6 to 8

a 5½-pound beef fillet, trimmed, tied
  crosswise at 1-inch intervals, and
  patted dry

salt and pepper
2 tablespoons softened unsalted butter
Blue Cheese Sauce (recipe follows)

Sprinkle the beef with salt and pepper to taste and rub it with the butter. Grill the fillet over a bed of glowing coals about 3 inches from the heat, turning it, for 20 to 25 minutes for rare meat. Transfer the fillet to a cutting board, let it stand for 15 minutes, and remove the string. Cut the fillet into ½-inch slices and serve it with the Blue Cheese Sauce.

Blue Cheese Sauce

Makes about 1½ cups

¾ cup Sercial Madeira
2 tablespoons minced shallot
1 cup heavy cream
½ cup brown stock (page 155) or
  canned beef broth

6 ounces blue cheese, crumbled and
  softened
1 stick (½ cup) unsalted butter, softened
salt to taste
cayenne to taste
paprika to taste

In a saucepan combine the Madeira with the shallot and reduce the mixture over moderately high heat to about 2 tablespoons. Add the cream and the stock or broth, and reduce the liquid over moderate heat to about 1 cup.

In a bowl cream together the cheese and the butter until smooth. Whisk the cheese mixture, a little at a time, into the saucepan and simmer the sauce for 3 minutes. Strain the sauce through a fine sieve into a bowl and add salt and cayenne to taste. Sprinkle the sauce with paprika before serving.

Buttered Sugar Snap Peas

1½ pounds sugar snap peas or snow peas, strings removed
2 tablespoons unsalted butter

salt and pepper
fresh lemon juice to taste

Serves 6

In a saucepan of boiling salted water blanch the sugar snap peas or snow peas for 5 seconds, drain them, and refresh them under running cold water. Pat the peas dry.

In a skillet melt the butter over moderately high heat, add the peas, and toss them until heated through. Season the peas with salt and pepper to taste and transfer them to a heated serving bowl. Sprinkle the peas with lemon juice to taste and toss.

Grilled Red Onions

1 tablespoon fresh thyme or
    1 teaspoon dried
salt and pepper

½ cup olive oil
6 red onions, halved lengthwise

Serves 6

In a large dish combine the thyme, salt and pepper to taste, and oil. Add the onions and let them marinate, turning them, for at least 2 hours.

Arrange the onions in a basket grill or on a 12-by-8½-inch hinged broiling rack fitted with a slide or directly on the grill. Grill the onions over a bed of glowing coals about 3 inches from the heat, brushing them lightly with the oil, for 6 to 8 minutes on each side, or until tender and browned.

Escarole, Orange, and Walnut Salad

Serves 6

2 tablespoons fresh lemon juice
1 tablespoon Dijon-style mustard
salt and pepper
½ cup olive oil
1 head of escarole, torn into bite-size
    pieces

2 oranges, peeled, halved lengthwise,
    and cut crosswise into ½-inch slices
½ cup coarsely chopped walnuts

In a salad bowl combine the lemon juice, mustard, and salt and pepper to taste, add the oil in a stream, beating, and beat the dressing until emulsified. Add the escarole, oranges, and walnuts, and toss the salad well with the dressing.

Snowballs

Serves 6

1 quart Vanilla Custard Ice Cream
    (page 29)
2 cups canned sweetened shredded
    coconut

1½ cups Hot Chocolate Sauce
    (recipe follows)

Scoop out 6 balls of the ice cream with a 2½-inch ice-cream scoop dipped in hot water, and freeze them on a baking sheet lined with wax paper for at least 1 hour. On another baking sheet toast the coconut in a preheated 350° F. oven, stirring occasionally, for 10 to 12 minutes, or until golden, and let cool. Roll the ice-cream balls in the coconut until well coated and freeze them on the baking sheet for at least 30 minutes. Serve the snowballs with the chocolate sauce.

Hot Chocolate Sauce

*Makes
1½ cups*

8 ounces semisweet chocolate,
    cut into small pieces

½ cup strong freshly brewed coffee
Cognac to taste (optional)

In the top of a double boiler set over hot water melt the chocolate with the coffee and keep the sauce warm over hot water. If the sauce becomes too thick, thin it with more coffee, water, or Cognac.

COOKING OUT ON THE FOURTH

Soft-Shelled Crab Sandwiches
Barbecued Smoked Pork Butt
Yankee Doodle Salad   Chopped Vegetable Salad
Blueberry Walnut Roll
Raspberry Ice Cream

California Johannisberg Riesling

SUGGESTIONS

You used to always be able to tell when soft-shelled crabs had come into season. You could see it in the expressions on the faces of certain individuals leaving the fish market. They looked flat-out contented but anticipatory. They had waited a year, one whole year; spring had returned and with it that spell, that short-lived moment in spring, when the crabs actually shed their shells and are delectable and sweet prior to the growing of a new harder outer cover. Now, thanks to technology, the soft-shelled-crab season is longer; the crabs are generally bigger and often less tender. We suggest buying only the smaller ones, and the fresher the better.

Do not be intimidated by cleaning crabs. Begin by holding the crab *behind* its claws. It's not folklore—a crab can deliver a nasty pinch! Remove the head and gills as directed in the recipe. The apron is the flap of matter on the white underside of the crab. It must be removed in full. If not apparent to you, ask someone in the fish market to point out the apron. After cleaning the crabs, be sure to wash them very well in cold water, then pat dry.

Unfortunately, the bacteria salmonella exists in most environments and can proliferate when the following factors—food, temperature, and moisture—combine over time. As a consequence, and particularly when it is hot, do not let *any* food remain unrefrigerated for any amount of time.

If the jelly roll cracks while you are rolling it, cover up the cracks with a *generous* dusting of powdered sugar. It's an age-old solution, and a pretty one, too.

Both salads and both desserts can be made in full 1 day in advance.

The pork should also start marinating that same day, which leaves only the marinating of the crabs and the grilling of them and the pork for the day of the cookout. That leaves a lot of time to celebrate!

Soft-Shelled Crab Sandwiches

Serves 8

8 live soft-shelled crabs, each weighing
   about 2 to 3 ounces (see Suggestions)
⅓ cup vegetable oil
2 garlic cloves, sliced
1 teaspoon Old Bay seasoning
   (available at some fish markets) or
   ⅛ teaspoon cayenne combined with
   ½ teaspoon sweet paprika and a
   ¼–½ teaspoon assorted dried herbs

salt and pepper
1 stick (½ cup) unsalted butter
2 tablespoons fresh lemon juice
2 tablespoons minced fresh parsley leaves
1 tablespoon minced shallot
8 English muffins, split in half and
   flattened with a rolling pin

Rinse the crabs under running cold water. With scissors cut off the heads about ¼ inch behind the eyes and cut off the white gills. Peel back the aprons, cut them off, and rinse the crabs again. Pat the crabs dry. In a dish combine the oil, garlic, Old Bay seasoning, and salt and pepper to taste. Add the crabs, turn them to coat them with the mixture, and let them marinate, covered and chilled, for at least 2 hours.

In a small saucepan combine the butter, lemon juice, parsley, shallot, and salt and pepper to taste. Heat the mixture over moderately low heat, stirring, until the butter is just melted, and remove the pan from the heat.

Drain the crabs, put them in a grill basket or arrange them directly on the grill, and cook them over glowing coals for 3 to 5 minutes on each side, or until they turn red. Grill the muffins, turning them once, until crisp and lightly browned, and brush the split sides with the herbed butter. Sandwich 1 crab between 2 muffin halves.

Barbecued Smoked Pork Butt

Serves 8

a 1¾-pound boneless smoked pork butt
1 cup bourbon marinade (page 78)*

watercress sprigs for garnish

*Increase bourbon to ⅓ cup, Worcestershire to
   1 teaspoon; use 1 onion, chopped (no scallion).

In a deep saucepan cover the pork with cold water, bring the water to a boil, and simmer for 5 minutes. Transfer the pork to a cutting board, remove the netting or casing, and return the pork to the pan. Simmer it, covered partially, adding more boiling water as necessary to keep it covered, for 45 minutes. Transfer the pork to a bowl just large enough to hold it, and pierce it all over with a sharp, thin skewer.

Pour the bourbon marinade over the pork, turn it to coat it well, and let it marinate, covered and chilled, turning it occasionally, overnight.

Barbecued Smoked Pork Butt and Chopped Vegetable Salad

Remove the pork from the marinade and pour the marinade into a small saucepan. Bring the marinade to a simmer on a grill over glowing coals and keep it at a simmer. Grill the pork, turning it and basting it with the marinade, for 20 to 30 minutes, or until browned and crisp. Slice the pork thin and arrange the slices on a heated platter. Brush any remaining marinade on the slices and garnish the platter with the watercress sprigs.

Yankee Doodle Salad

Serves 8

12 ounces tiny shell macaroni
1 cup Quick Mayonnaise (page 20)
⅓ cup sour cream
⅓ cup snipped fresh dill
1 tablespoon Dijon-style mustard
1 garlic clove, minced

1½ cups chopped radishes
1½ cups cooked corn
1 cup chopped green bell pepper
cayenne to taste
salt and pepper
additional snipped fresh dill for garnish

In a kettle of boiling salted water cook the macaroni for 6 to 8 minutes, or until tender. Drain it in a colander, and refresh it under running cold water. Drain the macaroni well.

In a large salad bowl combine the mayonnaise, sour cream, dill, mustard, and garlic. Add the macaroni and the radishes, corn, and green pepper with cayenne and salt and pepper to taste. Combine well and chill, covered, for at least 2 hours or overnight.

Just before serving, sprinkle the salad with the additional snipped dill.

Chopped Vegetable Salad

Serves 8

1 pound green beans

4 large stalks of celery, cut into ½-inch pieces (to measure 1 cup)

1 red onion, cut into ½-inch pieces (to measure 1 cup)

¾ pound tomatoes, cut into ½-inch pieces

¾ pound seedless cucumbers, cut into ½-inch pieces

For the dressing

⅔ cup olive oil

⅓ cup minced fresh parsley leaves

¼ cup fresh lemon juice

salt and pepper

In a saucepan of boiling salted water cook the beans for 6 to 8 minutes, or until just tender. Drain them in a colander, and refresh them under running cold water. Trim the beans and cut them into ½-inch pieces. In a salad bowl combine the beans, celery, red onion, tomatoes, and cucumber.

Make the dressing: In a small bowl combine the dressing ingredients with salt and pepper to taste.

Toss the salad with the dressing and chill it, covered, for at least 1 hour.

Blueberry Walnut Roll

Makes one 15-inch roll

4 large egg yolks

½ cup granulated sugar

1 cup walnuts, ground fine

3 tablespoons all-purpose flour

1 teaspoon double-acting baking powder

1 teaspoon vanilla

½ teaspoon cinnamon

4 large egg whites at room temperature

a pinch of cream of tartar

a pinch of salt

1 cup blueberry preserves or jam

confectioners' sugar for dusting the roll

Raspberry Ice Cream as an accompaniment (recipe follows)

Line a buttered 15½-by-10½-by-1-inch jelly-roll pan with wax paper, and butter and flour the paper. In a large bowl beat the egg yolks with ¼ cup of the sugar until the mixture is thick and lemon-colored and stir in the walnuts, the flour sifted together with the baking powder, the vanilla, and the cinnamon. In a bowl beat the egg whites with the cream of tartar and salt until they hold soft peaks. Add the remaining ¼ cup sugar, 1 tablespoon at a time, beating, and beat the whites until they hold stiff peaks. Stir one-fourth of the whites into the yolk mixture, fold in the remaining whites gently but thoroughly, and pour the mixture into the prepared pan, spreading it evenly. Bake the cake in a preheated 350° F. oven for 15 to 18 minutes, or until it shrinks from the sides of the pan. Invert it onto lightly buttered wax paper, and peel off the top sheet of wax paper. While the cake is still hot, beginning with a long side roll it up, lifting it with the wax paper, and let it cool, rolled.

When fully cool, unroll the roll, spread it with the preserves, and roll it up again. Transfer the roll, seam side down, to a plate, chill it, covered, for at least 1 hour, and sift the confectioners' sugar over it. Serve the roll with Raspberry Ice Cream.

Raspberry Ice Cream

Makes about 1 quart

two 10-ounce packages frozen raspberries
    packed in light syrup, thawed
1 to 2 tablespoons fresh lemon juice
3 cups half-and-half

½ cup sugar
4 large egg yolks
1 teaspoon vanilla

In a food processor fitted with the metal blade or in a blender purée the berries and force the purée through a fine sieve into a bowl. Stir in the lemon juice to taste and chill the purée, covered, for 2 hours.

In a heavy saucepan combine the half-and-half and sugar, and scald the mixture over moderate heat, stirring. In a bowl beat the egg yolks until light and thick, pour in the half-and-half mixture, whisking, and transfer the custard to the pan. Cook the custard over moderately low heat, stirring, until it coats the spoon. Transfer it to a metal bowl set in a bowl of ice, and stir in the vanilla. Let the custard cool, covered with a round of wax paper, chill it for 2 hours, then stir in the raspberry purée. Freeze the mixture in an ice-cream freezer according to the manufacturer's instructions.

INTIMATIONS OF INDIA

Chilled Indian Yogurt Drink
Curried Turkey Chutney Salad in Cantaloupe Halves
Assorted Condiments
Tomato Onion Sandwiches with Coriander Butter
Black Walnut Rose-Water Cake

California Chenin Blanc

SUGGESTIONS

The chilled Indian yogurt drink known as *lassi* in India, and very popular there, must be served ice-cold.

Curry mayonnaise is a delicious dipping sauce for steamed shrimp and/or mussels.

Coriander, also called *cilantro* or Chinese parsley in some markets, has a distinct, strong flavor. If you are unfamiliar with it, start by using less than is called for in the recipe.

Black walnuts are available at specialty-foods stores and some supermarkets. Because the wood of the black walnut tree is highly valued for making furniture and rare due to a recent blight, the nuts are expensive. Feel free to substitute regular walnuts. Rose water is most often found in pharmacies.

The components of this entire menu can be prepared in advance. Reserve combining the salad and making the sandwiches for the morning before the luncheon.

Chilled Indian Yogurt Drink

2 teaspoons cuminseeds
2 cups plain yogurt
2 cups ice water

1½ teaspoons salt
8 ice cubes

Makes about 5 cups

In a small dry skillet toast the cuminseeds over moderate heat, stirring, until they crackle and turn several shades darker. In a coffee or spice grinder grind the seeds.

In a blender or food processor fitted with the metal blade blend the yogurt, ice water, cuminseeds, and salt. With the motor on high add the ice cubes, 1 at a time, and blend the mixture until smooth.

Pour the drink into iced glasses and serve immediately.

Curried Turkey Chutney Salad in Cantaloupe Halves

Serves 6

a 3½- to 4-pound turkey breast, thawed if frozen
1 onion, halved and stuck with a clove
1 carrot, sliced
1 stalk of celery, sliced

Tie together in a cheesecloth bag
6 sprigs of parsley
1 bay leaf
1½ teaspoons minced fresh thyme or ½ teaspoon dried

1 cup Quick Mayonnaise (page 20)
2 teaspoons curry powder
¾ cup drained and chopped mango chutney

1½ cups thinly sliced celery
salt and pepper
3 cantaloupes, halved and seeded

For the condiments
½ pound toasted cashews
½ pound lean bacon, cooked and crumbled
¼ pound golden raisins
¼ pound chopped pitted dates
½ cup minced scallion

Combine
¼ cup chopped green bell pepper
¼ cup chopped red bell pepper

In a kettle bring to a boil enough water to cover the turkey breast with the onion, carrot, celery stalk, and the herbs in a cheesecloth bag. Add the turkey breast and boil it for 1 minute. Reduce the heat and poach the turkey, partially covered, at a bare simmer, skimming off the froth that rises to the surface, for 40 minutes, or until tender. Let the turkey cool completely in the liquid, discard the skin and bones, and cut the turkey into ½-inch cubes.

In a small bowl combine well the mayonnaise, curry powder, and chutney.

In a large bowl combine the turkey, the 1½ cups celery, curry mayonnaise, and salt and pepper to taste. Serve the curried turkey salad in the cantaloupe halves with the condiments in separate bowls.

Curried Turkey Chutney Salad in Cantaloupe Halves, Assorted Condiments,
and Tomato Onion Sandwiches with Coriander Butter

Tomato Onion Sandwiches with Coriander Butter

Makes 18 sandwiches

For coriander butter (makes about 1 cup)
1½ sticks (¾ cup) unsalted butter, softened
5 tablespoons minced fresh coriander leaves
1 tablespoon fresh lemon juice
¾ teaspoon ground coriander seed
salt and pepper

18 very thin slices of homemade-type white bread
18 very thin slices of whole-wheat bread
5 large plum tomatoes, cut into ¼-inch slices
2 small red onions, sliced thin

Make coriander butter: In a bowl cream together all the coriander-butter ingredients with salt and pepper to taste and let the butter stand, covered, for at least 1 hour.

With a 2½-inch cutter cut out 18 rounds from the white bread slices and 18 rounds from the whole-wheat slices. Spread the rounds with the coriander butter, top each white round with a tomato slice and an onion slice, then top with the whole-wheat slices.

Black Walnut Rose-Water Cake

Makes 2 cakes

1 stick (½ cup) unsalted butter, softened
1½ cups sugar
2 large eggs
1½ cups all-purpose flour
½ teaspoon double-acting baking powder
¼ teaspoon salt

⅓ cup milk
3 tablespoons brandy
1 cup ground black walnuts or ground walnuts (see Suggestions)
1 tablespoon rose water (see Suggestions)

In a large bowl cream together the butter and sugar until light and fluffy. Beat in the eggs, 1 at a time, beating well after each addition.

Into another bowl sift together the flour, baking powder, and salt and stir the mixture into the sugar mixture alternately with the milk and brandy. Stir in the walnuts and rose water. Divide the mixture between 2 buttered and floured loaf pans, 7½ by 3½ by 2 inches, and bake in the middle of a preheated 350° F. oven for 40 minutes, or until a cake tester comes out clean. Let the cakes cool in the pans on a rack for 10 minutes. Turn the cakes out onto the rack when cool, wrap in plastic wrap or foil to rest overnight.

A COOL LIGHT LUNCH ITALIAN STYLE

Cold Escarole Soup
Agnolotti Salad
Honeydew Spears and Almond Anise Biscotti

Bardolino

SUGGESTIONS

A lovely light lunch, with a beautiful theme of green throughout. Perfect for a hot, still summer day.

The pasta salad is made with filled *agnolotti*, little crescent-shaped pastas, or *tortellini*, both available frozen and sometimes fresh in many markets. If you want the fun of making your own, see pages 94–97.

Do try to find fresh mozzarella. Its texture is very unlike that of the commercial packaged variety—much more tender and toothsome.

If you don't have time to make *biscotti*, you can find good ones in Italian bakeries and Italian food stores.

Try *biscotti* in the morning, with a big cup of *café au lait*.

This menu is a do-aheader's dream. Everything can be readied in advance. In fact, remember this menu as a good candidate for a picnic. Take the soup in a wide-mouthed Thermos, the salad in a well-covered container, the cookies in a cookie tin, and the melon in a jar. You'll be traveling light, and deliciously.

If you are making your own *agnolotti*, know that the finished filled pasta can be stored in the refrigerator for no longer than 1 day or be frozen. Also, prepare them in stages: day 1, the filling; day 2, the dough; day 3, the forming.

Cold Escarole Soup

Makes 7 cups, serving 6

½ cup thinly sliced scallion
2 tablespoons olive oil
5 cups chicken stock (page 154) or
   canned chicken broth
1½ pounds escarole, well washed and
   shredded thin (enough to measure
   6 cups loosely packed)
1 tablespoon chopped fresh basil leaves
   or 1 teaspoon dried

1½ teaspoons minced fresh thyme
   or ½ teaspoon dried
2 garlic cloves
6 tablespoons minced fresh parsley leaves
½ teaspoon salt
pepper to taste

In a large saucepan cook the scallion in the oil over moderate heat, stirring, for 2 minutes, or until softened. Add the stock or broth, and bring the liquid to a boil. Stir in the escarole, the basil, and thyme, and simmer the soup for 10 minutes, or until the escarole is tender.

In a mortar with a pestle mash the garlic with 2 tablespoons of the parsley and the salt.

Remove the saucepan from the heat, stir in the garlic mixture, the remaining parsley, and salt and pepper to taste, and let the soup cool completely.

Agnolotti Salad

Agnolotti Salad

Serves 6

6 quarts water

1 tablespoon salt

1½ pounds prepared fresh or frozen
agnolotti or *tortellini* (available at
specialty-foods shops and some
supermarkets) or you can make your
own *agnolotti*; see A Pasta Primer,
pages 94–97.

1½ pounds whole-milk mozzarella,
preferably fresh, cut into ¼-inch slices
and halved

1 pint cherry tomatoes, halved

1 cup *niçoise* olives

For the dressing

¼ cup white-wine vinegar

2 tablespoons minced fresh basil leaves
or 2 teaspoons dried

1 teaspoon salt

¾ to 1 cup olive oil

In a kettle bring to a boil the water and add the salt. Stir in the *agnolotti*, and boil them,
stirring several times, for 3 to 5 minutes, or until *al dente*. Drain the pasta in a colander,
refresh it under cold running water, and drain it well.

In a large bowl combine the pasta, mozzarella, tomatoes, and olives.

Make the dressing: In a small bowl combine all the ingredients for the dressing, except the
oil. Add the oil in a stream, beating, and beat the dressing until emulsified. Add the dressing
to the salad and toss gently.

Honeydew Spears

Serves 6

1 honeydew melon, halved lengthwise,
seeded, and rind removed

Halve the melon halves crosswise, and cut the quarters into thin spears.

A PASTA PRIMER

Even though there are some very fine fresh pastas on the market in such compelling varieties as tomato, whole-wheat, spinach, and now even pumpkin, it is fun and a challenge to undertake making one's own fresh pasta. And, anyway, everyone ought to try making it once, just to see what it's like!

Here is a basic recipe for plain egg noodle dough and one for spinach dough. Either of them may be used for all sizes of noodles or for stuffed pastas or *lasagne* and *cannelloni*.

To demystify the undertaking, the process itself is really only threefold:

1. a dough must be made,
2. the dough must be kneaded and rolled, then
3. the dough must be cut.

The best machine for making pasta is the simple hand-cranked pasta machine, which is available at reasonable cost at almost any kitchenware or department store. Your work table should have a good "lip" on which to clamp the pasta machine.

Noodle Dough

Makes about 1 pound

2 cups fine semolina flour* or
   all-purpose flour
2 large eggs or more,* beaten lightly
1 tablespoon olive oil
1 tablespoon warm water
¾ teaspoon salt

*If you are using semolina flour, add half of *another* large egg, beaten lightly.

To make the dough by hand: Onto a work surface or into a large shallow bowl sift the flour and make a well in the center. Put the remaining ingredients into the well and, working from the inside of the well, incorporate the flour into the wet ingredients. Combine the mixture well and if necessary add more warm water, several drops at a time, to form a firm ball of dough. Knead the dough on a lightly floured surface for 5 minutes, or until smooth. Then let it rest, covered with an inverted bowl, for 1 hour.

To make the dough in a food processor: In a processor fitted with the metal blade combine the flour and salt. Add the eggs and combine well. With the motor running add the oil and enough of the warm water, several drops at a time, and process until a ball of dough forms. Then, with the motor still running, knead the dough in the bowl for 15 seconds. Dust the dough with flour and let it rest, covered with an inverted bowl, for 1 hour.

To Roll Pasta Dough

While the dough is resting, set the smooth rollers of a hand-operated pasta machine at the highest number. (The rollers will be wide apart.)

When the dough has fully rested, divide it into 6 pieces and flatten 1 piece into a rough rectangle. Cover the remaining pieces with an inverted bowl or plastic wrap.

Dust the dough with flour and start to feed it through the rollers. Fold the dough in half and feed it through the rollers 8 or 9 more times, folding it in half each time and dusting it with more flour to prevent it from sticking. You are preparing the dough for rolling by repeatedly pressing it between the rollers.

Now turn the dial that adjusts the width between the rollers down one notch and feed the dough through the rollers *without* folding it in half. You are in the process of rolling a longer and longer sheet of dough. Be careful that it does not rip, and if it does, seal the edges of the tear together firmly.

Continue to feed the dough through the rollers, without folding it, turning the dial down one notch each time, until the lowest or second-lowest notch is reached. The pasta will be a long sheet 4 or 5 inches wide and about $1/16$ inch thick. Transfer the sheet to a lightly floured baking sheet or tray. Continue to roll the remaining pieces.

Now, to make noodles, put the sheets of dough through either the narrow or wide cutting rollers. Hang the noodles over the backs of kitchen chairs for about 20 minutes. Then either cook them in a large pot of boiling salted water until *al dente* (only a few minutes) or toss the noodles in cornmeal and store in plastic bags.

NOTE: If you are making filled pasta—*agnolotti, tortellini,* or *capelletti*—with either plain or spinach noodle dough, roll out, cut, and fill *only one sheet of dough at a time* to prevent the remaining sheets from drying out.

NOTES ON MAKING AND FILLING
SPINACH AGNOLOTTI

What follow are the 3 steps involved in making *agnolotti*, crescent-shaped filled pasta, as called for on page 93. The filling is only a suggestion. If you have your own preferred cheese filling, for example, by all means use it.

Spinach Noodle Dough

Makes about ½ pound (about 80 finished, filled agnolotti)

¼ pound spinach, rinsed and
   tough stems removed
1 cup all-purpose flour
1 large egg, beaten lightly

¼ teaspoon salt
1½ teaspoons olive oil
about 1 tablespoon warm water

In a saucepan cook the spinach in the water clinging to its leaves over moderately high heat, covered, for 2 to 3 minutes, or until wilted. Drain, squeeze the spinach dry, and chop it.

To make the dough by hand: Onto a work surface or into a large shallow bowl sift the flour and make a well in the center. Add the egg and salt and, working from the inside of the well, incorporate some of the flour into the wet ingredients. Add the spinach and continue to incorporate the ingredients, adding the water, several drops at a time, until a firm ball of dough forms. Depending upon the amount of moisture in the flour you are using, you may have to add additional water, but do so sparingly. Knead the dough on a lightly floured surface for 5 minutes. As with plain noodle dough, let spinach dough rest, covered with an inverted bowl or plastic wrap, for 1 hour.

To make the dough in a food processor: In a processor fitted with the metal blade combine the dry ingredients. Add the spinach and the egg and combine well. With the motor running add the oil and enough of the warm water, several drops at a time, and process until a ball of dough forms. Then knead, with the motor running, the dough in the bowl for 15 seconds. Dust the dough with flour and let it rest, covered with an inverted bowl, for 1 hour.

While the spinach noodle dough rests, make

Makes about ¾ cup

Veal and Walnut Filling

2 ounces boneless lean veal, cubed

2 ounces prosciutto, chopped

1 tablespoon olive oil

2 tablespoons Marsala

¾ cup coarsely ground walnuts

½ cup freshly grated Parmesan

2 large egg yolks

1 tablespoon milk

freshly grated nutmeg to taste

salt and pepper

In a skillet sauté the veal and prosciutto in the oil over moderately high heat for 2 minutes. Add the Marsala, reduce the liquid until it is almost evaporated, and let the mixture cool.

In a food processor fitted with the metal blade grind the veal mixture fine in batches, transfer it to a bowl, and stir in the remaining ingredients with salt and pepper to taste.

Following the directions on page 95, roll spinach noodle dough, then make *agnolotti* with it and Veal and Walnut Filling as directed below.

To Make Agnolotti

Working with 1 sheet of dough at a time cut out as many rounds as possible with a 2-inch cutter. Save the scraps of dough to use in a soup.

Put ½ teaspoon of the filling in the center of each round. Moisten each round lightly with water halfway around the edge, fold it in half over the filling, and press the edges together firmly, sealing them. As they are shaped arrange the *agnolotti* in one layer on floured dish towels. They may be cooked immediately or left to dry, turning them once or twice on the towels, for 3 hours.

Store the *agnolotti* in a plastic bag in the refrigerator for up to 1 day. Or freeze them in airtight containers.

Pasta Possibilities

With the probability of homemade pasta now ever at the ready, whip up your own *pasta al pesto* (page 166) or pasta with Spinach *Pesto* (page 165), or noodles with uncooked tomato sauce (page 104). The possibilities are endlessly pleasing.

Almond Anise Biscotti

Makes about 65 cookies

1 stick (½ cup) unsalted butter, softened
¾ cup sugar
3 large eggs
2 tablespoons brandy
1 tablespoon grated lemon rind
3 cups all-purpose flour

2 teaspoons double-acting baking powder
½ teaspoon salt
1 cup blanched, toasted, and coarsely
  ground almonds
1 tablespoon aniseeds

In a large bowl cream the butter with the sugar until light and fluffy. Beat in the eggs, 1 at a time, beating well after each addition, the brandy, and lemon rind. Into a bowl sift together the flour, baking powder, and salt, and stir the mixture into the butter mixture with the almonds and aniseeds. Chill the dough, covered, for 1 hour.

Halve the dough and on a lightly buttered baking sheet shape each half into a log 16 by 2½ by ¾ inches. Bake the loaves in the middle of a preheated 350° F. oven for 15 to 20 minutes, or until lightly golden. Let the loaves cool on the baking sheet, cut them diagonally into ½-inch slices with a serrated knife, and arrange the slices close together in one layer on lightly buttered baking sheets. Bake the slices in the middle of the 350° F. oven for 15 to 20 minutes, or until dry. Transfer the cookies to racks, let them cool, and store them in airtight containers.

Honeydew Spears and Almond Anise Biscotti

A TERRACE BUFFET DINNER

Clams on the Half Shell
Smoked Mozzarella and Sun-Dried Tomato Salad
London Broil with Green Peppercorn Butter
Spaghetti Squash with Vegetables in Tomato Sauce
Assorted Seasonal Fruit

California Cabernet Sauvignon of a full, ripe year—
1978 or 1981, for instance

SUGGESTIONS

This terrace buffet menu is very definitely a special one, filled with the best of summer and her generous offerings.

Sun-dried tomatoes are available in bulk or packed in oil in jars. If you are using the latter, drain them before adding them to the olive-oil combination.

Be sure to serve a large crusty French bread with this meal, particularly to soak up the good dressing on the salad.

Mustard Chive Dressing is superb on a salad of cooked ham, chopped celery, a little red onion, grated smoked Gouda or Gruyère, spinach leaves, and *rugola* or endive.

Peperoncini are smallish green Italian peppers packed in jars. They are hot. Use fewer of them if that will serve the general good.

Like all good summer menus, short of the actual grilling of the meat, everything in this buffet can be prepared in advance. Be sure to have the London Broil at room temperature before grilling as well as the butter.

Clams on the Half Shell

*Enough for
6 servings*

36 cherrystone or other medium-size
   hard-shelled clams

lemon wedges

Scrub the clams with a stiff brush under running cold water, discarding any that have cracked shells or that are not shut tightly. Hold each clam in the palm of the hand with the hinge against the heel of the palm. Force a strong, thin, sharp knife between the shells, cut around the inside edges to sever the connecting muscles, and twist the knife slightly to open the shells. Release the clams completely from the shells, being careful not to spill any of the liquor, and discard the top shells. Arrange the clams on their bottom shells on a bed of crushed ice on a shallow platter and serve them with the lemon wedges.

Smoked Mozzarella and Sun-Dried Tomato Salad

Serves 6

⅔ cup olive oil
¼ cup dry white wine

Tie together in a cheesecloth bag
12 peppercorns
½ teaspoon dried basil
½ teaspoon dried orégano
1 bay leaf

½ teaspoon salt
¼ pound sun-dried tomatoes
   (available at specialty-foods stores)

½ pound smoked mozzarella, cut
   into cubes
6 large romaine leaves
½ pound small white radishes, peeled
2 red bell peppers, cut crosswise into
   ¼-inch rings
1 cup pitted black olives
1 cup drained bottled *peperoncini*
   (Tuscan peppers, see Suggestions)
parsley sprigs for garnish
Mustard Chive Dressing
   (recipe follows)

In a heavy saucepan bring to a boil the olive oil and the wine with the cheesecloth bag and the salt over moderate heat, stir in the tomatoes, and simmer the mixture for 7 minutes, or until the tomatoes are softened. Remove the pan from the heat, let the mixture stand, covered, for 30 minutes, and discard the cheesecloth bag. Drain the mixture, reserving the steeping liquid as a salad dressing, and in a bowl combine the tomatoes with the mozzarella.

Arrange the romaine leaves decoratively on a platter, top them with the tomato-mozzarella mixture, and arrange the radishes, red peppers, olives, and *peperoncini* decoratively over it. Garnish the platter with the parsley and serve the salad with the dressing.

Smoked Mozzarella and Sun-Dried Tomato Salad

Mustard Chive Dressing

¼ cup Dijon-style mustard
1 large egg yolk
3 tablespoons fresh lemon juice
1 garlic clove, minced

salt and pepper
1 cup olive oil
¼ cup snipped fresh chives

Makes about
1½ cups

In a bowl combine the mustard, egg yolk, lemon juice, garlic, and salt and pepper to taste. Add the oil in a stream, whisking, and whisk the dressing until thick. Stir in the chives and additional salt and pepper as needed.

London Broil with Green Peppercorn Butter

Serves 6

For the marinade
1 cup dry red wine
½ cup olive oil
1 scallion, minced
3 garlic cloves, minced
1 teaspoon salt
½ teaspoon black peppercorns, crushed
½ teaspoon dry mustard
½ teaspoon dried thyme
6 parsley sprigs
1 bay leaf

a 3-pound top round steak, about
  2 inches thick

For green peppercorn butter
  (makes about ½ cup)
1 stick (½ cup) unsalted butter, softened
¼ cup chopped fresh parsley leaves
1 tablespoon drained green peppercorns
  packed in water (available at specialty-
  foods stores)
1 teaspoon fresh lemon juice
½ teaspoon Dijon-style mustard,
  or to taste
Worcestershire sauce to taste

1½ tablespoons black peppercorns,
  crushed
salt

Make the marinade: In a large bowl combine all the ingredients. Add the steak, coating it completely, and let it marinate, covered and chilled, turning it occasionally, for at least 2 hours or overnight.

Make green peppercorn butter: In a food processor fitted with the metal blade blend all the peppercorn-butter ingredients until combined well. Transfer the butter to a bowl and chill it, covered, for at least 1 hour or overnight.

Drain the meat, pat it dry, and press the crushed black peppercorns into it. Let the meat stand for 30 minutes, season it with salt, and grill it over glowing coals for 8 to 10 minutes on each side for rare meat. Transfer the meat to a cutting board, brush it with some of the green peppercorn butter, and let it stand for 15 minutes. Cut the London broil into thin slices across the grain at a 45-degree angle and dot the slices with more of the butter.

Spaghetti Squash with Vegetables in Tomato Sauce and
London Broil with Green Peppercorn Butter

Spaghetti Squash with Vegetables in Tomato Sauce

Serves 6

For uncooked tomato sauce
 (makes about 3 cups)
2 cups peeled, seeded, and coarsely
 chopped tomato
½ cup olive oil
1 cup firmly packed fresh basil leaves,
 minced
1 cup firmly packed fresh parsley leaves,
 minced
3 tablespoons freshly grated Parmesan

3 garlic cloves, or to taste, minced
2 teaspoons salt

a 3½-pound spaghetti squash
2 cups broccoli flowerets
½ pound carrots, cut into 1-inch pieces
1 zucchini
½ cup minced scallions
3 tablespoons olive oil
salt and pepper

Make uncooked tomato sauce: In a bowl combine well all the sauce ingredients and let the sauce stand at room temperature, covered, for at least 1 hour.

Bake the squash in a preheated 350° F. oven for 1¼ to 1½ hours, or until it can be pierced easily with a metal skewer. Let stand for 15 minutes and halve lengthwise. Remove the seeds carefully and with a fork scrape the flesh into a large bowl.

While the squash is baking, prepare the vegetables. In a large saucepan of boiling salted water boil the broccoli for 1 minute, or until just tender. Remove with a slotted spoon, transfer it to a bowl of ice water, and let cool.

In the saucepan boil the carrots for 5 to 6 minutes, or until just tender. Transfer them to the ice water, and let cool.

In the saucepan boil the zucchini for 3 minutes, or until just tender. Transfer it to the ice water, and let cool. Drain the vegetables. Trim the zucchini, halve it lengthwise, and cut it crosswise into ¼-inch slices.

In a large skillet cook the scallions in the oil over moderate heat, stirring, until softened. Add the drained vegetables with salt and pepper to taste, and heat, tossing, for 3 to 4 minutes, or until heated through. Add the vegetable mixture to the spaghetti squash with the tomato sauce, toss, and transfer the mixture to a serving dish. Serve warm or at room temperature.

PICNICS

The beauty of a picnic is that it is food that can be taken anywhere. The beauty of a really good picnic is that it is *interesting* food that can *easily* be taken anywhere. The picnic menus that follow fit that bill to a T. We've A German Picnic, entirely doable ahead, that offers turnovers with a sauerkraut-and-sausage filling. We've A Chinese Picnic that combines homemade shrimp rolls and tea eggs. They are nutritious and inventive and light-years away from your sandwich in a bag with a few broken chips. Another outing offers spicy food, new American-style chicken wings with two savory sauces, and flavorful accompaniments—perfect for a Memorial or Labor Day gathering.

In fact, you could plan to have one or all of these menus on your back lawn or porch over the course of the summer. You'll find this kind of food is enjoyable anywhere.

A GERMAN PICNIC

Sauerkraut and Sausage Turnovers
Dilled Green Beans
Apples   Green Grapes

Beer

SUGGESTIONS

You can very easily substitute frozen puff pastry, available now in the frozen foods sections of most supermarkets, for flaky turnover dough. Follow the instructions on the package for softening and rolling the puff pastry, then cut it, make turnovers, and bake them as described in the recipe.

If you have a garden, you're accustomed to having your own supply of green beans on hand, which probably means you have your own supply of dilled green beans on hand! They make a good, to say nothing of healthful, hors d'oeuvre.

Make the filling and reserve in the refrigerator up to 2 days in advance.

THE DAY BEFORE:

Make dough and chill it. Fill and bake turnovers.

Sauerkraut and Sausage Turnovers

Serves 4

For flaky turnover dough

2½ cups all-purpose flour with additional
   flour for rolling the dough
1 teaspoon salt
½ cup cold vegetable shortening, cut
   into bits
1 large egg yolk, beaten lightly
1 tablespoon fresh lemon juice
¼ to ½ cup ice water
½ stick (¼ cup) cold unsalted butter

For the filling

½ pound sauerkraut (preferably not
   canned), drained and rinsed
1 onion, sliced very thin
3 tablespoons unsalted butter
¼ cup dry white wine

½ cup chicken stock (page 154) or
   canned chicken broth
1 tablespoon white-wine vinegar
2 teaspoons light brown sugar
½ bay leaf
salt and pepper to taste
¼ pound red-skinned potatoes, scrubbed
   and diced
¼ pound *kielbasa* (Polish sausage,
   available at meat markets and some
   supermarkets), diced
1 tablespoon Dijon-style mustard

egg wash: 1 egg yolk beaten with
   2 tablespoons water
2 teaspoons coarse salt, or to taste
1½ to 2 teaspoons caraway seeds

Make flaky turnover dough: Into a bowl sift together the flour and salt, add the vegetable shortening, and blend the mixture until it resembles coarse meal. Add the egg yolk, lemon juice, and enough of the ice water to make a soft dough, and form the dough into a ball. Dust the dough with flour and roll it into a 16-by-7-inch rectangle on a floured surface. Turn the rectangle so that a short side faces you and dot the top two-thirds of it with butter, pressing the butter gently into the dough. Fold the lower third of the rectangle up to meet the center of the buttered portion, fold the top of the rectangle over the bottom, and chill the dough, covered, for 30 minutes.

Sprinkle the dough with flour, turn it seam side down so that an open side faces you, and roll it into a 16-by-7-inch rectangle. With a short side of the rectangle facing you, fold in the short sides of the dough to meet the center of the rectangle and fold the top half over the bottom half. Chill the dough, covered, for 15 minutes. Roll out and fold the dough in the same manner one more time and chill it, covered, until ready to use.

Make the filling: In a saucepan of boiling salted water cook the sauerkraut for 10 minutes, drain it, and refresh it under running cold water. Squeeze out the water. In a non-aluminum skillet sauté the onion in the butter over moderately high heat, stirring, for 5 to 7 minutes, or until golden brown. Add the sauerkraut, wine, stock or broth, vinegar, sugar, bay leaf, and salt and pepper. Bring the liquid to a boil, stirring occasionally, and simmer the mixture, covered, stirring occasionally, for 30 minutes. Add the potatoes and *kielbasa*, and cook

Sauerkraut and Sausage Turnovers, Dilled Green Beans,
Shrimp Rolls, and Tea Eggs

the mixture, covered, over moderately low heat, stirring occasionally, for 15 minutes, or until the potatoes are tender. Transfer the filling to a bowl and let it cool. Discard the bay leaf and stir in the mustard.

To make turnovers: Divide the flaky turnover dough into fourths, roll one-fourth into an 8-inch square on a floured surface, and trim it to form a 7½-inch square. Arrange one-fourth of the filling on a diagonal half of the pastry, leaving a ½-inch border. Brush the edges lightly with the egg wash, and fold the pastry over the filling to form a triangle. Crimp the edges with a fork, brush the pastry with the egg wash, and cut two ¼-inch slits in the top for steam vents. Transfer the turnover carefully with a large spatula to a dampened baking sheet. Make 3 more turnovers with the remaining filling and dough in the same manner.

Sprinkle the turnovers with the coarse salt and caraway seeds, bake them in the upper third of a preheated 450° F. oven for 12 to 15 minutes, or until the pastry is golden, and let them cool on racks. Transfer the turnovers to portable containers.

Dilled Green Beans

Serves 4

½ pound green beans, trimmed
1 garlic clove, crushed
1 teaspoon red pepper flakes
8 sprigs of dill
¼ teaspoon dill seeds

¼ teaspoon mustard seeds
3 tablespoons sugar
1 cup cider vinegar
1 tablespoon salt
1 cup water

In a large bowl of ice water let the beans soak for 30 minutes and drain them. In a saucepan of boiling salted water simmer the beans for 5 minutes, drain them, and refresh them under running cold water. Drain the beans well.

In a shallow heatproof bowl combine the beans, garlic, pepper flakes, dill sprigs, dill seeds, and mustard seeds. In a saucepan combine the sugar, vinegar, salt, and water, bring the mixture to a boil, and pour it over the beans. Let the mixture cool and chill it, covered, overnight. Transfer the beans with the liquid to a portable container.

A CHINESE PICNIC

Shrimp Rolls
Tea Eggs
Carrots   *Snow Peas*
Kumquats

୬

Gewürztraminer d'Alsace

Shrimp Rolls

Serves 4

For the filling
¼ cup vegetable oil
½ pound shrimp, shelled, deveined, and
    chopped
1 stalk of celery, chopped
2 mushrooms, chopped
⅓ cup chopped red bell pepper
2 scallions, chopped
1 teaspoon peeled and minced gingerroot
red pepper flakes to taste
2 tablespoons minced fresh parsley leaves

1½ cups cooked rice
2 tablespoons fresh lemon juice
2 tablespoons Dijon-style mustard
1½ teaspoons dark brown sugar
2 tablespoons soy sauce
salt

8 egg-roll wrappers, thawed if necessary
egg wash: 1 egg yolk beaten with
    2 tablespoons water
¾ cup vegetable oil

Make the filling: In a skillet heat the oil over moderately high heat until hot and in it cook the shrimp, celery, mushrooms, red pepper, scallions, gingerroot, and pepper flakes, stirring, for 3 to 4 minutes, or until the shrimp turn pink. Transfer the mixture to a bowl and stir in the remaining filling ingredients with salt to taste. Let the filling cool.

Arrange 1 of the egg-roll wrappers so that a corner faces you, put ⅓ cup of the filling in a crosswise strip 1 inch from the corner facing you, and brush the edges of the wrapper with the egg wash. Roll up the wrapper until the filling is just enclosed, turn in the sides, and continue to roll up the wrapper tightly to enclose the filling completely. Cover the roll with a dampened dish towel. Make 7 more rolls in the same manner.

In a skillet heat the oil over moderately high heat until hot but not smoking. Fry the shrimp rolls in batches, turning them, for 5 to 7 minutes, or until golden brown. Transfer the rolls with tongs to paper towels to drain. Let the rolls cool on racks.

SUGGESTIONS

Egg roll wrappers are to be found in Oriental markets. Although they can be frozen, don't keep them in the freezer too long—and don't buy too large a supply—because they dry out quickly.

Simply blanch separately carrots, sliced, and snow peas, strings removed, in water to cover until just tender.

Kumquats, with their bright orange color and citrusy flavor, may not be easy to come by. If you do find them, eat them skin and all. If you can't, substitute clementines or tangelos, ugli fruit, or for a real zing, small pieces of candied ginger.

∽

Make the filling for the shrimp rolls 1 day in advance of serving, but roll and deep-fry them the day they are to be served. Be sure to allow enough time for them to drain well on paper towels.

If you make the eggs in advance, which you can do, simply store the eggs in the shells in a plastic bag overnight. If you are particularly fond of the flavor of tea, let them stand in the soaking liquid overnight. Be advised: the flavor the next day will be pronounced.

Tea Eggs

Serves 4

4 large eggs
8 cups water
1 tablespoon salt
4 slices of gingerroot, each the size
　of a quarter, crushed
a 3-inch cinnamon stick

2 whole star anise
3 tablespoons rice vinegar
2 tablespoons soy sauce
⅓ cup Formosa oolong tea leaves
　or black tea leaves

In a saucepan cover the eggs with 1 inch cold water, bring the water to a boil, stirring occasionally, and simmer the eggs, continuing to stir them occasionally, for 10 minutes. Rinse the eggs under running cold water, drain them, and crack the shells lightly all over but do not remove the shells.

In a saucepan combine the 8 cups water, salt, gingerroot, cinnamon stick, star anise, vinegar, and soy sauce. Bring the liquid to a boil and stir in the tea leaves. Simmer the mixture for 20 minutes, add the eggs, and simmer them for 45 minutes. Remove the pan from the heat and let the eggs cool in the tea mixture. (See Suggestions for storing the eggs.) Rinse the eggs and remove the shells. Transfer the eggs to a portable container.

A SPICY PICNIC

Spicy Hot Chicken Wings
Creamy Cucumber Dill Sauce   Apricot Mustard Sauce
Grilled Marinated Flank Steak
Curried Rice Salad   Sliced Tomatoes
Lemon Walnut Squares
Raisin Chocolate-Chunk Cookies
Green Grapes

∽

New York State Seyval Blanc
California Zinfandel

SUGGESTIONS

Summer get-togethers, unlike the more formal ones winter weather seems to inspire, have a very engaging way of starting, say, with six guests invited. Before you know it, the list is hovering at twelve and still climbing. As you know, some recipes lend themselves to doubling and tripling. Others do not. Fortunately, the ones that follow do. So, if you find yourself having a gala—number of guests unknown—double the chicken-wing recipe, whip up an extra batch of cookies or two, and lay in lots of fresh fruit.

Dividend: With only two slight exceptions, this menu constitutes perfect finger food. Instead of the sliced tomatoes, you could serve cherry tomatoes, and rather than arranging the rice salad on a bed of lettuce leaves, you might put small amounts of the salad down the center rib of each leaf.

Do not store Lemon Walnut Squares in the refrigerator. They will absorb moisture. Instead, wrap them in plastic wrap and keep at room temperature.

∽

Prepare Spicy Hot Chicken Wings up to 1 day ahead and keep covered and chilled. Reheat in one layer in a preheated 400° F. oven for 15 to 20 minutes.

Apricot Mustard Sauce can be made several days in advance of serving, whereas Creamy Cucumber Dill Sauce only 1 day ahead. Keep both covered and chilled.

Curried Rice Salad can also be prepared 1 day ahead. To serve, adjust the spices accordingly, once the salad has come to room temperature.

Spicy Hot Chicken Wings

Serves 4 to 6

1¾ pounds chicken wings
flour seasoned with salt and cayenne for
   dredging the wings
vegetable shortening for deep-frying
1 tablespoon red pepper flakes
½ stick (¼ cup) unsalted butter, melted

1 tablespoon fresh lemon juice
1 teaspoon Tabasco, or to taste
salt

Dipping sauces (recipes follow)
Creamy Cucumber Dill Sauce
Apricot Mustard Sauce

Cut off the tips of the chicken wings, reserving them for making stock (page 154). If desired, halve the wings at the joints, and dredge them in the flour, shaking off the excess. In a deep fryer or a kettle fry the wings in 3 batches in 2 inches of the hot shortening (375° F.), turning them, for 10 minutes, transferring them with a slotted spoon as they are fried to paper towels to drain.

   In a blender grind the pepper flakes to a powder and blend in the butter, lemon juice, Tabasco, and salt to taste. Transfer the chicken wings to a large bowl, toss them with the butter mixture, and pack them in a portable container. Serve with the dipping sauces.

Creamy Cucumber Dill Sauce

*Makes about
1½ cups*

1 cucumber, peeled, seeded, and minced
½ cup sour cream
½ cup plain yogurt

1 tablespoon snipped fresh dill
salt and white pepper

In a fine sieve set over a small bowl let the cucumber drain for 1 hour. Press out any remaining juice from the cucumber, and discard. In the bowl combine the cucumber with the remaining ingredients and salt to taste. Pour into a container and keep chilled.

Apricot Mustard Sauce

*Makes about
½ cup*

½ cup apricot preserves

2 tablespoons Dijon-style mustard

Force the preserves through a fine sieve into a small bowl and stir in the mustard. Transfer the sauce to a portable container and serve it at room temperature.

*Curried Rice Salad, Spicy Hot Chicken Wings with sauces,
and Grilled Marinated Flank Steak*

Grilled Marinated Flank Steak

Serves 4 to 6

For the marinade
1½ cups beer
4 scallions, minced
⅓ cup vegetable oil
3 tablespoons soy sauce
2 tablespoons light brown sugar
1 tablespoon peeled and minced
   gingerroot

2 garlic cloves, minced
1 teaspoon salt
1 teaspoon red pepper flakes

a 1½- to 1¾-pound flank steak
crusty white bread and flavored butter
   as accompaniments

Make the marinade: In a large dish combine all the marinade ingredients, add the steak, turning to coat it with the marinade, and let it marinate, covered and chilled, turning it occasionally, overnight or for up to 3 days.

Drain the steak, pat it dry, and grill it over a bed of glowing coals or broil it on the rack of a broiler pan under a preheated broiler about 2 inches from the heat for 5 minutes on each side for medium-rare meat. Let the steak cool on a cutting board and slice it diagonally across the grain into very thin slices. Serve with crusty white bread, sliced thin, and flavored butter.

Curried Rice Salad

Serves 4 to 6

5 quarts water
salt
1 cup long-grain rice
4 large mushrooms, sliced thin
1 tablespoon vegetable oil
2 small zucchini, scrubbed, quartered
   lengthwise, and cut into ½-inch slices
3 scallions, minced
⅓ cup minced red bell pepper
2 tablespoons minced fresh parsley leaves

For the dressing
1 tablespoon medium-dry Sherry
3 tablespoons fresh lemon juice
1 teaspoon salt
⅛ teaspoon cayenne
1 teaspoon curry powder
⅓ cup vegetable oil

romaine lettuce leaves for garnish

In a large saucepan bring the water to a boil with the salt to taste. Sprinkle in the rice, stirring until the water returns to a boil, and boil it for 10 minutes. Drain the rice in a large colander, and rinse it under running water. Set the colander over a pan of boiling water and steam the rice, covered with a dish towel and the lid, for 15 minutes, or until fluffy and dry. Spread the rice on a platter and let it cool completely.

In a skillet cook the mushrooms in the oil over moderate heat, stirring, for 2 minutes, add the zucchini and scallions, and cook the mixture, stirring, for 1 minute. In a large bowl combine the mixture well with the rice, red pepper, and parsley.

Make the dressing: In a small bowl combine all the ingredients except the oil. Add the oil in a stream, whisking, and whisk the dressing until emulsified.

Pour the dressing over the rice mixture and toss the salad well. Transfer it to a large portable container, garnish it with the lettuce, and serve it at room temperature.

Lemon Walnut Squares

¾ stick (6 tablespoons) cold unsalted
   butter, cut into bits
⅓ cup firmly packed light brown sugar
1 cup plus 3 tablespoons all-purpose flour
½ cup finely ground walnuts
2 large eggs

1 cup granulated sugar
2 tablespoons fresh lemon juice
2 teaspoons grated lemon rind
½ teaspoon double-acting baking powder
1 tablespoon confectioners' sugar,
   or to taste

Makes 9 squares

In a bowl blend the butter, brown sugar, 1 cup of the flour, and the walnuts until the mixture resembles coarse meal. Press all but ½ cup of the mixture evenly into the bottom of a 9-inch square baking pan, and bake the crust in a preheated 350° F. oven for 15 to 20 minutes, or until golden around the edges.

In a bowl beat the eggs lightly and stir in the granulated sugar, the remaining flour, the lemon juice, the lemon rind, and the baking powder. Pour the mixture over the baked crust, sprinkle it evenly with the remaining ½ cup walnut mixture, and bake the dessert in the oven for 25 to 30 minutes, or until the top is golden brown. Let the dessert cool in the pan on a rack and cut it into 3-inch squares. Sift the confectioners' sugar over the squares and transfer them to a portable container. If you've made these squares in advance, see Suggestions for storing them.

Lemon Walnut Squares and Raisin Chocolate-Chunk Cookies

Raisin Chocolate-Chunk Cookies

Makes about 48 cookies

2 sticks (1 cup) unsalted butter, softened
1 cup firmly packed light brown sugar
½ cup granulated sugar
1 teaspoon vanilla
2 large eggs
2 cups all-purpose flour combined
    with 1 teaspoon salt and 1 teaspoon
    baking soda

1 cup raisins plumped in boiling
    water to cover for 45 minutes and
    drained well
8 ounces semisweet chocolate,
    chopped coarse

In a large bowl cream the butter, add the brown sugar and granulated sugar, a little at a time, beating, and beat the mixture until fluffy. Stir in the vanilla and add the eggs, 1 at a time, beating well after each addition. Beat in the flour mixture in 3 batches, combine the mixture well, and stir in the raisins and chocolate. Chill the dough for 30 minutes, or until just firm. Put rounded teaspoons of the dough 3 inches apart on baking sheets. Bake the cookies in a preheated 375° F. oven for 8 minutes, or until the edges are golden, and transfer them with a spatula to racks to cool. The cookies keep in airtight containers with a slice of bread (to keep the cookies moist and chewy) for several days.

Chapter Three

Simple Suppers

∽

LENTEN ELECTIVES

We use the title Lenten Electives to mean menus without meat—not vegetarian menus *per se*—just meatless ones. And, while most Americans have always been meat and potato lovers, we are now coming around to the realization that a meal without meat can be not only interesting but significantly more varied as well as good for the health.

Note the variety among the menus of Lenten Electives: Spinach and Feta Loaf, Eggplant Soufflé with Red Pepper, Tomato, and Coriander Sauce, Meatless Moussaka, Mushroom-Stuffed Eggs in Mornay Sauce. These dishes are light by comparison to a steak dinner and innovative.

For an imaginative supper, try these menus. They'll make you feel good.

GRECIAN FLAVORS TO SAVOR

Spinach and Feta Loaf
Avgolemono Sauce
Celery, Radish, and Olive Salad
Kir-Poached Pears

Achaia Clauss Santa Helena

SUGGESTIONS

You want to be careful not to overheat *avgolemono* sauce as the eggs in it will curdle. Think of this light lemony sauce as a nice change from hollandaise and use it for green vegetables, as well—such as steamed broccoli spears or fresh asparagus.

Boxes of *phyllo* leaves, also spelled *filo* and called, in some instances, *strudel dough*, are available in most supermarkets in the frozen-baked-goods section. Follow the directions on the package for thawing the dough.

Also, if you have never worked with *phyllo* dough before you will discover very quickly that the sheets dry out almost immediately if not kept between sheets of wax paper and covered with a dampened dish towel. Be sure to keep the dough damp and pliable.

Phyllo is a boon to the kitchen adventurer, lending itself to quick starters, such as spinach triangles, and replacing puff pastry in some more complicated hors d'oeuvres. The dough keeps in the freezer for months.

Any type of pear is recommended for the dessert—Bosc, Bartlett, Anjou—and be sure they are firm. Otherwise they will collapse while poaching.

Grecian Flavors to Savor is one of those "finds" as a menu insofar as it paves the way to a good time. *You can serve everything at room temperature.* Therefore, go right ahead and prepare in advance in full as much of the menu as possible: the sauce, the components of the salad, the pears, even the filling for the loaf. All that will remain is the assembling and baking of the loaf on the day you intend to serve it. And even that can be done early.

Spinach and Feta Loaf with Avgolemono Sauce
and Celery, Radish, and Olive Salad

Spinach and Feta Loaf

Serves 6

1 large onion, minced
3 garlic cloves, minced
1¾ sticks (¾ cup plus 2 tablespoons) unsalted butter
four 10-ounce packages frozen spinach, thawed, drained, squeezed dry, and chopped
2 large eggs
¼ pound feta, crumbled fine

½ cup freshly grated Parmesan
¼ cup minced fresh parsley leaves
¼ teaspoon freshly grated nutmeg, or to taste
salt and pepper
10 sheets of *phyllo* (see Suggestions)
3 hard-boiled large eggs
Avgolemono Sauce (recipe follows)

In a large skillet sweat the onion and garlic in ¾ stick of the butter, covered, over moderately low heat, stirring occasionally, for 8 to 10 minutes, or until the onion is soft. Add the spinach and cook the mixture over moderate heat, stirring, for 3 minutes, or until the excess liquid is evaporated. In a food processor fitted with the metal blade blend the spinach mixture and the eggs to a coarse purée. In a bowl combine the purée, feta, Parmesan, parsley, nutmeg, and salt and pepper to taste.

Melt the remaining butter and let it cool to lukewarm. Stack the *phyllo* between sheets of wax paper and cover with a lightly dampened dish towel. Remove 1 sheet of *phyllo*, lay it on a sheet of wax paper, **and** brush it gently with some of the melted butter. Top the *phyllo* with another sheet **and** continue to butter and layer the *phyllo* in the same manner, using a total of 8 sheets. Fit the buttered *phyllo* crosswise into a buttered loaf pan, 9 by 5 by 3 inches, so that the edges hang over the long sides of the pan. Halve the remaining 2 *phyllo* sheets lengthwise, butter and stack them in the same manner, and fit them into the loaf pan lengthwise so that the edges hang over the short sides.

Spread half of the spinach filling in the pan, packing it, and arrange the hard-boiled eggs lengthwise down the center. Spread the remaining spinach filling over the eggs, packing it, and fold the overhanging *phyllo* over the filling to enclose it completely. Brush the top with some of the melted butter and bake the loaf in the middle of a preheated 375° F. oven for 1 hour and 10 minutes to 1 hour and 15 minutes, or until it is flaky and golden. Let the loaf cool in the pan on a rack for 10 minutes and then invert it onto a platter. Let the loaf cool to room temperature and serve it, sliced, with the sauce.

Avgolemono Sauce

Makes about 2 cups

½ cup dry white wine
½ cup water
3 large eggs

⅓ cup fresh lemon juice
salt and pepper

In a heavy saucepan combine the wine and water and bring the liquid to a boil. Simmer the liquid for 3 minutes and keep it warm.

In a bowl beat the eggs until thick and foamy and add the lemon juice, drop by drop, beating. Add the wine mixture in a stream, beating, and beat the mixture until combined well. Season the sauce with salt and pepper to taste, return it to the pan, and cook it over moderately low heat, stirring constantly, until thickened, *but do not let it boil.* Strain the sauce through a fine sieve into a serving bowl and let it cool to room temperature, covered. Stir the sauce before serving.

Celery, Radish, and Olive Salad

Serves 6

5 cups celery, strings discarded and stalks cut into 2-by-¼-inch matchsticks
2 cups thinly sliced radishes
1½ cups Kalamata or other Greek-style olives, pitted and cut into slivers

3 tablespoons wine vinegar
salt and pepper
½ cup olive oil
2 tablespoons snipped fresh dill

In a salad bowl combine the celery, radishes, and olives. In a food processor fitted with the metal blade or in a blender blend the vinegar with salt and pepper to taste, with the motor running add the oil in a stream, and blend the dressing until emulsified. Pour the dressing over the salad, add the dill, and toss the salad well.

Kir-Poached Pears

Serves 6

4 firm pears (see Suggestions)
the juice of 1 lemon
2½ cups dry white wine

½ cup *crème de cassis* (black currant liqueur)
½ cup sugar

Peel, core, and halve each pear lengthwise. Quarter each half lengthwise, dropping the pieces into a bowl of cold water acidulated with the lemon juice.

In a saucepan combine the remaining ingredients, bring the liquid to a boil, stirring until the sugar is dissolved, and simmer the syrup for 5 minutes. With a slotted spoon transfer the pears to the syrup, and poach them at a simmer, covered, for 10 to 20 minutes, or until slightly translucent and tender. With the slotted spoon transfer the pears to a bowl, bring the syrup to a boil, and reduce it over moderately high heat to about 2 cups. Pour the syrup over the pears and let the dessert cool to room temperature. The pears may be served at room temperature or chilled.

A SOUFFLÉ-AND-SALAD SUPPER

Eggplant Soufflé with Red Pepper, Tomato,
and Coriander Sauce
Shredded Romaine with Garlic Vinaigrette
Pita Bread
Assorted Fruit

Rioja from Spain, Corbières from France,
or a hearty red jug from California

SUGGESTIONS

There are dishes and various cunning culinary presentations, but the soufflé stands in a league by itself. It is magic; it is defiance of gravity; it is short-lived but splendid; and its success depends upon nothing more or less than the beating and folding in of egg whites. See page 124 for pointers.

Either Poached Pears in Orange Syrup (page 329) or Sliced Oranges with Rum (page 163) would be a good candidate for a prepared dessert, an easy one at that, for this menu.

ᔆ

You can prepare the soufflé through the point of spooning it into the prepared dish up to 2 hours in advance. Chill, uncovered. Do watch the clock, however: 2 hours is the maximum time the mixture should stand because of the egg whites.

The sauce can be made 1 day in advance and kept covered and chilled.

Eggplant Soufflé with Red Pepper, Tomato, and Coriander Sauce
and Shredded Romaine with Garlic Vinaigrette

NOTES ON EGG WHITES

Always start with egg whites at room temperature to achieve maximum volume, and always beat them in a spanking-clean bowl, preferably a copper one, but failing that a metal one. Never use a plastic bowl as it can retain a greasy film, which will impede the whites' inflation. Glass bowls are also not recommended because the whites tend to "weep," meaning exude liquid, in them.

A pinch of cream of tartar and/or salt helps stabilize the foam as the whites are beaten. Contrary to popular myth, neither the cream of tartar nor salt do anything to increase the volume of the finished product. It is advisable, however, to use cream of tartar if you're not using a copper bowl in order to promote stability.

Start beating slowly by hand with a large metal whisk or by machine, and increase your speed as the whites increase in volume. You'll see the whites go from a foamy, spumy stage to soft peaks (billowy mounds form when the whisk or mixer is lifted) to stiff peaks (shiny, dense by comparison to the previous stage, but still moist). Stop beating at that point, or you run the risk of overbeating. Your first clue to this mishap will be a dry, curdy look to the whites. (The giveaway will be later, when the whites collapse when combined with other ingredients.) Unfortunately, there is no way to "bring back," correct, overbeaten whites.

Never try to beat whites in advance and reserve them. They deflate quickly and cannot be revived. Also, try, if you possibly can, to avoid beating egg whites on a humid day. They will almost invariably refuse to expand.

Work quickly when folding in egg whites. Start by stirring one-third of the beaten whites into the base—be it a soufflé base, cake batter, or so on—to lighten it. Then, using your hand or a spatula, place some of the whites on top of the base. Using a cutting motion and turning the bowl slightly with each cut, incorporate the whites by scooping the heavier base up and over them. Keep scooping and turning the bowl until all the whites have been added. Don't be alarmed if you see traces of white in the base—it's better that than overworking the whites so that they deflate by the time they have been incorporated.

Egg whites, as you collect them, freeze splendidly in a plastic airtight container. Just be sure to remember to note on the top of the container the number of whites within. And if by any chance you have bits of yolk in the whites, use an egg shell to scoop out the strands.

Eggplant Soufflé with Red Pepper, Tomato, and Coriander Sauce

For the sauce

1 small onion, minced
1 garlic clove, minced
2 tablespoons unsalted butter
a 6½-ounce jar roasted red peppers, drained and chopped
½ cup canned tomato purée
½ cup water
1 teaspoon minced fresh coriander leaves
a pinch of sugar
salt and pepper

For the soufflé

1 large eggplant (about 1 pound), peeled and cut crosswise into ¼-inch slices
2 tablespoons vegetable oil
2 garlic cloves, minced
4 scallions, minced
½ stick (¼ cup) unsalted butter
5 tablespoons flour
1½ cups milk
5 large egg yolks
1 tablespoon Worcestershire sauce
salt and pepper
6 large egg whites at room temperature
a pinch of cream of tartar
¼ cup fine fresh bread crumbs

fresh whole coriander leaves for garnish

Serves 6

Make the sauce: In a saucepan cook the onion and garlic in the butter over low heat, stirring, for 5 minutes. Add the red peppers, tomato purée, and water, and simmer the sauce, stirring occasionally, for 3 minutes. Stir in the minced coriander, sugar, and salt and pepper to taste. To serve, reheat the sauce if necessary over low heat, transfer to a serving bowl, and garnish with the whole coriander leaves.

Make the soufflé: In a colander set over a bowl let the eggplant slices stand, sprinkled with salt, for 1 hour. Discard the liquid in the bowl, rinse the eggplant under cold water, and pat it dry. Arrange the eggplant slices in one layer on lightly oiled jelly-roll pans and brush them lightly with the oil. Broil the eggplant under a preheated broiler about 2 inches from the heat for 3 to 5 minutes, or until browned lightly, turn, and broil for 3 to 5 minutes more, or until very tender. In a food processor or blender purée the eggplant.

In a heavy saucepan cook the garlic and scallions in the butter over moderately low heat, stirring, for 3 minutes. Stir in the flour, and cook the mixture, stirring, for 3 minutes. Whisk in the milk, heated, and simmer the mixture, whisking, for 5 minutes. Transfer the mixture to a large bowl, let it cool for 5 minutes, and whisk in the egg yolks, Worcestershire sauce, eggplant purée, and salt and pepper to taste.

In a bowl with an electric mixer beat the egg whites with a pinch of salt until frothy, add the cream of tartar, and beat the whites until they just hold stiff peaks. Stir one-third of the whites into the eggplant mixture and fold in the remaining whites gently but thoroughly. Butter a 1½-quart soufflé dish and sprinkle it with the bread crumbs, shaking out the excess. Spoon the soufflé mixture into the dish, smooth the top gently, and bake the soufflé in a preheated 400° F. oven for 40 to 45 minutes, or until a skewer comes out clean. Serve the soufflé immediately with the sauce.

Shredded Romaine with Garlic Vinaigrette

Serves 6

2 garlic cloves
¼ teaspoon salt
1 teaspoon Dijon-style mustard
2 tablespoons white-wine vinegar
½ cup olive oil

1 large head of romaine, rinsed, spun dry, and shredded
freshly ground pepper to taste
¼ cup freshly grated Parmesan
¼ cup pine nuts, toasted lightly

In a small saucepan of boiling water boil the garlic for 10 minutes and drain it well. In a large salad bowl mash it to a paste with the salt and whisk in the mustard and vinegar. Add the oil in a stream, whisking, and whisk until emulsified. Add the romaine, toss the salad to combine it well, and season it with the pepper. Sprinkle the salad with the Parmesan and the pine nuts.

A MOUSSAKA MENU

Meatless Moussaka
Avocado, Cucumber, and Carrot Salad
Pita Bread
Pineapple with Honey and Yogurt

Napa Valley Fumé Blanc of recent vintage

SUGGESTIONS

Moussaka is a great party dish, and if you should decide to serve it in that fashion, to a gathering, a thoughtful touch might be to offer both a meat and meatless version. For the meat version, simply have 1 pound of lean ground lamb or beef on hand. Start tomato sauce as directed in the recipe, and when the onions are softened add the meat and cook until no longer pink. Finish the sauce and continue with the recipe as instructed.

Cottage cheese can be substituted for the ricotta.

For tips on preparing a *roux,* the base of all cream sauces, see page 132.

Moussaka can be prepared fully in advance and be reheated in a 350° F. oven for 20 minutes, or until heated through. To make it really simple for yourself, make the tomato sauce early in the week and store, chilled. Prepare the eggplant in the morning of the day you intend to assemble the dish. Making the custard sauce, which should take only 20 minutes, will be all that remains.

Dessert will take no time at all if you prepare it up to the point of running it under the broiler.

Meatless Moussaka

For the tomato sauce
2 cups minced onion
2 garlic cloves, minced
¼ cup olive oil
a 2-pound-3-ounce can tomatoes,
    drained and chopped
1 tablespoon tomato paste
1 teaspoon salt
¾ teaspoon cinnamon
¼ teaspoon dried orégano
¼ teaspoon ground allspice

4 pounds eggplant
salt
1 cup olive oil

For the custard
½ stick (¼ cup) unsalted butter
¼ cup flour
1½ cups milk
freshly grated nutmeg to taste
white pepper and salt
4 large eggs, beaten lightly
2 cups ricotta

⅔ cup freshly grated Parmesan

Serves 8

Make the tomato sauce: In a saucepan cook the onion and garlic in the oil over moderately low heat, stirring, until softened. Add the remaining sauce ingredients and simmer the sauce over low heat, stirring occasionally, for 25 minutes.

While the sauce is simmering, prepare the eggplant: peel it decoratively by removing lengthwise strips of peel at ½-inch intervals all the way around each eggplant. Cut the eggplant crosswise into ½-inch slices, stand the slices in a colander set over a bowl, sprinkling each layer generously with salt, and let them drain for 30 minutes. Pat the slices dry and arrange them in one layer in lightly oiled jelly-roll pans. Brush the slices with half of the oil and broil them in batches under a preheated broiler about 4 inches from the heat for 3 to 5 minutes, or until golden. Turn the slices, brush them with the remaining oil, and broil them for 3 to 5 minutes, or until golden. Transfer to paper towels and reserve.

Make the custard: In a saucepan melt the butter, add the flour, and cook the *roux* over low heat, stirring, for 3 minutes. Remove the pan from the heat, add the milk in a stream, whisking, and whisk the sauce until smooth. Add the nutmeg, white pepper and salt to taste, simmer the sauce for 15 minutes, or until thickened, and let it cool.

In a large bowl combine the eggs and ricotta, add the sauce in a stream, whisking, and whisk the custard until it is combined well.

To assemble the moussaka: Spread half the tomato sauce in the bottom of a gratin dish, 15 by 10 by 3 inches, top it with half the eggplant slices, and sprinkle the eggplant with half the Parmesan. Add the remaining tomato sauce, top it with the remaining eggplant, and spoon the custard over the top. Sprinkle the remaining Parmesan over the top and bake the dish in a preheated 325° F. oven for 50 minutes, or until the top is set. Let the moussaka stand for 20 minutes before serving.

Meatless Moussaka with Avocado, Cucumber, and Carrot Salad

Avocado, Cucumber, and Carrot Salad

Serves 8

4 avocados
¼ cup plus 2 tablespoons fresh
    lemon juice
1 seedless cucumber, cut into
    ⅛-inch slices

3 carrots, grated coarse
½ teaspoon salt
1 teaspoon Dijon-style mustard
½ cup olive oil
freshly ground pepper for garnish

Halve the avocados lengthwise, peel them, and cut each half lengthwise into 6 slices. Toss them in a bowl with ¼ cup of the lemon juice, then arrange the slices decoratively in a shallow glass bowl. Mound the cucumber and carrots around the avocado slices.

In a small bowl whisk together the remaining lemon juice, salt, and mustard, add the oil in a stream, whisking, and whisk the dressing until emulsified. Spoon the dressing over the salad and grind the pepper generously over the top.

Pineapple with Honey and Yogurt

Serves 8

a 3½-pound pineapple
½ stick (¼ cup) unsalted butter, melted
⅓ cup honey

1 cup chilled plain yogurt or
    Crème Fraîche (page 13)

Peel, core, and cut the pineapple into ½-inch rings. Pat the rings dry. Arrange the rings in one layer in a buttered jelly-roll pan, brush them with the butter, and drizzle them with the honey. Broil the slices about 4 inches from the heat for 2 to 3 minutes, or until bubbly. Serve the pineapple on heated dessert plates and top each serving with 2 tablespoons of the yogurt or *crème fraîche*.

CREAMED STUFFED EGGS IN CASSEROLE

Mushroom-Stuffed Eggs in Mornay Sauce
Potato and Snow Pea Salad
Almond Crescent Cookies
Chocolate-Covered Strawberries

Vouvray

SUGGESTIONS

For notes on making white sauces, see page 132.

When hard-boiling the eggs for Mushroom-Stuffed Eggs in Mornay Sauce, add 2 more to the pot. You will need the hard-cooked yolks for the Almond Crescent Cookies. The yolks make the cookies richer and shorter.

Moutarde de Meaux is one very recommendable coarse-grain mustard. There are an incredible variety of these mustards on the market these days, however. Experiment to find what you like best.

Almond Crescent Cookies keep well in an airtight container. You might even consider freezing them for freshness.

You want to avoid overheating chocolate when melting it, as too high a temperature will cause it to scorch, altering the texture. A truly foolproof method: heat the chocolate in a heatproof bowl in a preheated 250° F. oven until barely melted.

For preparing Mornay Sauce in advance, see page 132.

Steam and season the potatoes in Potato and Snow Pea Salad up to 8 hours ahead and keep covered and chilled. However, add the snow peas and dressing *just before serving*.

Chocolate-Covered Strawberries, like Frosted Grapes (page 142), can be prepared no more than several hours in advance. Any longer than that and even with good, strong refrigeration, the strawberries will begin to turn mushy.

NOTES ON THE MAKING OF WHITE SAUCES

There are two important points in making a white sauce. First cook the *roux*—the mixture of butter and flour that acts as the thickening agent—and pay attention adding the liquid.

Always combine the *roux* over low heat, stirring with a wooden spoon or whisk, for 2 to 3 minutes. The easiest way to insure a smooth sauce is to warm the liquid before adding and whisk vigorously as you pour it in. If you are experienced at sauce making you can add cold liquid, but first remove the pan from the heat, whisk in the liquid, and return the pan to moderate heat, continuing to whisk, until the sauce is thickened. Whichever method you use, the sauce should be brought to a boil, then *simmered* to the desired consistency. Stir every now and then to keep the sauce from sticking on the bottom. Finally, if you are worried that there are a few lumps, strain the sauce. If you are not using it at once, cover its surface—not the pan—with a buttered round of wax paper.

Once you have made a white sauce known as *béchamel* you have only to add cheese and there is your Sauce Mornay. Add onion purée and there is your Sauce Soubise. A *gratiné*, to say nothing of a soufflé, becomes second nature with a fully mastered *béchamel*.

Another butter-and-flour combination that is used specifically to thicken sauces goes by the name of *beurre manié*. Knead together an equal amount of butter and flour to a paste with your fingertips, then whisk it bit by bit into simmering cooking liquid, such as a stew sauce. Keep cooking, stirring the sauce over medium heat, until it is as thick as you want it. If you have put too much in, thin with whatever liquid you have used for that recipe.

Mornay Sauce

For the béchamel (makes about 2 cups)
1 tablespoon minced onion
3 tablespoons unsalted butter
3 tablespoons all-purpose flour
2 cups milk, scalded
¼ teaspoon salt
white pepper to taste

2 tablespoons freshly grated Parmesan
2 tablespoons grated Gruyère
2 tablespoons unsalted butter,
   cut into bits

Make the béchamel: In a saucepan cook the onion in the butter over moderately low heat, stirring, until softened. Stir in the flour and cook the *roux* over low heat, stirring, for 3 minutes. Remove the pan from the heat and add the hot milk in a stream, whisking vigorously until the mixture is smooth and thick. Add the salt and white pepper to taste, and simmer the sauce for 5 minutes, or until thickened to the consistency of a medium cream sauce.

In a saucepan combine 2 cups of the béchamel, the Parmesan, Gruyère, and butter, and cook the mixture over moderately low heat, stirring, until the cheese and butter are just melted. Remove the pan from the heat, and if not using immediately cover the surface of the sauce with a buttered round of wax paper.

Mushroom-Stuffed Eggs in Mornay Sauce

Serves 4

2 cups Mornay Sauce (preceding recipe)
6 hard-boiled large eggs
  (see Suggestions, page 4)
2 tablespoons minced shallots
7 tablespoons unsalted butter
¼ pound mushrooms, chopped fine and
  squeezed gently dry

salt and pepper
2 tablespoons minced fresh parsley leaves
1 teaspoon Dijon-style mustard
a pinch of cayenne
2 tablespoons freshly grated Parmesan

Have ready the Mornay Sauce.

Halve the eggs lengthwise, scoop out the yolks, and sieve them into a bowl. Reserve the whites.

In a skillet cook the shallots in 3 tablespoons of the butter over moderate heat, stirring, until softened, add the mushrooms and salt and pepper to taste, and cook the mixture, stirring, until the liquid is evaporated. Add the mixture to the yolks and stir in the parsley, mustard, cayenne, 2 tablespoons of the Mornay Sauce, and salt and pepper to taste.

Mound the filling into the whites and stir any excess filling into the Mornay Sauce. Spoon ½ cup of the sauce into the bottom of a buttered 1½-quart gratin dish, arrange the stuffed eggs, filled sides up, in the dish, and spoon the remaining sauce over them. Sprinkle the Parmesan over the top, dot the dish with the remaining 4 tablespoons butter, and bake in a preheated 425° F. oven for 25 to 30 minutes, or until the sauce is bubbling and the top is golden brown.

Potato and Snow Pea Salad

Serves 4

¾ pound red boiling potatoes, quartered lengthwise and cut crosswise into ½-inch pieces

¾ pound white boiling potatoes, quartered lengthwise and cut crosswise into ½-inch pieces

3 tablespoons fresh lemon juice

salt

½ pound snow peas, strings discarded and the pods halved crosswise diagonally

1 tablespoon coarse-grain mustard

⅓ cup olive oil

In a steamer set over boiling water steam the red and the white potatoes separately, covered, for 8 to 12 minutes, or until just tender, and then transfer them to a large bowl. Toss the potatoes with 1 tablespoon of the lemon juice and salt to taste and let them cool for 15 minutes.

In a saucepan of boiling water blanch the snow peas for 5 seconds, drain them in a colander, and refresh them under cold water.

In a small bowl whisk together the remaining 2 tablespoons lemon juice and the mustard, add the oil in a stream, whisking, and whisk the dressing until emulsified. Add the snow peas to the potatoes, drizzle the mixture with the dressing, and toss gently. Serve the salad at room temperature.

Almond Crescent Cookies and Chocolate-Covered Strawberries

Almond Crescent Cookies

*Makes about
48 cookies*

1 stick (½ cup) unsalted butter, softened
6 tablespoons sugar
the yolks of 2 hard-boiled eggs, sieved
1 raw large egg yolk
½ teaspoon vanilla
¼ teaspoon almond extract
1½ cups all-purpose flour
1 large egg white, beaten lightly
¼ cup finely chopped blanched almonds
    combined with 2 tablespoons sugar

In a bowl cream the butter, add the sugar, and beat the mixture until light and fluffy. Add the sieved yolks, raw yolk, vanilla, and almond extract, and beat the mixture until combined well. Add the flour, combine the mixture to form a stiff dough, and chill the dough, wrapped in wax paper, for 1 hour.

Working with half the dough at a time, roll each half into a round ¼ inch thick on a floured surface and cut out cookies with a crescent-shaped cutter. Brush 1 side of each crescent with the egg white, and dip the glazed side of each cookie into the almond mixture, shaking off the excess. Bake the cookies 1½ inches apart on buttered baking sheets in a preheated 325° F. oven for 15 to 20 minutes, or until lightly golden. Let the cookies cool on racks.

Chocolate-Covered Strawberries

Serves 4

6 ounces semisweet chocolate, preferably imported, cut into pieces
1½ pints strawberries with the stems intact

In the top of a double boiler set over hot water melt the chocolate, stirring, or melt it in a preheated 250° F. oven.

Spear each strawberry onto a toothpick, pat the berries dry, and dip each berry into the chocolate, coating the lower two-thirds and letting the excess drip back into the pan. If the chocolate becomes too thick, return the pan to the heat to thin the mixture. As the berries are coated, stick the picks in a sieve set upside down on a flat surface lined with wax paper. Let the chocolate cool and chill the berries until the chocolate is hardened. Remove the picks before serving.

SOUP FOR SUPPER

Soup. It's warming. It's nourishing. It can be light or hearty. It comes in astonishing variety. It can be blissfully economical like the one made with lentils and brown rice on page 145. It can also be show-stopping and stunning like *Zuppa di Pesce* on page 153.

A really fine soup lends itself to simple partnering, requiring little more than a crust of bread, a salad, and a dessert. Depending upon how rich your soup is, you might even omit dessert, as we did with Smoked Fish Chowder on page 137, in favor of fruit and cheese. What could be easier?

Finally, how can you argue with a course that can be made in full in advance, which waits patiently on the back burner to be reheated? That's reason enough to serve soup for supper!

CHOWDER FOR SIX

Smoked Fish Chowder

Walnut Wheat Muffins   *Broccoli Salad*

Fruit and Cheese

Saint-Véran, Montagny, or a California Chardonnay with a touch
of ruggedness to support the smoky flavors and cream

SUGGESTIONS

Smoked haddock, also known as finnan haddie, is almost always available at better fish markets. But call ahead to make sure it is in stock, particularly in summer, when the production of smoked fish decreases.

Fruit and cheese ideas: apples and sharp Cheddar; pears and a creamy Brie; raisins and sweet Gorgonzola.

Be sure to remove the cheese from the refrigerator 1 hour before serving.

§

From start to finish, the chowder should take 1 hour, plus or minus, to prepare. If you prepare it in full in advance, reheat it over moderate heat.

The muffins can also be baked early in the day. Reheat in a warm oven.

Broccoli Salad should be fresh, so don't make it more than 3 or 4 hours ahead.

Smoked Fish Chowder

1½ pounds smoked haddock
   (finnan haddie)
2¼ cups bottled clam juice
2 cups water
4 slices of bacon, chopped
1 large onion, chopped
3 tablespoons flour
1½ pounds red potatoes, quartered and
   cut crosswise into ½-inch pieces

2 stalks of celery, chopped
1 bay leaf
1½ cups heavy cream
1 cup milk
salt and pepper
1 tablespoon snipped fresh dill

Makes 10 cups,
serving 6

In a large, heavy saucepan cover the haddock with the clam juice and water. Bring the liquid to a simmer and poach the haddock at a bare simmer, covered, for 10 to 15 minutes, or until it just flakes. Transfer the haddock to a bowl, strain the stock through a fine sieve into another bowl, and reserve it.

In another large, heavy saucepan cook the bacon over moderate heat, stirring, until it is crisp, transfer it to a small bowl, and discard all but 3 tablespoons of the fat. Cook the onion in the fat, covered, over moderately low heat, stirring occasionally, for 5 minutes, or until softened, add the flour, and cook the mixture, stirring, for 3 minutes. Add the reserved stock in a stream, whisking, and bring the mixture to a boil, whisking. Add the potatoes, celery, and bay leaf, and simmer the mixture, covered, stirring occasionally, for 15 to 20

Broccoli Salad and Smoked Fish Chowder

minutes, or until the potatoes are tender. Stir in the cream, milk, and salt and pepper to taste, and bring the mixture to a simmer. Add the haddock, flaked into large pieces, and the dill. Heat the mixture over moderately low heat, stirring gently, until the haddock is heated through, and discard the bay leaf. Serve in heated bowls.

Walnut Wheat Muffins

Makes 12 muffins

1½ cups whole-wheat flour
2¼ teaspoons double-acting baking
    powder
1 teaspoon salt
3 tablespoons wheat germ
1 large egg, beaten lightly

1 cup milk
½ stick (¼ cup) unsalted butter,
    melted and cooled
1 tablespoon honey
1 cup walnuts, toasted lightly and
    chopped

Into a large bowl sift together the flour, baking powder, and salt and stir in the wheat germ. In a small bowl beat together the egg, milk, butter, and honey. Add the mixture to the flour mixture with the walnuts and stir until just combined. Spoon the batter into 12 buttered ⅓-cup muffin tins, filling them three-fourths full. Bake the muffins in the middle of a preheated 400° F. oven for 20 minutes, or until puffed and golden brown, and turn them out onto a rack.

Broccoli Salad

Serves 6

1 large bunch of broccoli
    (about 2 pounds), trimmed
3 tablespoons distilled white vinegar
1 teaspoon Oriental sesame oil*

Tabasco to taste
⅓ cup olive oil
salt and pepper

*Available at Oriental markets and some
supermarkets.

Peel the broccoli stalks and cut the broccoli into small flowerets. Cut the stalks crosswise into ¼-inch slices. In a large saucepan of boiling salted water boil the broccoli for 2 to 3 minutes, or until barely tender. Drain and plunge it into a bowl of ice and water. Drain well again.

In a small bowl whisk together the vinegar, sesame oil, and the Tabasco, add the olive oil in a stream, whisking, and whisk the dressing until emulsified. In a bowl toss the broccoli with the dressing and season it with salt and pepper. Serve the salad at room temperature.

A TRIESTE-STYLE SOUP FOR SUPPER

Bean, Potato, and Sauerkraut Soup
Mild Garlic Bread
Chicory Salad with Hot Shallot Dressing
Frosted Grapes

Full-bodied, dry, but mild-flavored wine:

an Alexander Valley Chardonnay or White Chateauneuf-du-Pape,

for examples

SUGGESTIONS

This Bean, Potato, and Sauerkraut Soup, which goes under the name of *jota* in Italy, derives from Trieste, a seaport at the head of the Adriatic, very near the Yugoslav border. Nourishing and hearty, it combines several salient culinary influences. One item should be noted, however: Do not try to substitute canned red kidney beans for the dried variety called for in the recipe. The long, slow cooking of the dried beans imparts intrinsic flavor and thickness and cannot be speeded up in favor of haste. Therefore, anticipate soaking the beans, starting a day or two ahead of when you want to serve the soup.

Chicory, with its slightly bitter flavor, goes under the name of curly endive in many greengrocers. They are not exactly the same, but are cousins. If chicory is not available, look for escarole, another relative.

For the salad dressing, if you do not have shallots on hand, substitute the white part of 2 scallions. Speaking of shallots, store them as you would onions—loose, in a cool, dry, well-ventilated spot.

Prepare Frosted Grapes no more than 2 hours ahead of serving and store them in the refrigerator. If made way in advance, the sugar coating will absorb moisture in the refrigerator and the grapes will begin to "sweat"—a terrible turn of events given their pretty crunchiness and charm.

Bean, Potato, and Sauerkraut Soup

Makes about 16 cups, serving 8 to 10

1½ cups red kidney beans, picked over and rinsed
8 cups water
4 cups chicken stock (page 154) or canned chicken broth
2 ham hocks
1 large onion, chopped
3 garlic cloves, minced
3 tablespoons yellow cornmeal

1 bay leaf
1 teaspoon crumbled dried sage
a 1-pound package sauerkraut, rinsed well and squeezed dry
1 pound red potatoes, quartered and cut crosswise into ½-inch pieces
⅓ cup minced fresh parsley leaves
salt and pepper

In a bowl let the beans soak in 5 cups cold water overnight.

Drain the beans and in a heavy kettle combine them with the water, stock, ham hocks, onion, and garlic. Bring the liquid to a boil, add the cornmeal gradually, whisking, and add the bay leaf and sage. Simmer the mixture, covered, stirring occasionally, for 2 hours and remove the ham hocks to a cutting board. Add the sauerkraut and the potatoes to the bean mixture and simmer, covered, stirring occasionally, for 20 minutes, or until the potatoes are tender. Remove the meat from the ham hocks and chop it. Add the meat to the soup with the parsley and salt and pepper to taste, and discard the bay leaf.

Mild Garlic Bread

3 garlic cloves, peeled
½ stick (¼ cup) unsalted butter, melted
salt and pepper

1 long loaf of Italian bread, preferably whole-wheat, halved lengthwise

In a small saucepan of boiling water boil the garlic for 15 to 20 minutes, or until soft. Drain the garlic, and in a small bowl mash it to a paste. Stir in the butter, add salt and pepper to taste, and spread the mixture on the cut sides of the bread. Re-form the bread into a loaf, wrap it in foil, and heat it in a preheated 350° F. oven for 15 minutes. If desired, unwrap the bread and broil the halves cut side up on a baking sheet under a preheated broiler about 2 inches from the heat for 1 minute, or until golden.

Chicory Salad with Hot Shallot Dressing

Serves 8

1 large head of chicory, torn into
    bite-size pieces
2 hard-boiled large eggs, chopped
2 shallots, minced

½ cup olive oil
⅓ cup red-wine vinegar
salt and pepper

In a heatproof salad bowl combine the chicory with the eggs.

In a heavy skillet cook the shallots in the oil over low heat for 3 minutes, or until softened. Let cool slightly, add the vinegar carefully, and bring the mixture to a boil, whisking. Drizzle the hot dressing over the salad, toss the salad, and season with salt and pepper. Serve immediately.

Frosted Grapes

Serves 8

2 large egg whites
1 pound seedless green grapes, separated
    into small bunches

1 pound seedless red grapes, separated
    into small bunches
superfine granulated sugar for coating
    the grapes

In a bowl beat the egg whites until they are just frothy, and brush the grapes lightly but thoroughly with the whites. Arrange the grapes on racks and sift the sugar over them, turning them to coat them evenly. Chill the grapes until the sugar is set, and arrange them carefully in a serving bowl.

WARMING VICTUALS

Lentil and Brown Rice Soup
Parmesan Toasts
Mushroom Salad with Scallions and Celery
Minted Oranges in Wine Syrup

Côtes du Rhône—Villages Rouge

SUGGESTIONS

This soup is a quintessential stick-to-the-ribs combination, marrying all the nutritional value of a legume with brown rice. It cooks up quickly, needs no special tender loving care, and improves in flavor as it stands. Count on it for sustenance on a windy, wintry day.

Vary Mushroom Salad with Scallions and Celery by the addition of endive and/or watercress sprigs.

By all means, if you've an opened bottle of red wine just begging to be used, substitute it for the white wine in Minted Oranges in Wine Syrup. It makes for beautiful coloration. Also, this dessert is a superb one to remember in the heat of summer. Serve it icy cold, with a chocolate cookie or a brownie.

In a menu that can otherwise be prepared fully in advance, one note of caution: Leave combining the salad for the last minute. Mushrooms, particularly in dressing, do not improve in texture if left to wait and develop a rather unappealing, slippery quality. This is not to say that the dressing cannot be made and the celery and scallions already cut. Just before serving, simply slice up the mushrooms, combine, and toss.

Lentil and Brown Rice Soup

5 cups chicken stock (page 154) or
    canned chicken broth
3 cups water
1½ cups lentils, picked over and rinsed
1 cup brown rice
a 2-pound can tomatoes, drained and
    chopped, juice reserved
3 carrots, halved lengthwise and cut
    crosswise into ¼-inch pieces
1 onion, chopped

1 stalk of celery, chopped
3 garlic cloves, minced
½ teaspoon crumbled dried basil
½ teaspoon crumbled dried orégano
¼ teaspoon crumbled dried thyme
1 bay leaf
½ cup minced fresh parsley leaves
2 tablespoons cider vinegar, or to taste
salt and pepper

*Makes about
14 cups,
serving 6 to 8*

In a heavy kettle combine the stock, water, lentils, rice, tomatoes, reserved juice, carrots, onion, celery, garlic, basil, orégano, thyme, and bay leaf, bring the liquid to a boil, and simmer the mixture, covered, stirring occasionally, for 45 to 55 minutes, or until the lentils and rice are tender. Stir in the parsley, vinegar, and salt and pepper to taste, and discard the bay leaf. The soup will be thick and will thicken as it stands. Thin the soup, if desired, with additional hot chicken stock or water.

Parmesan Toasts

1 long loaf of Italian bread, cut into
    ½-inch slices
1 garlic clove, halved crosswise

olive oil for brushing the slices
about 1 cup freshly grated Parmesan

*Makes about
25 toasts*

Bake the bread slices on baking sheets in a preheated 350° F. oven for 7 to 8 minutes, or until crisp but not yet golden. Rub the cut sides of the garlic over the slices, brush the slices generously with the oil, and sprinkle them with a thin layer of the Parmesan. Bake the toasts in the 350° F. oven for 7 to 8 minutes, or until the cheese is melted and the toasts are crisp.

    They are best when served immediately.

Lentil and Brown Rice Soup with Parmesan Toasts

Mushroom Salad with Scallions and Celery

Serves 6

1 pound mushrooms, trimmed
8 scallions, minced
3 stalks of celery, minced
6 tablespoons fresh lemon juice

1 teaspoon ground cumin
salt and pepper
⅔ cup olive oil

Cut the mushroom stems crosswise into thin slices until they are flush with the caps, slice the caps thin, and in a salad bowl combine the mushrooms, scallions, and celery.

In a small bowl whisk together the lemon juice, cumin, and salt and pepper, add the oil in a stream, whisking, and whisk the dressing until emulsified. Toss the salad with the dressing and more salt and pepper if necessary. Serve immediately.

Minted Oranges in Wine Syrup

Serves 6 to 8

6 navel oranges, peeled, pith removed, and sliced horizontally into ¼-inch slices
½ cup sugar
½ cup water
1½ cups dry white wine (see Suggestions)

4 thin slices of lemon
a 3-inch cinnamon stick
4 cloves
2 tablespoons Cognac
3 tablespoons minced fresh mint leaves

In a shallow glass serving dish arrange the orange slices.

In a saucepan combine the sugar and water, bring the mixture to a boil over moderate heat, stirring, and cook it, stirring, until the sugar is dissolved. Add the remaining ingredients, except the Cognac and mint, bring the syrup to a boil, and simmer it for 15 minutes. Remove the pan from the heat, stir in the Cognac, and pour the syrup over the orange slices. Sprinkle the dessert with the mint leaves and chill, covered, for at least 3 hours.

A GREEK MEAT SOUP SUPPER

Arni Soupa Avgolemono
Sesame-Seed Whole-Wheat Bread
Greek Salad
Dried-Fruit Compote

∽

Carafes of Greek dry white wine

SUGGESTIONS

Avgolemono in Greek means with egg and lemon, and it is a favorite combination in the cuisine of that country. You've already seen it used as a sauce for Spinach and Feta Loaf (page 120), and here it is further enriched with cream to form the base of a nourishing lamb soup/stew, if you will. Given the richness of the soup, all you need to fill out this menu is a simple bread, a salad, and a straightforward dessert.

It goes without saying that the lamb for *Arni Soupa Avgolemono* should be particularly well trimmed of all visible fat.

Orzo, a rice-shaped pasta, is sold in boxes at most supermarkets. Don't hesitate to substitute the same amount of rice if you've no *orzo* on hand, and adjust the cooking time accordingly. Or use spaghetti, broken into small pieces.

As with any soup that is cream-based, and especially with eggs added, reheat carefully over moderate heat, stirring.

Substitute plain brandy in the Dried-Fruit Compote if apricot brandy is not in stock.

If you have a cache of pine nuts, also known as *pignoli*, *pignolia*, and *piñons*, know that they spoil easily owing to their high fat content. As a preventative, store them in a well-sealed jar in the refrigerator or freezer. A garnish of slivered almonds on the compote is a nice alternative.

∽

This entire menu can be prepared in advance. Feel free to make the bread at an earlier date and freeze it. We would not suggest doing that with the soup, however.

Arni Soupa Avgolemono

Makes about 12 cups, serving 6 to 8

3 pounds lean boneless shoulder of lamb, cut into 1½-inch pieces
2 pounds lamb bones, cut into 1½-inch pieces
¼ cup olive oil
2 stalks of celery, sliced
1 large onion, sliced
1 carrot, sliced
10 cups cold water

Tie together in a cheesecloth bag
2 teaspoons dried rosemary
1 teaspoon dried thyme
1 bay leaf
8 peppercorns
6 sprigs of parsley

salt
½ cup *orzo* (see Suggestions)
5 large eggs
½ cup fresh lemon juice
½ cup heavy cream
¼ cup snipped fresh dill
white pepper to taste

In a kettle brown lightly the lamb and lamb bones in batches in the oil over moderately high heat, transferring them to a plate with a slotted spoon as they are browned. Add the celery, onion, and carrot and cook the vegetables for 5 minutes. Return the lamb and bones to the kettle, add the water, the cheesecloth bag, and 1 teaspoon salt, and bring the liquid to a boil. Simmer the soup, covered, skimming off the froth as it rises to the surface, for 2 hours, or until the lamb is tender. Strain the stock through a fine sieve into a large saucepan, pressing hard on the solids. Discard the bones and vegetables, reserve the meat, and chill the stock. Remove the fat from the surface of the chilled stock, bring the stock to a boil, and add the reserved lamb and the *orzo*. Simmer the soup, covered, for 15 minutes, or until the *orzo* is tender.

In a glass bowl beat the eggs until they are thick and light. Add the lemon juice, drop by drop, beating constantly, and 1 cup of the hot stock in a slow stream. Add the egg mixture to the saucepan with the cream, stirring, and heat the soup, stirring, for 7 to 10 minutes, or until thick enough to coat a spoon, *but do not let it boil*. Stir in the dill and season the soup with salt and white pepper. Serve the soup in heated bowls.

Sesame-Seed Whole-Wheat Bread

Makes 1 loaf

1 package active dry yeast
   (For suggestions on baking with yeast,
   see A Bread Box, pages 22–23.)
¼ cup lukewarm water
1 teaspoon sugar
½ cup lukewarm milk
¼ cup unsulfured molasses

1 large egg at room temperature,
   beaten lightly
1½ cups whole-wheat flour
1½ cups or more unbleached flour
2 teaspoons salt
egg wash: 1 egg, beaten lightly
sesame seeds as needed

In a bowl proof the yeast in the water with the sugar for 15 minutes, or until foamy. Add the milk, molasses, and egg and combine the mixture well.

In a large bowl combine the flours and salt. Beat the yeast mixture into the flour mixture, adding more unbleached flour if necessary to make a soft but not sticky dough. Transfer the dough to a floured surface and knead it for 15 minutes, or until smooth and satiny, adding more flour as necessary. Form the dough into a ball, put it in a buttered bowl, and turn it to coat it with the butter. Let the dough rise, loosely covered, in a warm place for 1½ hours, or until it is almost double in bulk. Punch down the dough, form it into a loaf, and fit it into a buttered loaf pan, 8½ by 4½ by 2⅝ inches. Let the loaf rise, covered loosely, in a warm place for 1 hour, or until it is almost double in bulk. Brush the loaf with the egg wash and sprinkle it with the sesame seeds. Bake the loaf in a preheated 400° F. oven for 30 minutes, or until it sounds hollow when the bottom is tapped. Turn the loaf out of the pan and let it cool on a rack.

Greek Salad

Serves 4 to 6

4 heads of Bibb lettuce, separated into
   leaves, rinsed and patted dry
4 tomatoes, cut into wedges
2 cucumbers, peeled, halved lengthwise,
   and cut into ¼-inch slices
2 green bell peppers, halved lengthwise,
   and cut into ¼-inch slices
¼ pound feta cheese, broken into large
   chunks

16 Greek olives
olive oil
red-wine vinegar
salt and pepper
1 tablespoon minced fresh parsley leaves
   for garnish

Line a salad bowl with the lettuce leaves and arrange the tomatoes, cucumbers, bell peppers, feta, and olives decoratively on top. Sprinkle the salad with the oil and vinegar, add salt and pepper to taste, and garnish it with the parsley.

Dried-Fruit Compote

two 11-ounce packages mixed dried fruit
1⅔ cups dry white wine
1⅔ cups water
a 3-inch cinnamon stick
3 tablespoons apricot brandy
1 cup fresh orange juice
⅓ cup fresh lemon juice

¼ cup honey
¼ teaspoon ground allspice
¼ teaspoon ground ginger
¼ teaspoon cinnamon
blanched julienne strips of orange rind
   for garnish
lightly toasted pine nuts for garnish

Serves 4 to 6

In a saucepan combine the dried fruit, wine, water, and cinnamon stick, bring the liquid to a boil, and simmer the mixture for 15 to 20 minutes, or until the fruit is tender. Transfer the fruit with a slotted spoon to a serving bowl and sprinkle it with the brandy.

Add to the saucepan the orange juice and lemon juice, the honey, and spices, and reduce the liquid over high heat by half. Let the liquid cool, pour it over the fruit, and garnish the dessert with the orange rind and pine nuts. Serve chilled or at room temperature.

Dried-Fruit Compote

AN ITALIAN FISH SOUP SUPPER

Zuppa di Pesce
Tuscan Bread   *Mixed Salad*
Assorted Cheese and Fruit

∽

Vernaccia di San Gimignano

SUGGESTIONS

You can reduce considerably the time needed for preparing *Zuppa di Pesce* by buying cultivated grit-free mussels, a new addition to the seafood market. Grit-free mussels are seeded on ropes that extend into the ocean and, as a consequence, have no contact with the ocean bottom and its silt and seaweed and sand. These mussels are more expensive than the regular ocean-bottom mussels, but they are so much easier to clean.

Tuscan bread is saltless and has an interesting, unusual flavor that for some might take getting used to. In the recipe that follows you will see that we have added salt, a mere pinch, for flavoring. Add more if you want to.

Speaking of Tuscan bread, you will see that it is made with a sponge: part of the flour is added to the yeast and liquid mixture and left to rise. Then the remaining ingredients are incorporated and the dough is kneaded and left to rise again. A sponge makes for flexibility. If you like, prepare it the night before and let it rise overnight. Finish the free-form loaf at your convenience the next day.

Consider these options for dessert: *mascarpone*, a delicate white triple-cream cheese, with strawberries; *taleggio*, a mild-flavored semisoft cheese, with fresh figs; *torta*, a soft cheese layered with ingredients such as basil, prosciutto, or nuts.

∽

A clue as to how not to overcook the shellfish and fish in *Zuppa di Pesce*: Prepare the soup base up to the point of adding the seafood hours in advance and let it come to a rich garlicky headiness. About 50 minutes before you intend to serve the soup, bring it to a boil, add the squid and proceed with the recipe. In that way you almost insure perfectly cooked seafood.

Zuppa di Pesce

1 pound squid, cleaned and cut into
   ¼-inch rings
¾ pound mussels, cleaned
   (For procedure, see page 324.)

For the stock
2 cups sliced onions
¾ pound mushrooms, sliced
¼ cup olive oil
1½ cups dry white wine
3 pounds heads and bones of sea bass
   and red snapper or other white fish,
   rinsed well
12 cups cold water
12 sprigs of parsley
2 teaspoons dried thyme
6 peppercorns
1 large bay leaf

1 cup minced fennel bulb
1 cup well-washed minced leek

3 large garlic cloves, minced
¼ cup minced fresh parsley leaves
1 teaspoon dried orégano
1 teaspoon dried basil
1 teaspoon dried thyme
¼ cup olive oil
¾ cup dry red wine
a 2-pound-3-ounce can Italian plum
   tomatoes, including the juice, chopped
salt and pepper
a ¾-pound lobster tail, cut crosswise into
   1-inch slices
1½ pounds sea bass fillets or other
   firm-fleshed white fish, cut into
   2-inch pieces
1½ pounds red snapper fillets, cut into
   2-inch pieces
½ pound shrimp, shelled, the tail shells
   intact, and deveined
additional minced fresh parsley leaves
   for garnish
grated lemon rind for garnish

Have ready the squid and mussels, both cleaned well.

Make the stock: In a kettle cook the onions and mushrooms in the ¼ cup oil over moderate heat for 5 minutes, or until the onions are softened. Add the white wine, bring it to a boil, and boil it for 2 minutes. Add the fish heads and bones, the water, parsley sprigs, thyme, peppercorns, and bay leaf and bring the liquid to a boil. Reduce the heat to moderate and skim off the froth that rises to the surface. Cook the stock for 20 minutes, strain it through a fine sieve into a bowl, and reserve it.

In another kettle cook the fennel, leek, garlic, minced parsley leaves, orégano, basil, and thyme in the ¼ cup oil over moderate heat for 5 minutes. Add the red wine and boil the liquid for 2 minutes. Add the tomatoes and juice and the reserved fish stock and bring the liquid to a boil. Add the squid and salt and pepper to taste and simmer the mixture, covered, for 25 to 30 minutes, or until the squid is tender. Bring the mixture to a boil, add the mussels and lobster tail, and cook the shellfish, covered, over moderately high heat for 5 minutes. Add the bass and snapper fillets and shrimp, and cook the soup, covered, for 8 to 10 minutes, or until the mussel shells have opened and the fillets are firm when tested with a fork. Discard any unopened mussels. Season the soup with salt and pepper if needed, transfer it to a heated tureen, and garnish it with the additional minced parsley and lemon rind.

A STOCK FILE

We recommend always having a good supply of homemade stock on hand, either in the refrigerator or freezer. If you run out, it is no calamity, however. Canned broth, be it chicken or beef, in almost every instance is an acceptable substitute. Look for a brand that is not too salty. And if you should need to reduce canned broth for a specific preparation, *be sure* to taste the reduction before adding any salt.

One point: Do not try to substitute consommé for brown stock or beef broth. Consommé has a highly concentrated flavor, and if added as beef stock it will knock off the balance of the other ingredients in the recipe.

Recipes for both chicken stock and brown stock (meaning beef) follow. Both freeze beautifully and can be put to use most handily if frozen in amounts that can be readily incorporated into recipes: a 2-cup container, for example.

Chicken Stock

Makes about 6 cups

about 4 pounds wings, necks, backs, and other assorted chicken parts*
12½ cups cold water
1 large onion stuck with 2 cloves
2 leeks, halved lengthwise and washed well
2 carrots
1 stalk of celery, halved
2 teaspoons salt

Tie together in a cheesecloth bag
6 sprigs of parsley
½ teaspoon dried thyme
1 unpeeled garlic clove
1 bay leaf

*If you are the kind of cook who cuts up her own chickens, save the waste parts, including the gizzards (not livers) and freeze until you have enough to make stock.

In a kettle combine the chicken parts and 12 cups water, bring the water to a boil, and skim off the froth. Add ½ cup more cold water, bring the stock to a simmer, and skim off the froth. Add the remaining ingredients and simmer, skimming off the froth, for 2 to 3 hours.

Remove the chicken (and give the meat to the dog or cat). Strain the stock through a fine sieve into a bowl, pressing hard on the solids, and let cool, uncovered. Chill the stock and remove the fat on the surface.

If you store the stock in the refrigerator, keep it from spoiling by bringing it to a boil every several days. Another way to keep stock is to *not* skim off the fat, which, in turn, then acts as a natural sealant. Stock stored in this manner lasts at least 1 week without boiling.

Makes about 8 cups   ## Brown Stock

2 pounds meaty beef shanks,   2 stalks of celery
  sawed into 1-inch slices   1½ teaspoons salt
2 pounds meaty veal shanks,
  sawed into 1-inch slices   *Tie together in a cheesecloth bag*
2 unpeeled onions, quartered   4 sprigs of parsley
1 carrot, quartered   ½ teaspoon dried thyme
a total of 16½ cups cold water   1 bay leaf

Spread the beef shanks, veal shanks, onions, and carrot in a flameproof baking pan. Brown them well in a preheated 450° F. oven, and transfer them to a kettle. Add 2 cups of the water to the pan, deglaze the pan over high heat, scraping up the brown bits, and add the liquid with the remaining ingredients, including 14 cups water, to the kettle. Bring the water to a boil and skim off the froth. Add ½ cup more cold water, bring the mixture to a simmer, and skim off the froth. Simmer the mixture, adding boiling water to keep the ingredients barely covered, for 2 hours. Remove the shanks, strip off the meat, and reserve for use as a stew or in hash or salad. Return the bones to the pot and continue cooking 3 to 4 hours, or until the stock is reduced to about 8 cups.

Strain the stock through a fine sieve, pressing hard on the solids, and let cool. Chill the stock and remove the fat on the surface. Store as you would chicken stock.

Makes about 3 cups   ## To Clarify Stock

4 cups cool liquid stock,*   2 scallions, chopped
  fat removed   salt and pepper
the crushed shells of 2 large eggs
2 large egg whites, beaten lightly

In a kettle combine all the ingredients, with salt and pepper to taste. Bring to a boil, stirring constantly, and simmer, undisturbed, for 20 minutes. *It is very important not to stir the mixture at this point.* Impurities collecting in the egg white and egg shell float on the surface of the stock, and stirring would only incorporate them back into the mixture.

Turn off the heat, then ladle the stock through a fine sieve lined with a double thickness of rinsed and squeezed cheesecloth into a bowl. The stock is now ready to be used for making aspic.

*NOTE: If you are using canned broth, the same clarifying method applies.

Tuscan Bread

Makes 1 loaf

1 package active dry yeast
　(For suggestions on baking with yeast,
　see A Bread Box, pages 22–23.)
1 cup lukewarm water

a pinch of sugar
3 cups unbleached or bread flour
a pinch of salt

In a bowl proof the yeast in ½ cup of the water with the sugar for 15 minutes, or until foamy. Add 1 cup of the flour and combine the mixture well. Let the sponge rise, covered loosely, in a warm place for about 1½ hours, or until it is double in bulk.

In another bowl combine the remaining 2 cups flour, the ½ cup lukewarm water, and the salt. Transfer this mixture to a floured surface, add the sponge, and knead the dough for 15 minutes, or until it is smooth and elastic. Form the dough into a round loaf, put it on a floured baking sheet, and sprinkle it with flour. Let the loaf rise, covered loosely, in a warm place for 1½ hours, or until it is double in bulk. Make 3 slashes on the top of the loaf with a razor blade, and bake the loaf in a preheated 400° F. oven for 50 to 55 minutes, or until it sounds hollow when the bottom is tapped. Let the loaf cool on a rack.

Mixed Salad

Serves 8

1 head of Boston lettuce, separated into
　leaves, rinsed, and patted dry
1 head of romaine, separated into leaves,
　rinsed, and patted dry
1 head of escarole, separated into leaves,
　rinsed, and patted dry
1 fennel bulb, quartered and sliced thin
2 carrots, grated

4 large mushrooms, sliced thin
a 2-inch piece of the white part of leek,
　well washed and cut into julienne strips
olive oil
red-wine vinegar
salt and pepper
minced fresh parsley leaves for garnish

Tear the Boston lettuce, romaine, and escarole into bite-size pieces and in a salad bowl combine them with the remaining vegetables. Sprinkle the salad with the oil and vinegar, add salt and pepper to taste, and garnish the salad with the parsley leaves.

SALAD SUPPERS

We have deliberately assembled this mix of menus for salad suppers with the hotter weather in mind, when time in the kitchen standing over a stove should be kept to a minimum, when each meal should be light and surprisingly refreshing. These are meals when your garden is thriving or the green market in your neighborhood is filled with fresh herbs and plenty of vine-ripened tomatoes.

We have also organized these salad menus beginning with the more informal and relaxed ones, graduating to the not necessarily more complicated but more elegant—those appropriate for entertaining. A Special Supper for Six (page 177), for instance, combines cold beef, *ratatouille*, Cracked-Wheat Salad, and raspberry sherbet with honeydew melon. A regal supper, in fact.

None of this is to say, however, that you should restrict these menus to only the times when the temperatures soar and the dog days set in. A salad entrée can always be preceded by a hearty, rich soup. You're simply realigning an emphasis when you mix and match that way, and there are no hard rules.

It goes without saying that a salad supper should be simple. We're passing on a secret here: salad suppers are wonderful Sunday-night suppers, year round. And, as we all know, Sunday is a day of rest.

WITH ORIENTAL OVERTONES

Peanut and Chili Pepper Soup
Beef, Snow Pea, and Bean Sprout Salad
Ginger Custards

ℭ

Saumur Blanc Sec

SUGGESTIONS

An entrée salad is meant to be simplicity itself, and you can plan for the one that follows by either grilling or broiling the steak earlier in the week. Then it is just a matter of assembling and serving.

Know that Peanut and Chili Pepper Soup is spicy and that it is much easier to add spice than it is to remove it. (Almost impossible in some cases.) Therefore, start off with fewer peppers if you don't like too fiery a flavor.

Poached chicken can be easily substituted for the beef in the salad. See pages 170–71 for poaching technique.

The flavor of ginger in Ginger Custards is a deliberate complement to the Eastern intent of the beef, snow pea, and bean sprout combination. If the time needed for cooking custard has eluded you and you want that same effect, try vanilla ice cream with either bits of crystallized ginger or preserved ginger swirled in.

There is absolutely no reason not to prepare the soup, all components of the salad, and the dessert in advance. The finishing touches can be accomplished in a matter of minutes.

Peanut and Chili Pepper Soup

Serves 6

3 cups dry-roasted peanuts, with several additional peanuts for garnish
a 4-ounce can whole green chili peppers, including the liquid, more or less

2 tablespoons Worcestershire sauce
3 cups chicken stock (page 154) or canned chicken broth
1 cup milk

In a food processor fitted with the metal blade blend the peanuts, about two-thirds of the chili peppers, and Worcestershire sauce until smooth, with the motor running add the stock or broth in a stream, and blend the mixture until smooth. Taste: if you wish to add the remaining chilies—some or all—blend them in the food processor with a little of the soup and add them to the soup pot. Transfer the soup base to a heavy saucepan, stir in the milk, and heat the soup, stirring, until hot. Serve the soup in heated bowls and garnish each serving with some of the reserved peanuts.

Beef, Snow Pea, and Bean Sprout Salad

Serves 6

a 2-pound flank steak, scored lightly on the diagonal across the grain on both sides
¼ cup fresh lemon juice
3 tablespoons soy sauce
2 tablespoons peanut oil or vegetable oil
1 tablespoon Oriental sesame oil*
2 slices of gingerroot, each the size of a quarter, peeled and shredded fine

salt
½ pound snow peas, trimmed and strings removed
½ pound mung-bean sprouts, rinsed and drained well
1 teaspoon thinly sliced red hot pepper (optional)

*Available at Oriental markets and some supermarkets.

Broil the steak on the rack of a broiler pan under a preheated broiler about 2 inches from the heat for 3 to 4 minutes on each side for rare meat, transfer it to a cutting board, and let it stand for 10 minutes.

In a large bowl combine the lemon juice, soy sauce, peanut or vegetable oil, sesame oil, gingerroot, and salt to taste. Holding the knife at a 45° angle to the cutting surface cut the steak across the grain into ¼-inch slices, add it to the bowl, and toss it with the dressing.

In a saucepan of boiling salted water blanch the snow peas for 30 seconds, drain them, and refresh them under running cold water. Pat the snow peas dry. Add the snow peas and bean sprouts to the bowl and toss the salad. Transfer the salad to a serving bowl and sprinkle it with the hot pepper, if desired. Serve the salad at room temperature.

Ginger Custards

Serves 6

1½ cups milk
½ cup heavy cream
½ cup sugar
1 teaspoon ground ginger

3 large eggs
a pinch of salt
½ teaspoon vanilla

In a saucepan scald the milk and cream with the sugar and ginger.

In a bowl beat the eggs with the pinch of salt until just combined, strain the milk mixture through a fine sieve into the egg mixture, stirring, and stir in the vanilla. Skim the froth from the surface and divide the mixture among six ¾-cup custard cups. Put the cups in a baking pan, add enough hot water to the pan to reach halfway up the sides of the cups, and bake the custards, covered with a baking sheet, in a preheated 300° F. oven for 45 minutes, or until just set. Remove the cups from the pan and let them cool to room temperature.

WITH INTERNATIONAL OVERTONES

Sliced Tomatoes with Gorgonzola
Sausage, Mushroom, and Potato Salad
Sliced Oranges with Rum
Molasses Cashew Cookies

Chinon, Bourjueil, or Anjon Rouge—a brusque, red wine
with stout flavor and a little bite

SUGGESTIONS

If tomatoes are out of season, for the first course either roast your own red peppers or use jarred pimientos, drained.

A tomato salad is always best served at room temperature. Chilling decreases the flavor and wonderful sweetness of that fruit.

To achieve an attractively peeled orange, with no traces of membrane or pith, use a serrated knife and, beginning at the top of the orange, cut the peel away in strips. This is an ideal method if you intend to serve the oranges whole, in a candied syrup, for example.

The menu for this salad supper could easily be one of the simplest in this book. By all means ready all of it in advance.

Sliced Tomatoes with Gorgonzola

6 tomatoes, sliced thin
¼ pound Gorgonzola, frozen for 30
   minutes, or until firm enough to grate
¼ cup minced fresh parsley leaves
3 tablespoons thinly sliced shallot
2 tablespoons minced fresh basil leaves
   or 2 teaspoons dried

2 tablespoons fresh lemon juice
2 teaspoons Dijon-style mustard
⅓ to ½ cup olive oil
salt and pepper

Serves 6

Pasta Salad with Spinach Pesto; Beef, Snow Pea, and Bean Sprout Salad;
and Sausage, Mushroom, and Potato Salad

Arrange the tomatoes, overlapping the slices slightly, in a circle on a large platter.

Into a bowl grate the Gorgonzola, add the parsley, shallot, and basil, and combine well. Sprinkle the mixture over the tomatoes.

In a small bowl combine the lemon juice and mustard, add the oil in a stream, whisking, and whisk the dressing until emulsified. Pour the dressing over the tomatoes and sprinkle the salad with salt and pepper to taste.

Sausage, Mushroom, and Potato Salad

Serves 6

3 pounds small red potatoes
1 tablespoon Dijon-style mustard
salt
white pepper
¼ cup dry white wine
¼ cup chicken stock (page 154) or
   canned chicken broth

½ cup olive oil
⅓ cup dried wood ears, also called
   tree ears and cloud ears*
6 ounces *chorizo* (Spanish sausage)
½ cup chopped scallion

*Available at Oriental markets and some
   supermarkets.

In a large saucepan combine the potatoes with enough salted cold water to cover them by 2 inches, bring the water to a boil, and simmer the potatoes, covered, for 20 to 25 minutes, or until tender. Drain the potatoes, return them to the pan, and steam them, covered, over moderate heat, shaking the pan, for 1 minute, or until dry.

In a small bowl combine the mustard, ¾ teaspoon salt, and white pepper to taste, whisk in the wine and stock or broth, and add the oil in a stream, whisking. While the potatoes are still warm slice them in ⅓-inch slices and arrange them in layers in a shallow bowl, drizzling them with half of the dressing. Let the potatoes cool completely, turning to coat them with the dressing two or three times.

In a small bowl let the wood ears soak in hot water to cover for 20 minutes, or until softened. Drain, trim off any hard edges, and slice into strips.

Prick the *chorizo* with a needle and put it in a small skillet with ¼ inch water. Bring the water to a simmer and simmer the sausage, covered, for 10 minutes. Cook it, uncovered, over moderate heat, turning it, for 5 minutes. Transfer the sausage to a cutting board, let cool, and cut it into ¼-inch slices.

In a large bowl combine the sausage, wood ears, potatoes, scallion, and salt and white pepper to taste, add the remaining dressing, and toss. Chill the salad, covered, for at least 1 hour or overnight. Serve the salad at room temperature.

Sliced Oranges with Rum

Serves 6

4 navel oranges, peeled and pith removed,
   sliced crosswise into ⅓-inch slices

2 tablespoons dark rum
2 tablespoons sugar

In a glass serving dish arrange layers of the orange slices, sprinkling each layer with some of the rum and sugar. Chill, covered, for at least 2 hours or overnight.

Molasses Cashew Cookies

Makes 36 cookies

1½ sticks (¾ cup) unsalted butter,
   softened
1 cup plus 3 tablespoons sugar
1 large egg, beaten lightly
1 teaspoon vanilla
¼ cup unsulfured dark molasses

2 cups all-purpose flour
2 teaspoons baking soda
1 teaspoon cinnamon
a pinch of salt
1½ cups chopped unsalted cashews

In a large bowl with an electric mixer cream the butter, add 1 cup of the sugar, and beat the mixture until light and fluffy. Beat in the egg, vanilla, and molasses.

Into the bowl sift together the flour, baking soda, cinnamon, and salt and stir the mixture until combined well. Chill the dough, covered, for 2 to 3 hours, or until firm.

In a shallow dish combine the cashews and the remaining 3 tablespoons sugar. Roll rounded tablespoons of the dough into balls and roll the balls in the cashew mixture, pressing the cashews gently into them. Arrange the cookies 3 inches apart on buttered baking sheets and bake in the middle of a preheated 350°F. oven for 8 to 10 minutes, or until they are firm around the outside but still slightly soft in the center. Transfer the cookies to racks, let them cool, and store in airtight containers.

WITH ITALIAN OVERTONES

Red Bean Soup
Pasta Salad with Spinach Pesto
Rugola, Fennel, and Pine Nut Salad
Peach Mousse

White Penadés

SUGGESTIONS

For the fun of it and for variety's sake, we have included in this menu a recipe for both Spinach *Pesto* and the real McCoy. One combines spinach and walnuts; the other, the classic, basil and pine nuts. Depending upon the splendor of your garden or green market, make one or both. Note that both freeze remarkably well, too.

To freeze *pesto*: Combine as directed in the recipes, but omit the Parmesan in each case. Blend in the cheese when the *pesto* is thawed.

Use *pesto* not only on pasta, be it hot or cold, but as a dipping sauce for *crudités* or on steamed vegetables. It is lovely with baby new potatoes.

Use the ham from the ham hock that is removed from Red Bean Soup (recipe follows) shredded in omelets, diced atop green salad or steamed beans, or ground with mayonnaise, a touch of mustard, and a few herbs as a mouth-watering sandwich spread.

This menu, like the one that precedes it, can be prepared entirely in advance. The salad will need to be brought to room temperature before serving, and remember to remove the mousses to the refrigerator if they run the risk of becoming too chilled in the freezer.

Red Bean Soup

1 cup chopped onion
1 cup chopped carrot
2 garlic cloves, minced
3 tablespoons olive oil
6 cups water
1½ cups dried red kidney beans,
   rinsed and picked over
1 meaty ham hock

a 2-pound-3-ounce can Italian plum
   tomatoes, drained
1 tablespoon tomato paste
salt and pepper
2 tablespoons unsalted butter, cut
   into bits and softened
minced scallion top for garnish

*Makes 8 cups,
serving 6*

In a large saucepan cook the onion, carrot, and garlic in the oil over moderately low heat, stirring, for 5 minutes, or until the vegetables are softened. Add the water, beans, and ham hock, bring the water to a boil, and simmer the soup, partially covered, for 45 minutes, or until the beans are barely tender. Add the tomatoes, tomato paste, and salt and pepper to taste, and simmer the soup, breaking up the tomatoes with a spoon, for 45 minutes more, or until the beans are very soft. Remove the ham hock and reserve it for another use.

Purée the mixture in batches through the fine disk of a food mill into another large saucepan, add salt and pepper to taste, and bring the soup to a simmer. Remove the pan from the heat and swirl in the butter. Ladle the soup into heated bowls and garnish each serving with some of the scallion.

Pasta Salad with Spinach Pesto

1 red bell pepper, cut into ½-inch pieces
½ pound *rotelle* (corkscrew-shaped pasta)
1 cup Spinach *Pesto* (page 166)
a 10-ounce package frozen peas, thawed,
   or 2 pounds fresh peas, shelled and
   blanched

a 7-ounce can light tuna packed in oil,
   drained
salt and pepper

Serves 6

In a saucepan of boiling water blanch the red pepper for 30 seconds, drain it, and refresh it under running cold water.

In a kettle of boiling salted water boil the pasta for 7 minutes, or until *al dente*. Drain the pasta, refresh it under running cold water, and drain it well.

In a large bowl combine the pasta with the *pesto*, peas, tuna, red pepper, and salt and pepper to taste. Chill the salad, covered, for at least 1 hour or overnight. Let the salad come to room temperature before serving.

Spinach Pesto

Makes about 2 cups

1 pound spinach, tough stems removed, blanched, and squeezed well, or a 10-ounce package frozen chopped spinach, thawed and squeezed well
1 cup fresh parsley leaves
⅔ cup freshly grated Parmesan
½ cup walnut pieces

4 flat anchovy fillets
2 garlic cloves, mashed to a paste
1 tablespoon dried basil
1 teaspoon salt
¼ teaspoon ground fennel seeds
1 cup olive oil

In a food processor fitted with the metal blade blend until smooth all the ingredients except the olive oil. With the motor running add the oil in a stream. The sauce keeps about 1 week, covered and chilled. NOTE: If you intend to freeze *pesto,* see Suggestions before starting the recipe.

Pesto

Makes about 2 cups

4 cups coarsely chopped fresh basil
1 cup chopped fresh parsley leaves
1 cup pine nuts
¾ cup olive oil
1 cup freshly grated Parmesan

½ stick (¼ cup) unsalted butter, cut into bits and softened
2 garlic cloves, crushed
salt and pepper

In a food processor fitted with the metal blade or in a blender purée all the ingredients with salt and pepper to taste. NOTE: If you intend to freeze *pesto,* see Suggestions before starting the recipe.

Rugola, Fennel, and Pine Nut Salad

1 teaspoon Dijon-style mustard
2 tablespoons wine vinegar
½ teaspoon salt
½ cup olive oil

2 bunches of *rugola*, trimmed
1 fennel bulb, stems and strings
   removed and the bulb cut crosswise
   into ⅛-inch slices
⅓ cup pine nuts, toasted lightly
   (see Suggestions, page 147)
salt and pepper

Serves 6

In a bowl whisk together the mustard, vinegar, and salt, add the oil in a stream, whisking, and whisk the dressing until emulsified.

    Add the *rugola*, fennel, pine nuts, and salt and pepper to taste, toss gently, and serve the salad on chilled plates.

Peach Mousse

2 very ripe peaches (about ¾ pound)
2 tablespoons fresh lemon juice
1 cup well-chilled heavy cream
2 large egg whites at room temperature
a pinch of salt

a pinch of cream of tartar
¼ cup sugar
amaretti (Italian almond macaroon
   cookies, available at specialty-foods
   shops), crumbled, for garnish

Serves 6

In a saucepan of boiling water blanch the peaches for 30 seconds, or until the skins will peel off easily. Plunge them into cold water, and remove the skins. Cut the peaches into chunks, discarding the pits, and in a food processor fitted with the metal blade purée them with the lemon juice until the mixture is smooth.

    In a bowl beat the cream until it holds stiff peaks.

    In another bowl beat the egg whites with the salt until they are frothy, add the cream of tartar, and beat the whites until they hold soft peaks. Beat in the sugar, a little at a time, and beat the meringue until it holds stiff glossy peaks. Transfer the peach purée to a large bowl, fold in the whipped cream and the meringue, and spoon the mousse into 6 wine glasses. Freeze the mousse in the freezer compartment of the refrigerator for 1 hour, transfer it to the refrigerator for 2 hours, and serve it chilled but not hardened. Garnish the mousse with the *amaretti*.

AN ELEGANT CHICKEN SALAD SUPPER

Chilled Herb Soup
Tarragon Chicken Salad with Vegetables in Aspic
Cantaloupe Ice Cream

ରୁ

Bardeaux Sauvignon Blanc of recent vintage

SUGGESTIONS

This menu is the perfect solution to that one week in the summer when your garden is bursting at its seams. The soup, salad, and dessert—all three courses—employ fresh produce. And the fresher the better, of course.

For information on clarifying stock, see page 155.

You can fill the center of the aspic mold with any salad of your choosing. One alternative might be Curried Turkey Chutney Salad (page 88), without the melon boats. If you take that route, serve smaller portions of the creamed soup.

ରୁ

Like any cold soup, chilled herb soup has to be prepared well ahead. Check the seasonings before serving, though.

If you are preparing the aspic mold, which is entirely optional, by the way, you absolutely have to do so in advance!

Tarragon Chicken Salad with Vegetables in Aspic

Chilled Herb Soup

*Makes about
5 cups,
serving 4*

3 cups chicken stock (page 154) or
   canned chicken broth
¾ cup minced fresh parsley leaves
⅓ cup minced fresh basil leaves
⅓ cup snipped fresh chives

2 tablespoons minced fresh mint leaves
2 large egg yolks
1½ cups heavy cream
salt and white pepper to taste
additional minced herbs for garnish

In a saucepan combine the stock or broth and all the herbs, and simmer the mixture for 20 minutes.

In a bowl beat the egg yolks lightly with the cream, add 1 cup of the stock in a stream, whisking, and add the mixture to the pan, whisking. Simmer the soup, stirring, for 5 minutes, or until thickened, *but do not let it boil*. Add the salt and white pepper, let the soup cool, and chill it, covered, for 2 hours.

Before serving, season the soup again with salt and white pepper, ladle it into chilled bowls, and sprinkle each serving with minced herbs.

Tarragon Chicken Salad with Vegetables in Aspic

Serves 4

8 plum tomatoes, peeled
1 unwaxed cucumber, cut on the
   diagonal into 20 thin slices,
   the slices patted dry

For the aspic
1 envelope unflavored gelatin
   (if using canned broth,
   use 2 envelopes gelatin)
4 cups chicken stock (page 154)
   or canned chicken broth, clarified
   (for procedure see page 155) and
   cooled to room temperature

For the chicken salad
three 1-pound whole chicken breasts
6 sprigs of fresh tarragon or
   2 tablespoons dried
1 pound fresh peas, shelled
3 tablespoons tarragon wine vinegar
2 tablespoons minced fresh tarragon or
   2 teaspoons dried
2 teaspoons Dijon-style mustard
¾ teaspoon salt
⅔ cup olive oil
2 stalks of celery, cut on the diagonal
   into thin slices
thin slices of cucumber and sprigs of
   fresh tarragon for garnish

Cut ½-inch slices from the stem ends of the tomatoes and squeeze out the seeds gently. Put 1 tomato in the corner of a dish towel, enclose it, and twist the towel around it, squeezing out the excess juice and forming the tomato into a compact ball. Repeat with the remaining tomatoes and chill.

Make the aspic: In a small bowl sprinkle the gelatin over ½ cup of the chicken stock and let it soften for 15 minutes. Set the bowl in a bowl of hot water and stir the mixture until the gelatin is dissolved. Stir the gelatin mixture into the remaining clarified stock. Pour a ½-inch layer of the aspic into a rinsed and chilled 4-cup ring mold, and chill it for 1 hour, or until set.

Arrange the tomatoes and the cucumber slices decoratively on the aspic, ladle 1 cup more of the aspic carefully over them, and chill the mold for 1 hour, or until the aspic is set. Ladle the remaining aspic into the mold and chill for 6 hours.

Prepare the chicken salad: In a deep large saucepan of simmering salted water poach the chicken breasts with the tarragon sprigs for 20 to 25 minutes, or until they are just springy to the touch, and let them cool in the liquid for 2 hours. Remove the chicken from the liquid, discard the skin and bones, and cut the chicken into bite-size pieces.

While the chicken is cooking, in a saucepan of boiling salted water cook the peas for 5 minutes, or until tender, drain, and refresh under running cold water.

In a bowl combine the vinegar, minced tarragon, mustard, and salt, add the oil in a stream, whisking, and whisk the dressing until emulsified. Add the chicken, peas, and celery, toss the salad well, and chill it, covered, for 1 hour.

Run a thin knife around the edges of the mold and dip the mold into hot water for 1 or 2 seconds. Invert a serving plate over the mold and invert the aspic onto it. Fill the center of the ring with the chicken salad and garnish the salad with the cucumber slices and tarragon sprigs.

Cantaloupe Ice Cream

a 1-pound cantaloupe, seeded, rind removed, and cut into 2-inch pieces
1 cup sugar

⅔ cup water
1½ cups well-chilled heavy cream

*Makes about
1 quart*

In a food processor fitted with the metal blade purée the cantaloupe coarse.

In a saucepan combine the sugar and water, and bring the mixture to a boil over moderate heat, stirring until the sugar is dissolved. Add the purée and boil the mixture for 5 minutes. Let cool.

In the processor purée the mixture until smooth and transfer it to a bowl.

In a chilled bowl beat the cream until it just holds soft peaks and fold it into the cantaloupe purée. Freeze the mixture in an ice-cream freezer according to the manufacturer's instructions.

A COOLING COMBINATION

Dilled Shrimp
Layered Vegetable Salad with Herb Mayonnaise
Walnut Quick Bread
Thin Peach Tart

Sancerre or Pouilly-Fumé from the Loire

SUGGESTIONS

Although there is nothing like homemade mayonnaise, if time is short, add minced herbs and a touch of lemon juice to commercial mayonnaise.

For suggestions on stock making and clarifying, see page 155.

Quick breads are so called because they are just that: breads that do not rely on yeast for leavening but rather on baking soda and/or baking powder to raise them. They are fun, extraordinarily easy to make, and usually keep very well, wrapped securely in plastic. They are good as accompaniments to soup suppers or salad luncheons, or as a sweet with coffee or tea.

Substitute plums or nectarines or a combination of both for the peach in Thin Peach Tart. Or, for that matter, use any beautiful sweet summer fruit.

Make Walnut Quick Bread up to 2 days in advance. Store at room temperature in plastic wrap.

Dilled Shrimp, the Layered Vegetable Salad, as well as Herb Mayonnaise, can all be made 1 day in advance and kept, covered and chilled.

Have a recipe of basic pastry dough wrapped in plastic chilling in the refrigerator. You will then have dough on hand to roll out. While the round is baking, you can blanch the peach and prepare the glaze. A simple tart to assemble.

Dilled Shrimp

Serves 4

a 12-ounce can beer
3 dill sprigs
10 parsley stems
1 garlic clove, crushed
a pinch of ground allspice
1½ pounds shrimp

2 tablespoons snipped fresh dill
2 to 3 tablespoons fresh lemon juice,
   or to taste
¼ cup olive oil
coarsely ground pepper to taste

In a large skillet combine the beer, dill sprigs, parsley, garlic, and allspice and bring the beer to a boil. Add the shrimp and cook them, covered, over moderately high heat for 1 to 2 minutes, or until pink and just firm. Drain the shrimp, refresh them under cold water, and shell them.

    In a bowl toss the shrimp with the snipped dill, lemon juice, oil, and pepper. Serve warm or at room temperature.

Layered Vegetable Salad
with Herb Mayonnaise

Serves 4

1 pound carrots, sliced thin diagonally
3 cups canned chicken broth, chilled
1½ tablespoons unflavored gelatin
4 dill sprigs

1½ cups cooked fresh peas or a
   10-ounce package thawed frozen
1½ cups cooked fresh corn kernels or a
   10-ounce package thawed frozen
Herb Mayonnaise (recipe follows)

In a saucepan of boiling salted water cook the carrots for 5 to 6 minutes, or until just tender. Drain the carrots in a colander, refresh them under cold water, and pat dry.

    Strain the broth through a sieve lined with a triple thickness of rinsed and squeezed cheesecloth into a bowl to remove any fat, and put 1 cup of it in a small saucepan. Sprinkle the gelatin over the 1 cup broth and let it soften for 5 minutes. Heat the gelatin mixture over low heat, stirring, until the gelatin is dissolved, and stir the mixture into the remaining broth. Set the bowl of broth in a bowl of ice and cold water and stir the mixture until it is cold but not thickened.

    Ladle a very thin layer of the liquid aspic into the bottoms of four 1-cup glass dishes and chill the dishes until the aspic is set. Put 1 dill sprig in the bottom of each dish and arrange the carrots decoratively in the dishes. Into each dish ladle enough of the remaining liquid aspic to just cover the carrot layer and chill the dishes for 5 to 10 minutes, or until the aspic begins to set. Divide the peas, patted dry, among the dishes, pressing down on them gently. Just cover them with a layer of the liquid aspic, and chill the dishes until the aspic is just set. Form the final layers with the corn, patted dry, and aspic and chill the dishes for 4 hours. Dip the dishes in hot water for a few seconds and run a thin knife around the edge of each dish. Unmold the layered vegetables onto a platter and serve them with the Herb Mayonnaise.

Herb Mayonnaise

*Makes about
2 cups*

2 large egg yolks
1 teaspoon white-wine vinegar
1 teaspoon Dijon-style mustard
salt
white pepper to taste
1½ cups olive oil
1 teaspoon fresh lemon juice plus
    additional to taste

3 tablespoons snipped fresh dill
1 scallion, chopped
3 tablespoons chopped fresh parsley
    leaves
1 tablespoon chopped celery leaves
3 tablespoons chopped fresh basil

Rinse a bowl with hot water and dry it well. In the bowl combine the egg yolks, vinegar, mustard, salt, and white pepper. With an electric mixer at high speed beat the mixture until it is combined and add ½ cup of the oil, drop by drop, beating constantly. Add the 1 teaspoon lemon juice and the remaining 1 cup oil in a stream, beating constantly. Beat in additional salt and pepper to taste and thin the mayonnaise, if desired, with water.

In a blender or food processor fitted with the metal blade mince the dill, scallion, parsley, celery leaves, and basil, add the mayonnaise, and blend the mixture to combine it. Season the mayonnaise with the additional lemon juice if desired.

Walnut Quick Bread

*Makes 3
small loaves*

1 cup plus 2 tablespoons all-purpose flour
2 tablespoons sugar
1 teaspoon double-acting baking powder
½ teaspoon salt
2 tablespoons unsalted butter, melted
    and cooled

1 large egg, beaten lightly
½ cup milk
½ cup coarsely ground, lightly toasted
    walnuts

In a bowl combine the flour, sugar, baking powder, and salt, stir in the butter, egg, and milk, and stir the batter until it is combined well. Stir in the walnuts. Spoon the batter into 3 buttered 6-ounce metal juice cans or a buttered 8-inch loaf pan, and bake the breads on a baking sheet in a preheated 375° F. oven for 30 minutes, or until the tops are golden brown and a skewer comes out clean. Let the breads cool in the cans on a rack for 5 minutes, rap the cans gently on the side to loosen, and remove the breads. Serve sliced, with softened butter.

Thin Peach Tart

One 8-inch tart

Basic Pastry Dough (page 202)
1 large peach
1 tablespoon fresh lemon juice

½ cup peach or apricot jam, heated
   and strained
2 teaspoons confectioners' sugar
whipped cream as an accompaniment

On a lightly floured baking sheet roll out the dough ⅛ inch thick, cut out a round from the center of it using the fluted rim of an 8-inch tart pan as a cutter, and remove the trimmings. Cover the dough with a round of wax paper, weight it with the flat bottom of the tart pan, and bake it in a preheated 425° F. oven for 8 minutes. Remove the bottom of the pan and the wax paper, reduce the heat to 375° F., and bake the round for 8 to 10 minutes more, or until golden.

In a saucepan of boiling water blanch the peach for 1 to 2 minutes, or until the skin will peel off easily. Plunge it into cold water, and remove the skin. Cut the peach lengthwise into ¼-inch slices, and in a bowl toss the slices with the lemon juice.

Brush the pastry round with half the jam, arrange the peach slices, patted dry, on the round in a circle, overlapping them slightly, and brush them with the remaining jam. Sift the confectioners' sugar evenly over the top, and glaze the tart under a preheated broiler about 3 inches from the heat for 3 to 4 minutes, or until the top is bubbling. Serve the tart immediately with the whipped cream.

A SPECIAL SUPPER FOR SIX

Cold Beef with Mustard Sauce
Ratatouille with Croutons in Eggplant Shells
Cracked-Wheat Salad
Melon with Raspberry Sherbet

Bardolino

SUGGESTIONS

Mustard sauce goes well not only with roast beef or steak but with grilled butter-flied leg of lamb.

Ratatouille, heady with flavors of the Mediterranean, can also be used as a filling for a *pita* bread, as a bed for poached eggs, or as a garnish, hot or cold, with something as simple as scrambled eggs or hamburger. Try freezing it. Some believe it improves in flavor when frozen.

You'll recognize *bulgur*, partially cooked and dried cracked-wheat berries, if you're fond of *tabbouleh*, the Lebanese salad of *bulgur* and fresh herbs, including lots of minced mint and parsley. Serve the Cracked-Wheat Salad that follows as you would *tabbouleh*—scooped into romaine leaves. An appealing summer hors d'oeuvre.

For dessert, if you've no Chambord in your bar, sprinkle the melon with *cassis*.

Some people maintain that there are no conceivable improvements that could possibly be wrought on a ripe, lush raspberry. If making sherbet with them is unthinkable to you, serve them plain, with a chocolate wafer, perhaps.

The menu for A Special Supper for Six was devised with the interests of the cook at heart: to maximize the pleasure of a congenial gathering by eliminating all concerns as to schedule and timing. Prepare everything ahead. Then serve the menu as a buffet, or seated if you choose. Bring it to table early or late. There are no restraints as to the amount of relaxation and fun that can be had on an evening like this.

Cold Beef with Mustard Sauce

Serves 6

2 tablespoons red-wine vinegar
2 tablespoons coarse-grain mustard,
 or to taste
salt and pepper
⅓ cup olive oil

2 scallions, minced
¼ cup minced watercress leaves
½ cup Quick Mayonnaise (page 20)
1½ pounds rare roast beef or leftover
 steak at room temperature, thinly sliced

In a small bowl whisk together the vinegar, mustard, and salt and pepper to taste, whisk in the oil, and whisk the dressing until emulsified. Whisk in the scallions, watercress, and mayonnaise.

Arrange the beef on a platter and serve it with the mustard sauce.

Ratatouille with Croutons in Eggplant Shells

Serves 6

6 small eggplants, each about ½ pound
5 tablespoons fresh lemon juice
salt
3 small onions, sliced
2 garlic cloves, minced
½ cup plus 2 tablespoons olive oil
1 zucchini, quartered lengthwise and cut
 into 1-inch pieces
3 tablespoons minced fresh basil

5 plum tomatoes, seeded and chopped
a 6-ounce jar roasted red peppers, drained
 and chopped
¼ cup minced fresh parsley leaves
6 thin slices of homemade-type white
 bread, crusts discarded and the crumb
 cut into small cubes
salt and pepper

Cut off a ¼-inch-thick slice from along the length of each eggplant and with a small spoon or melon-ball cutter scoop out the flesh from each eggplant, leaving ¼-inch-thick shells. Chop the flesh, toss it with 1 tablespoon of the lemon juice, sprinkle it with salt, and in a colander let it drain for 30 minutes. Rub the shells with 1 tablespoon of the remaining lemon juice, sprinkle them with salt, and let them drain, inverted on paper towels, for 30 minutes.

In a large skillet cook the onions and the garlic in ¼ cup of the oil over moderately low heat, stirring, until the onions are just softened, and transfer the mixture to a bowl. Add ¼ cup of the remaining oil to the skillet, heat it over moderate heat until hot, and in it cook the eggplant flesh, squeezed dry, the zucchini, and the basil, stirring, until the eggplant is

just tender. Transfer the mixture to the bowl and stir in the tomatoes, red peppers, parsley, and remaining 3 tablespoons lemon juice.

Brush a jelly-roll pan with the remaining 2 tablespoons oil, add the bread cubes, and toss them with the oil. Toast the bread in a preheated 375° F. oven, stirring occasionally, for 8 to 9 minutes, or until the croutons are golden. Season the *ratatouille* with salt and pepper, mound it in the eggplant shells, and serve it at room temperature with the croutons served separately. NOTE: The eggplant shells serve as containers only and are not meant to be eaten.

Cracked-Wheat Salad

Cracked-Wheat Salad

Serves 6

an 18-ounce box *bulgur**
1 cup raisins
2 navel oranges
6 tablespoons fresh lemon juice
2 tablespoons fresh orange juice
1 tablespoon Dijon-style mustard
1¼ cups olive oil

*Available at natural-foods stores.

⅓ cup minced fresh mint
1 teaspoon cinnamon
½ teaspoon cumin
1 tablespoon sugar, or to taste
salt and pepper
4 scallions, sliced thin
½ cup minced fresh parsley leaves
1 cup salted roasted cashew nuts
a mint sprig for garnish

In a large bowl let the *bulgur* soak in enough cold water to cover it by 1 inch for 1 hour, or until just tender. Squeeze the water from the *bulgur* by handfuls and transfer the *bulgur* to another large bowl.

In a small bowl let the raisins soak in warm water to cover for 15 minutes, then drain.

Grate enough of the rind from the oranges to measure 2 tablespoons. Then peel the oranges, removing the pith, and section them over a bowl.

In another small bowl whisk together the lemon juice, orange juice, and mustard, add the oil in a stream, whisking, and whisk the dressing until emulsified. Whisk in the orange rind, mint, cinnamon, cumin, sugar, and salt and pepper to taste.

Add the raisins to the *bulgur,* stir in the scallions, parsley, cashews, and orange sections, reserving 2 for garnish, and toss the mixture until it is combined well. Pour the dressing over the salad and toss gently. Season the salad with salt and pepper if necessary, transfer it to a serving bowl, and garnish it with the reserved orange sections and the mint sprig. Serve at room temperature.

Melon with Raspberry Sherbet

For the sherbet
1⅓ cups sugar
1⅓ cups water
a 1-pound package frozen raspberries,
    thawed, reserving the juice
2 tablespoons fresh lemon juice,
    or to taste

a 4-pound honeydew melon, seeded, cut
    into 6 wedges, and rind removed
2 tablespoons fresh lemon juice
6 tablespoons Chambord
    (black raspberry liqueur)
1½ cups fresh raspberries, or to taste

Serves 6

Make the sherbet: In a small saucepan combine the sugar with the water, bring the water to a boil over moderate heat, stirring, and cook, stirring, until the sugar is dissolved. Pour the syrup into a bowl set in a bowl of cracked ice, and chill it for 1 hour.

In a food processor fitted with the metal blade or in a blender in batches purée the frozen raspberries with the juice, and strain the purée through a fine sieve into the syrup. Add the lemon juice and combine well. Chill in the refrigerator for at least 2 hours, then freeze in an ice-cream freezer according to the manufacturer's instructions.

Sprinkle each melon wedge with 1 teaspoon of the lemon juice and 1 tablespoon of the Chambord and chill, covered, for at least 1 hour. Divide the melon pieces among plates, put 1 scoop of the sherbet on each plate, and garnish each serving with some of the fresh raspberries.

A COLLECTION OF CASSEROLE MENUS

There is something very reassuring about casserole cookery. Once assembled and safe in the oven, a casserole makes no demands. It fills the house with wonderful aromas. And with the exception of about two weeks in the summer, when only an ice cube will do, it is appropriate to any season of the year. Casserole cookery is comfort food.

Add the collection of casseroles that follows to your own list of personal favorites. You will see that each has a decidedly foreign influence: there is a layered, luscious baked *ziti*, which kids love; a pepper-filled veal stew; a fragrant lamb curry. Each dish has an intriguing set of accompaniments, and ends with an impossible-to-pass-up dessert (see Walnut Butterscotch Tart, page 196).

FOR ALL AGES

Antipasto
Baked Ziti with Sausage
Spinach and Lettuce Salad with Tarragon French Dressing
Herbed Garlic Pita Toasts
Praline Ice-Cream Log
Cider

Antipasto

½ pound sliced *mortadella,* rolled
½ pound sliced *soppressata* or other
   Italian salami, rolled
½ pound sliced provolone, rolled

6 stalks of celery, cut into 4-inch sticks
½ cup black olives for garnish
½ cup pimiento-stuffed olives for garnish

Serves 8

Arrange the *mortadella,* the *soppressata,* and the provolone in a spokelike pattern on a platter, add the celery stalks, and garnish the dish with the olives.

Antipasto and Baked Ziti with Sausage

SUGGESTIONS

There is really no substitute for freshly grated Parmesan, and with a food processor it can be prepared on demand. Failing that, do take the time to grate it by hand. You'll find there is absolutely no comparison between the fresh-grated and jarred variety.

If a food mill—a hand-cranked metal container with disks that purées food fine, medium, or coarse—is not part of your kitchen equipment, consider adding it to your collection. It has the invaluable attribute of separating out any solids (seeds, cores) in the food as it purées it. But, if upon making winter tomato sauce you still don't have a food mill, simply force the cooked sauce through a sieve. Do not just decide to purée it in a food processor. Once it is sieved, you can then, if you like, purée it in the processor to synthesize the texture.

∽

You can prepare *ziti* casserole 24 hours in advance, up to the point when it is to be baked. Bring to room temperature before baking.

Simplify your schedule by preparing Praline Ice-Cream Log in stages:

Phase 1. Begin with praline powder. It keeps beautifully in an airtight container in the refrigerator.

Phase 2. Next, make the cake. Remove it from its original baking sheet as directed in the recipe and keep it, wrapped very well in plastic, on the second baking sheet. If the space in your freezer allows, consider freezing the sheet cake.

Phase 3. Purely optional. If time and inclination permit, make caramel cutouts. If they don't, go to a confection store and see if there isn't some candy there that will serve a decorative end.

Phase 4. Fluff up the ice cream, roll the log, and chill the cake for 2 hours.

Phase 5. Whip the cream, then ice and freeze the log for 1 hour.

Phase 6. Enjoy!

Postscript: Of course, if you're feeling terrifically ambitious, you can also make your own ice cream. . . .

Baked Ziti with Sausage

Serves 8

For winter tomato sauce
  (makes about 6 cups)
2 cups minced onion
1 small carrot, minced
½ stalk of celery, sliced thin
salt and pepper
3 tablespoons unsalted butter
2 tablespoons olive oil
½ cup dry white wine
two 2-pound-3-ounce cans plum
  tomatoes, drained, 2 cups of
  the juice reserved
a 6-ounce can tomato paste
1 cup canned beef broth
1 tablespoon minced garlic
1 tablespoon sugar

1 teaspoon dried thyme
1 teaspoon dried basil
1 bay leaf
½ teaspoon fennel seeds, crushed
4 cloves
6 parsley sprigs

1 pound sweet Italian sausages,
  pricked all over
1 pound *ziti* (tubular pasta)
1 pound ricotta
1 large egg
¼ cup minced fresh parsley leaves
1 pound mozzarella, grated
1½ cups freshly grated Parmesan

Make the sauce: In a large saucepan cook the onion, carrot, and celery with salt and pepper in the butter and oil over moderate heat, stirring occasionally, until the onion is softened. Add the wine, and cook over high heat for 1 minute. Add the remaining ingredients, bring the liquid to a boil, and simmer the mixture, covered, stirring occasionally, for 1 hour. Discard the bay leaf and force the mixture through the medium disk of a food mill into a bowl.

In a lightly oiled baking pan bake the sausages in a preheated 400° F. oven, turning them and discarding the fat, for 30 minutes, or until browned. Transfer the sausages to a cutting board, let cool for 15 minutes, and cut them into ⅛-inch slices.

Cook the *ziti* in a large pot of boiling salted water until *al dente*. Drain and refresh under cold water. Drain again thoroughly.

In a bowl combine the ricotta, egg, and parsley.

Coat the bottom of a baking pan, 15 by 10½ by 2½ inches, with 2 cups of the tomato sauce. On the sauce layer half the *ziti,* half the ricotta mixture, half the sausages, half the mozzarella, and half the Parmesan, and cover the mixture with 2 more cups of the sauce. Layer the remaining *ziti,* ricotta, sausage, and mozzarella. Cover the mixture with the remaining sauce, and sprinkle it with the remaining ¾ cup Parmesan. Bake the mixture in a preheated 325° F. oven for 1¼ hours, or until bubbling.

Spinach and Lettuce Salad

Serves 8

⅔ cup Tarragon French Dressing
　(recipe follows)
½ pound spinach, stems removed,
　washed, patted dry, and torn into
　bite-size pieces
1 head of soft-leaf lettuce, rinsed, dried,
　and torn into bite-size pieces

1 cucumber, peeled (if waxed) and sliced
1 red bell pepper, halved lengthwise
　and cut into thin strips
6 radishes, sliced
2 scallions, minced

In a large bowl combine the spinach, lettuce, cucumber, bell pepper, radishes, and scallions, and toss the salad with the dressing.

Tarragon French Dressing

Makes about
⅔ cup

3 tablespoons tarragon vinegar
¼ teaspoon salt
¼ teaspoon freshly ground pepper

½ cup olive oil
3 tablespoons minced fresh tarragon or
　1 tablespoon dried

In a bowl combine the vinegar, salt, and pepper. Add the oil, whisking, and whisk the dressing until emulsified. Stir in the tarragon and additional salt and pepper to taste.

Herbed Garlic Pita Toasts

Makes
24 toasts

1½ sticks (¾ cup) unsalted butter,
　softened
1 tablespoon snipped fresh dill
1 tablespoon minced fresh parsley leaves
1 large garlic clove, minced

fresh lemon juice to taste
salt and pepper
6 large *pita* loaves, halved horizontally
　and each half separated into 2 pieces

In a bowl cream the butter with the dill, parsley, garlic, lemon juice, and salt and pepper and let stand, covered, for at least 1 hour.

Spread the inside of each *pita* piece with some of the butter mixture, arrange the *pita* buttered side up in one layer on a baking sheet, and bake it in the upper third of a preheated 450° F. oven for 5 minutes, or until browned lightly and crisp.

Praline Ice-Cream Log

For the cake
½ pound dark sweet chocolate,
   broken into bits
¼ cup cold strong brewed coffee
7 large egg yolks
¾ cup sugar
7 large egg whites at room temperature
a pinch of salt
a pinch of cream of tartar

For the praline powder
   (makes about 2 cups)
1½ cups sugar
a pinch of cream of tartar
¼ cup water
1 cup blanched whole almonds

1 quart vanilla ice cream, softened slightly
1 cup well-chilled heavy cream
3 tablespoons confectioners' sugar

*For the caramel cutouts for garnish,
   optional* (makes 6 cutouts)
flavorless vegetable oil for coating the
   cookie cutters and jelly-roll pan
1½ cups sugar
a pinch of cream of tartar
¼ cup water

Make the cake: Butter a 15½-by-10½-by-1-inch jelly-roll pan, line it with wax paper, and butter the paper.

In the top of a double boiler set over hot water stir the chocolate with the coffee until it is just melted, and let the mixture cool.

In a bowl with an electric mixer beat the egg yolks until they are combined, beat in ½ cup of the sugar, a little at a time, and beat the mixture until it ribbons when the beater is lifted.

In another bowl with an electric mixer beat the egg whites with the salt until they are frothy, add the cream of tartar, and beat the whites until they hold soft peaks. Beat in the remaining ¼ cup sugar, a little at a time, and beat the whites until they hold stiff peaks.

Add the chocolate mixture to the egg-yolk mixture and combine well. Stir in one-fourth of the whites and fold in the remaining whites gently but thoroughly. Spoon the batter into the pan, spread it evenly with a spatula, and bake the cake in a preheated 350° F. oven for 15 to 20 minutes, or until a cake tester comes out clean. Transfer the pan to a rack and let the cake cool completely, covered with dampened paper towels. Remove the towels and run a knife around the sides of the pan to release the wax paper. Cover the top of the cake with wax paper and a baking sheet, invert the cake onto the baking sheet, and peel off the wax paper on top.

Make the praline powder: In a heavy saucepan bring to a boil the sugar with the cream of tartar and water over moderately high heat, stirring and washing down any sugar crystals clinging to the sides of the pan with a brush dipped in cold water. Cook the syrup over high heat without stirring, swirling the pan, until it is a light caramel, add the almonds, and swirl the pan until the nuts are coated with the caramel and begin to make a popping sound.

Pour the mixture onto an oiled marble surface or jelly-roll pan and let it cool until it is hard. Transfer the praline to a cutting board, chop it coarse, and in a food processor or blender pulverize it in batches. Store the praline powder in an airtight container.

In a bowl with an electric mixer beat 1½ cups of the praline powder with the ice cream until it is just soft enough to spread, and spread it over the cake, leaving a 1-inch border. Starting with a long side, roll up the cake jelly-roll fashion, lifting it with the wax paper and finishing with the seam side down. Transfer it to a platter, and freeze it for at least 2 hours, or until the ice cream is frozen.

In a chilled bowl beat the cream with the confectioners' sugar until it just holds soft peaks. Spoon three-fourths of it into a pastry bag fitted with a ribbon tip, and pipe it over the cake. Spoon the remaining cream into a pastry bag fitted with a ¼-inch plain round tip, and pipe it onto the ends of the cake. Or spread all the cream over the cake with a spatula. Freeze the cake for 1 hour more. Sprinkle the cake with the remaining ½ cup praline powder and garnish it with the caramel cutouts, if desired.

Make the caramel cutouts: Coat 6 metal "open" cookie cutters with the oil and arrange them 2 inches apart on a well-oiled jelly-roll pan.

In a heavy saucepan bring to a boil the sugar with the cream of tartar and the water over moderately high heat, stirring and washing down any sugar crystals clinging to the sides of the pan with a brush dipped in cold water. Cook the syrup over high heat without stirring, swirling the pan, until the syrup is caramel-colored. Let it cool for 1 minute and spoon enough of it carefully into each cookie cutter to measure ⅛ inch. Let the cutouts cool until they are hard and release them from the pan and cutters with the tip of a knife. Arrange them fancifully on the ice-cream log.

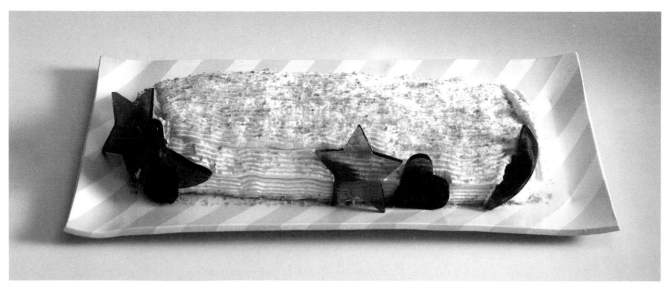

Praline Ice-Cream Log

AFTER A DAY'S HIKE IN THE COUNTRY

Veal Stew with Peppers and Mushrooms
Green Bean Salad with Horseradish Dressing
Salted Knots
Prune Whip

☙

A Kabinett-quality Rhine—a Hattenheimer,
Olstricher, or Erbacher wine especially

SUGGESTIONS

For optimum return on your stew, you will want to find veal from the center cut of the shoulder. It is not inexpensive, but the results will prove well worth the investment. As a second choice, but one that is only slightly less costly, try veal from the back cut of the shoulder. Any other cut, the leg, for example, will be too tender and will either dry out or fall apart during cooking.

☙

The stew can be prepared up to 2 days in advance and can be refrigerated. Reheat over moderately low heat, stirring occasionally.

Blanch the beans for the salad well in advance and store in the refrigerator. Prepare the salad dressing only 1 day ahead, however. Any longer in storage and the horseradish will lose its zip.

Allow about 3½ hours for making and baking salted knots. If you like, start the dough the day before and simply let it rise in the refrigerator overnight.

Veal Stew with Peppers and Mushrooms

Serves 6

6 onions, sliced thin
¼ cup lard or vegetable oil
2 garlic cloves, minced
2 tablespoons sweet Hungarian paprika
1½ teaspoons salt
3 pounds boneless veal shoulder,
  cut into 1-inch cubes

6 canned plum tomatoes, seeded and
  chopped
3 green bell peppers
3 red bell peppers
1 pound mushrooms

In a large flameproof casserole cook the onions in the lard or oil over moderate heat, stirring, for 8 to 10 minutes, or until golden, and remove the casserole from the heat. Add the garlic, paprika, salt, and veal, combine the mixture well, and cook it in a preheated 325° F. oven, stirring occasionally, for 30 minutes. Stir in the tomatoes and bake the stew, stirring occasionally, for 30 minutes. Stir in 2 of the green peppers, chopped fine, 2 of the red peppers, chopped fine, and ¾ pound of the mushrooms, chopped fine, and bake the mixture for 30 minutes. Add the remaining green and red peppers, both cut into ¾-inch pieces, and the remaining ¼ pound mushrooms, quartered, and cook the stew, stirring occasionally, for 30 minutes.

Transfer the casserole to the top of the stove and reduce the sauce over moderate heat, stirring, for 15 minutes, or until thickened.

Green Bean Salad with Horseradish Dressing

Serves 6

1 pound green beans, trimmed
1 tablespoon drained bottled horseradish,
  or to taste
½ teaspoon Dijon-style mustard
2 tablespoons vegetable oil

¼ cup sour cream
salt and pepper
4 slices of bacon, cut crosswise into
  ½-inch pieces

In a large saucepan of boiling salted water cook the beans for 6 to 8 minutes, or until tender, drain them, and refresh them under running cold water. Chill the beans, covered, for at least 1 hour or overnight.

In a small bowl whisk together the horseradish, mustard, oil, sour cream, and salt and pepper to taste and chill the dressing, covered, for at least 1 hour or overnight.

In a skillet cook the bacon over moderate heat, stirring, until brown and crisp, and transfer it with a slotted spoon to paper towels to drain. Arrange the beans in a salad bowl, spoon the dressing over them, and sprinkle the bacon over the top.

Veal Stew with Peppers and Mushrooms and Salted Knots

Salted Knots

Makes 10 rolls

1 package active dry yeast
  (For suggestions on baking with yeast,
  see A Bread Box, pages 22–23.)
1½ cups milk, heated to lukewarm
1 teaspoon sugar

4 cups all-purpose flour
1 teaspoon table salt
egg wash: 1 egg yolk beaten with
  1 teaspoon water
2 teaspoons kosher salt

In a small bowl proof the yeast in ¼ cup of the milk with the sugar for 15 minutes.

In a large bowl combine the yeast mixture, the flour, the table salt, and enough of the remaining milk to form a soft dough. Knead the dough on a floured surface for 6 to 8 minutes, or until smooth and elastic, put it in a lightly oiled bowl, and turn it to coat it with the oil. Let rise, covered loosely, in a warm place for 1 hour, or until double in bulk.

Punch down the dough, divide it into 10 equal portions, and roll each portion into a 12-inch rope. Tie each rope into a loose knot, arrange the knots 3 inches apart on buttered baking sheets, and let them rise, uncovered, in a warm place for 1 hour, or until double in bulk. Brush the knots with the egg wash, sprinkle them with the coarse salt, and bake them in a preheated 400° F. oven for 15 to 20 minutes, or until golden.

Prune Whip

Serves 6

For the purée
½ pound (about 1¼ cups) pitted prunes
a ½-inch lemon slice
a 2-inch strip of orange peel
a 1-inch cinnamon stick
2 tablespoons sugar

1 cup well-chilled heavy cream
1 large egg white at room temperature
a pinch of cream of tartar
a pinch of salt

Make the purée: In a saucepan soak the prunes in hot water to cover for 2 hours. Add the lemon slice, orange peel, and cinnamon stick. Bring the water to a boil over moderate heat, stirring occasionally, and simmer the mixture, stirring occasionally, for 25 minutes. Stir in the sugar and cook the mixture, stirring occasionally, for 20 minutes. Discard the lemon slice, orange rind, and cinnamon stick and purée the mixture in a food processor fitted with the metal blade. Let the purée cool in a large bowl.

In a chilled large bowl beat the cream until it holds soft peaks, and fold it into the purée. In a bowl beat the egg white with the cream of tartar and salt until it holds stiff peaks, and fold it into the prune mixture. Chill, covered, for 1 hour or overnight.

A WARMING WINTER SUPPER

Lamb Curry
Steamed Rice
Twice-Cooked Green Beans
Walnut Butterscotch Tart

ໜ

A dry Saumur Blanc, a Muscadet,
or even cold beer

SUGGESTIONS

Toasted shredded coconut, mango chutney, and sliced bananas are also superb accompaniments to curry. For something even more Indian-style, try preparing a *raita*—a refreshing and very cooling yogurt and vegetable combination.

It is particularly important when deep-frying the green beans that they be absolutely dry. Otherwise they will splatter furiously when put in contact with the hot oil.

An old-fashioned but very reliable way of measuring beans without actually going over to the scale and weighing them out: 1 large healthy handful per diner.

ໜ

Lamb Curry can be made well in advance and frozen. Reheat over moderate heat, stirring.

Roll, cut, and shape the shell for the tart in advance and either refrigerate or freeze, unbaked. You can even complete the "blind baking" of the shell in entirety. Then, all that will remain is the filling preparation and 20-minute baking. Store the baked shell at room temperature.

Remember: You will need at least 2 hours for the filling in the tart to set.

For other suggestions on working with pastry, see page 202.

Lamb Curry

Serves 8

3 Granny Smith apples, cored and
   chopped
3 large onions, chopped
1 stick (½ cup) unsalted butter
1½ tablespoons *garam masala*
   (recipe follows, or available at
   specialty-foods stores)
1½ tablespoons curry powder
4 pounds boneless leg of lamb, trimmed
   and cut into 1½-inch pieces
a 17-ounce can Italian plum tomatoes,
   including the juice

1 cup golden raisins
2 teaspoons red pepper flakes
salt and pepper
fresh lemon juice to taste

Accompaniments
steamed rice
peeled, pitted, and cubed avocado
chopped dry-roasted peanuts
chopped scallion

In a kettle cook the apples and onions in the butter over moderate heat, stirring, until softened. Add the *garam masala* and curry powder, and cook the mixture, stirring, for 5 minutes. Add the lamb, tomatoes with their juice, raisins, red pepper flakes, enough water to cover the mixture by 1 inch, and salt and pepper to taste. Cook the curry, partially covered, at a bare simmer for 1½ to 2 hours, or until the lamb is tender. Stir in the lemon juice and salt and pepper to taste. Serve the curry over the rice with the avocado, peanuts, and scallion.

Garam Masala
(Indian Mixed Spice)

*Makes about
3 tablespoons*

20 to 25 cardamom pods
a 2-inch piece cinnamon stick, broken
1 teaspoon cuminseed

1 teaspoon cloves
1 teaspoon peppercorns
½ teaspoon freshly grated nutmeg

Break open enough of the cardamom pods to measure 1 tablespoon seeds. In a spice or coffee grinder pulverize to a powder the cardamom seeds and the remaining ingredients. The spice keeps in an airtight container indefinitely.

Twice-Cooked Green Beans

Serves 8

4 cups peanut oil
2 pounds green beans, trimmed

1 tablespoon Oriental sesame oil
salt and pepper

In a deep fryer or deep heavy saucepan heat the peanut oil to 375° F. If you have rinsed the beans, dry them thoroughly. In the hot oil fry them in batches for 45 seconds, or until they just blister, transferring them with a skimmer as they are done to paper towels to drain. In a large, heavy skillet sauté the beans with the sesame oil and salt and pepper to taste over moderately high heat, stirring, for 30 seconds, or until heated through but still crisp.

Walnut Butterscotch Tart

One 8½-inch tart

For the shell
1½ cups all-purpose flour
¾ stick (6 tablespoons) cold butter,
    cut into bits
2 tablespoons cold vegetable shortening
¼ teaspoon salt
1 to 2 tablespoons ice water
raw rice for weighting the shell

For the filling
¾ stick (6 tablespoons) unsalted butter,
    softened
¾ cup sugar
4 tablespoons all-purpose flour
3 tablespoons heavy cream
1 teaspoon vanilla
1¼ cups walnut pieces, toasted lightly

Make the shell: In a bowl blend the flour, butter, shortening, and salt until the mixture is the consistency of meal. Add just enough of the ice water to form the dough into a ball, knead the dough lightly with the heel of the hand against a smooth surface for a few seconds to distribute the fat evenly, and re-form the dough into a ball. Flatten the ball slightly, dust it with flour, and chill it, wrapped in wax paper, for 1 hour.

On a floured surface roll the dough into a round ⅛ inch thick, fit it into an 8½-inch fluted flan pan with a removable bottom, and trim off the excess dough. Prick the shell with a fork and chill it for 30 minutes. Line the shell with wax paper, fill the paper with the rice, and bake the shell in the lower third of a preheated 400° F. oven for 10 minutes. Remove the rice and paper carefully and bake the shell for 10 to 15 minutes more, or until lightly golden. Transfer the shell to a rack and let it cool.

Make the filling: In a bowl cream the butter, add the sugar and flour, a little at a time, beating, and beat the mixture until fluffy. Beat in the cream and vanilla and stir in the nuts.

Spread the filling in the shell and bake in the lower third of a preheated 425° F. oven for 20 minutes. (The filling will not be set.) Let cool on a rack for at least 2 hours.

LEFTOVER MAGIC

We are making certain assumptions in this menu, Talking Turkey. One, that you have had turkey, maybe on either Thanksgiving or Christmas; two, that you have ample leftovers, meaning meat, stuffing, and gravy, even mincemeat; and three, that the prospect of another hot or cold turkey sandwich, delicious as it is, does not particularly thrill you. Enter our menu.

To take full advantage of all of the above we have included *two* possibilities for leftover turkey: a cottage pie as well as a creamed combination that is served on croustades. Each option can be increased in volume should your home be teeming with holiday visitors. Each is honest, home fare. Each is very easy to prepare.

TALKING TURKEY

Two Pea Soup
Turkey Cottage Pie or Creamed Turkey Croustades
Mincemeat Parfaits

Sonoma County Gamay Beaujolais or
California dry white wine

Two Pea Soup

1 large onion, chopped
2 stalks of celery, chopped
2 carrots, chopped
2 garlic cloves, minced
½ stick (¼ cup) unsalted butter
1 smoked ham hock (about ¾ pound)
½ pound dried green split peas, picked over and rinsed

4 cups chicken stock (page 154) or canned chicken broth
1 bay leaf
2 cups water
salt and pepper
1½ cups fresh peas, cooked, or a 10-ounce package frozen peas, thawed

Makes about 7 cups, serving 4 to 6

In a kettle cook the onion, celery, carrots, and garlic in the butter, covered, over moderately low heat, stirring occasionally, for 10 minutes, or until the vegetables are softened. Add the ham hock, split peas, stock, bay leaf, and water, bring the liquid to a boil, skimming the froth, and cook the soup, covered partially, in a preheated 400° F. oven for 1 hour. Transfer the ham hock to a cutting board and cut the meat into small pieces, discarding the bone and trimmings. Stir the ham into the soup, add the soup with salt and pepper to taste, and discard the bay leaf. Just before serving stir in the peas.

SUGGESTIONS

Two Pea Soup, with a wonderful homemade bread and simple salad, constitutes a simple but fine Sunday night supper. Croutons (page 31) would be good sprinkled over the top.

For Turkey Cottage Pie, if you've run out of stuffing, which so often is the case, just eliminate the stuffing as an ingredient.

We would not suggest "mashing" potatoes in the food processor—they turn to glue. Either rice the potatoes by hand or mash with a potato masher. About 3 all-purpose medium-size potatoes will yield 2 cups mashed.

A good turkey gravy is a homemade delight, and though it should not be all that difficult to execute, there are good gravies and many not so good ones. What follows is a method for a good one:

Remove the cooked turkey from the roasting pan and keep it warm on a platter. With a spoon skim the fat from the surface of the pan juices and discard. Allow sufficient time to really do this. The turkey is not going anywhere, nor at this point are your guests. And, quite practically, a turkey, like beef, should rest before carving. When all but about 3 tablespoons of fat have been removed, return the roasting pan to the burner and over low heat scrape the bottom of the pan to dislodge the brown bits. Stir in 3 tablespoons flour and cook, stirring constantly, for 2 to 3 minutes. Then add gradually either 2 cups of boiling water or hot chicken or turkey stock if you've put neck and giblets on to make a broth, and stir the gravy until thickened and smooth. The tricks are to remove the fat and not to stir in too much flour. Serve in a heated sauceboat.

∽

The soup may be prepared to the point of stirring in the fresh or frozen peas 1 day in advance. Reheat over moderate heat.

Turkey Cottage Pie can be fully assembled in advance and then baked before serving. Bring to room temperature before putting in the oven.

If you've prepared creamed turkey in advance, reheat it in a double boiler.

Turkey Cottage Pie

Serves 4

1 cup ½-inch pieces celery
1 cup ½-inch pieces carrot
1 cup ½-inch pieces onion
2 teaspoons minced garlic
3 tablespoons unsalted butter
3 tablespoons flour
1 cup turkey gravy (see Suggestions)
1 cup chicken stock (page 154) or
    canned chicken broth

Tie together in a cheesecloth bag
6 parsley stems
½ teaspoon dried thyme
1 bay leaf

2½ cups bite-size cooked turkey pieces
1 cup turkey stuffing
    (don't use one containing shellfish)
1 cup cooked peas
salt and pepper
2 cups mashed potatoes (see Suggestions)
melted unsalted butter as needed

In a saucepan sweat the celery, carrot, onion, and garlic in the butter, covered with a buttered round of wax paper and the lid, over moderately low heat for 5 minutes. Add the flour and cook the mixture over moderate heat, stirring, for 3 minutes. Add the gravy, stock or broth, and cheesecloth bag, and cook over moderate heat, stirring, for 20 minutes. Discard the cheesecloth bag, add the turkey, stuffing, peas, and salt and pepper to taste, and bring the mixture to a simmer. Transfer the mixture to a flameproof 1½-quart baking dish, and with a spatula spread the potatoes over it. Drizzle the potatoes with some melted butter. Bake the pie in a preheated 350° F. oven for 30 minutes, or until bubbling, and put it under a preheated broiler until the top is golden brown.

Creamed Turkey Croustades

Serves 4

four 1½-inch slices from an unsliced
    loaf of homemade-type white bread,
    1 or 2 days old, crusts removed and
    corners trimmed
Clarified Butter (page 37)
2 cups water
½ pound mushrooms, sliced
2 tablespoons unsalted butter
2 teaspoons fresh lemon juice
salt and white pepper to taste
¾ cup dry white wine
¼ cup minced scallion, including the
    green and white parts

3 tablespoons minced fresh tarragon or
    1 tablespoon dried
3 tablespoons minced fresh chervil or
    1 tablespoon dried
1 cup chicken stock (page 154) or
    canned chicken broth
2 cups heavy cream
1½ cups bite-size cooked turkey pieces
¼ cup sour cream
¼ cup minced fresh parsley leaves
¼ cup minced scallion tops

With a sharp knife hollow out each bread square halfway down, leaving the sides ¼ inch thick. Brush the croustades inside and out with clarified butter. Arrange them on a jelly-roll pan and bake them in a preheated 325° F. oven, turning them occasionally, for 20 to 25 minutes, or until golden.

In a saucepan combine the water, mushrooms, butter, lemon juice, and salt and white pepper. Bring the water to a boil and simmer the mixture for 3 to 5 minutes, or until the mushrooms are cooked but still firm. Transfer the mixture to a bowl.

In a saucepan combine the wine, minced scallion green and white parts, tarragon, and chervil, and reduce the wine over moderately high heat to about 1 tablespoon. Strain the mushroom cooking liquid into the pan, reserving the mushrooms, add the stock or broth, and reduce the liquid to about ½ cup. Strain the liquid through a fine sieve into a bowl, pressing hard on the solids, transfer it to the pan, and add the heavy cream. Reduce the sauce over moderately high heat to about 2 cups and add the reserved mushrooms and the turkey. Cook the mixture over moderate heat, stirring, until heated through. Remove the pan from the heat, and stir in the sour cream, parsley, and scallion tops. Bring the mixture just to a simmer and season it with salt and white pepper. Arrange the croustades on plates and divide the creamed turkey among them.

Mincemeat Parfaits

1 cup well-chilled heavy cream
2 tablespoons confectioners' sugar
1⅓ cups mincemeat

¼ cup Cognac, or to taste (optional)
1 pint vanilla ice cream

Serves 4

In a chilled bowl beat the cream with the sugar until it holds soft peaks. In a bowl combine the mincemeat with the Cognac, if desired.

Have ready 4 parfait glasses. Put 2 tablespoons of the mincemeat in each glass, divide half the whipped cream among the glasses, and put 1 scoop of ice cream atop the whipped cream. Make another layer in each glass with the remaining ingredients, reserving a dollop of mincemeat to garnish each parfait.

A PASTRY PRIMER

Basic pastry dough can be made by hand or in the food processor fitted with the metal blade, the latter being far and away the fastest method. Remember: be careful not to overprocess the dough; it will turn tough very quickly.

Basic Pastry Dough (Processor Version)

1¼ cups all-purpose flour
¼ teaspoon salt
¾ stick (6 tablespoons) cold unsalted
    butter, cut into bits

2 tablespoons vegetable shortening
3 tablespoons ice water

In the bowl of a food processor fitted with the metal blade put the flour and salt. Lay the butter and shortening in pieces over the dry ingredients and cover the bowl. Turn on and off 8 or 10 times, until the mixture is crumbly. With the motor running, add the water in a stream through the feed tube until the mixture just starts to hold together. Do not process to the point where the dough forms a ball.

Remove the dough to a piece of wax paper, form it into a ball, and chill, covered, in the refrigerator for at least 30 minutes.

೮

The recipe for pastry dough calls for both butter and shortening—butter abetting the flavor, shortening creating texture. Depending upon the filling you are using and the flavor you want to achieve, you can also make the dough with *all* butter or *all* shortening. The other measurements in the recipe remain the same.

In rolling out basic pastry dough, do it on a lightly floured surface and roll the dough from the center out, turning it a quarter turn after each roll, to achieve a well-shaped round. You want to avoid excessive working of the dough.

To transfer the round to the tart shell, pie pan, or aluminum pan in which it will bake, roll it loosely around the rolling pin, then unroll it evenly over the pan. Press the dough gently but firmly into the pan, well into the bottom edge, trim, then crimp the top edge decoratively.

Basic pastry dough can be frozen, either in batches or rolled into rounds or in the pan in which it will bake. Bake it frozen. Do not let it thaw.

Certain tarts must be partially prebaked, otherwise the bottom crust when filled with a wet mixture will turn into a soggy, sodden mess. This is called "blind baking" a shell and can be done well ahead of time, the day before even. Prick the raw dough in the pan all over with the tines of a fork, lay a round of wax paper or parchment paper on top of the dough extending up the sides of the shell, and fill the shell with raw rice or beans. Bake as directed in the individual recipe. Save the rice or beans in a coffee can to use again.

Chapter Four

A Dozen Dinners

∽

INVITATIONS TO DINE . . .

WITH EASE

Of the twelve varied dinner menus in this chapter the first four have one characteristic very much in common: true ease of preparation. Basic cooking techniques have been used on good ingredients in inventive ways to render smart and pleasing menus that in no way tax the cook. For example, chicken breasts are sautéed quickly in butter, then sprinkled with cheese and wine and baked. Sirloin steak is simply broiled and served with a glorious combination of diced potatoes, green peppers, and onions. Southwestern flavors come into play in one dish—tamale pie—beef, tomatoes, olives, and other good things topped with a batter of cornmeal, cheese, and chili peppers. Veal, a meat that must never be overcooked, is browned quickly, then combined with ham and mushrooms in a flavorful Madeira sauce. Because each of the main courses in these menus is straightforward, the other courses seem to fall naturally into place.

What these four menus as well as the others in this chapter prove will come as no surprise: basic food can not only be good and forthright, but it can be easy to prepare and fun to eat.

A BUSY DAY DINNER

Parmesan Chicken Breasts
Sautéed Cherry Tomatoes
Scallion Rice
Grapefruit, Radish, and Romaine Salad
Mocha Pudding

∽

Verdicchio dei Castelli di Jesi

SUGGESTIONS

If you don't even want to have to think about preparing Mocha Pudding while finishing three other dishes on the stove, replace it with Angel Food Cake with Bitter Chocolate Sauce (page 238), which can be prepared entirely in advance.

∽

Even though the individual courses of this doable good dinner after a busy day are really very simple, a little skillful timing is needed to get each of them on the plate at the same moment! For flawless clockwork:

Well ahead of time, wash and chill the salad greens and prepare the dressing.

About 45 minutes before serving, start the pudding. (We assume the use of a glass double boiler or a metal one. If you have a porcelain-lined copper double boiler, you will have to double the cooking time. See recipe.) Prepare through covering and starting to cook for 20 minutes.

About 30 minutes before serving, start the rice. With that underway, then start the chicken breasts and prepare them through putting them in the oven to bake.

About 15 minutes before serving, dress and plate the salad.

At about this point in the preparation of the dinner, the pudding should be set. Remove the double boiler from the burner and let the pudding stand in the top of the double boiler until ready to serve. Serve warm or at room temperature.

About 5 minutes before serving, sauté the tomatoes. Arrange them, the rice, and chicken breasts on heated plates.

There's only one thing left to do. Sit, eat, and enjoy.

Parmesan Chicken Breasts, Sautéed Cherry Tomatoes, Scallion Rice,
and Grapefruit, Radish, and Romaine Salad

Parmesan Chicken Breasts

Serves 2

a 1-pound chicken breast, skinned, boned, and halved
½ cup plus 1 tablespoon freshly grated Parmesan (preferably grated by hand)

½ cup all-purpose flour
3 tablespoons unsalted butter
¼ cup dry vermouth or dry white wine

Dredge the chicken breasts, rinsed and patted dry, in ½ cup of the Parmesan, patting the cheese into the flesh, and dredge them in the flour, lightly shaking off the excess.

In a non-stick skillet just large enough to hold the chicken without crowding heat the butter until the foam begins to subside and in it sauté the chicken over moderately high heat until golden on each side. Transfer the chicken to a baking dish, pour the vermouth over it, and sprinkle the chicken with the remaining 1 tablespoon Parmesan. Bake the chicken, covered loosely, in a preheated 325° F. oven for 15 minutes.

Sautéed Cherry Tomatoes

Serves 2

10 cherry tomatoes, rinsed and patted dry
1 tablespoon unsalted butter
1 tablespoon olive oil

1 teaspoon Worcestershire sauce
salt and pepper

In a small heavy skillet sauté the tomatoes in the butter and oil over moderately high heat, stirring, for 3 minutes, or until the skins begin to split. Swirl in the Worcestershire sauce and salt and pepper to taste, and cook the tomatoes, stirring for 1 minute.

Scallion Rice

Serves 2

⅔ cup long-grain rice
¼ cup minced scallion

2 tablespoons melted unsalted butter
salt and white pepper

Into a saucepan of boiling salted water sprinkle the rice, stirring until the water returns to the boil and boil for 12 minutes. Drain and steam the rice in a colander set over simmering water, covered with a folded dish towel and the lid, for 15 minutes. Transfer the rice to a heated bowl, add the scallion, butter, salt and white pepper to taste, and toss the mixture to combine it well.

Grapefruit, Radish, and Romaine Salad

Serves 2

1 tablespoon fresh grapefruit or
   lemon juice
¼ teaspoon sugar
salt
3 tablespoons olive oil

6 grapefruit sections
4 radishes, cut into sixths
the pale inner leaves from 1 head of
   romaine, rinsed, spun dry, and torn
   into bite-size pieces

In a small bowl whisk together the grapefruit juice, sugar, and salt to taste, add the oil in a stream, whisking, and whisk the dressing until emulsified.

In a bowl combine the grapefruit sections, the radishes, and the romaine and toss the salad with the dressing.

Mocha Pudding

Serves 4

1 cup milk
½ cup sugar
2 ounces unsweetened chocolate
1 tablespoon instant espresso powder
½ teaspoon cinnamon

⅛ teaspoon salt
3 whole large eggs
1 large egg white
1 teaspoon vanilla
heavy cream as an accompaniment

In the top of a 1½-quart glass double boiler or a metal or porcelain-lined copper one set over boiling water combine the milk, sugar, chocolate, espresso powder, cinnamon, and salt and cook the mixture, stirring, until the chocolate is melted. Then beat the mixture with an electric mixer or rotary beater until smooth. Add the eggs and egg white, 1 at a time, beating well after each addition, and the vanilla and beat the mixture at high speed for 2 minutes. Cook the pudding, covered tightly with foil and the lid, for 20 minutes in the glass double boiler or the metal one, or for 40 minutes in the porcelain-lined double boiler, or until set. Serve the pudding with the heavy cream.

A DINNER OF EUROPEAN FLAVORS

Veal, Ham, and Mushrooms in Madeira Sauce
Rösti
Orange and Olive Salad
Chocolate Raisin Cake

ల

Red Bordeaux, preferably a small Médoc chateau
of the 1978 or 1979 vintages

SUGGESTIONS

Note that the batter for Chocolate Raisin Cake is made in the same pan in which the cake is actually baked. Now *there's* convenience. To make this dessert even easier, eliminate the icing entirely and serve with billows of whipped cream either lightly sweetened or flavored with brandy, or both. And do follow the directions in the recipe for icing the cake in the pan. To invert this cake onto a rack, to be iced later, will not work.

ల

In this menu you want to finish the veal dish and the potato cake at the same moment. If coordinating that seems difficult, try this: Prepare the veal up to the point of the final combination. Then completely finish the potato cake and keep warm, covered. You will then have the time and peace of mind to heat and thoroughly combine the veal with the ham and mushrooms.

For the record: Most chocolate cakes improve in flavor with time. Chocolate Raisin Cake is no exception.

Rösti; Veal, Ham, and Mushrooms in Madeira Sauce;
and Chocolate Raisin Cake

Veal, Ham, and Mushrooms in Madeira Sauce

Serves 6

1 pound veal scallops, flattened slightly and cut into 4-by-1-inch strips
salt and pepper
flour
3 tablespoons olive oil
¾ stick (6 tablespoons) unsalted butter
¾ cup minced onion
½ cup plus 3 tablespoons Sercial Madeira
2½ teaspoons crumbled dried sage
1 bay leaf

2 cups brown stock (page 155) or canned beef broth
1 tablespoon arrowroot
¾ pound mushrooms, sliced thick
6 ounces baked ham, cut into julienne strips
½ cup drained roasted red peppers, cut into julienne strips
minced fresh parsley leaves for garnish

Sprinkle the veal strips with salt and pepper and dust them with flour. Heat a large, heavy skillet over high heat until very hot. In it combine the oil and 2 tablespoons of the butter, and swirl the skillet until the foam subsides. Brown the veal in batches for 3 minutes, transferring it to a plate with a slotted spoon as it is browned, and keep it warm, covered. Add the onion to the skillet and cook it over moderate heat, stirring, for 3 minutes, or until softened. Add the ½ cup Madeira, sage, and bay leaf, and reduce the mixture over high heat by half. Add the stock or broth and reduce the mixture to about 2 cups. Strain the mixture through a fine sieve into a saucepan, pressing hard on the solids, and bring the liquid to a boil. In a small bowl stir the arrowroot into the remaining Madeira, whisk the mixture into the stock mixture, and simmer the sauce, stirring vigorously, until thickened. Keep the sauce warm over low heat.

In a large, heavy skillet cook the mushrooms in 2 tablespoons of the butter over high heat for 3 minutes, or until golden. Add the ham, peppers, and veal, heat the mixture, tossing it, until heated through, and transfer it to a heated platter. Swirl the remaining 2 tablespoons butter, cut into bits, into the sauce, season the sauce with salt and pepper, and pour it over the veal. Sprinkle the dish with the parsley and serve it with the *Rösti* (recipe follows).

Rösti (Swiss Potato Cake)

Serves 6

2½ pounds boiling potatoes
salt and pepper

5 tablespoons unsalted butter
4 tablespoons olive oil

Put the potatoes in a large saucepan and add enough cold water to cover them by 2 inches. Bring the water to a boil and simmer the potatoes, covered partially, for 10 minutes. Drain, let the potatoes cool, and chill them for at least 2 hours or overnight. Peel the potatoes, grate them coarse, and sprinkle them with salt and pepper to taste.

In a 7-inch non-stick pan or iron skillet heat 3 tablespoons of the butter and 2 tablespoons of the oil over moderately high heat until the fat is hot and add the potatoes, spreading them evenly and tamping them down with a metal spatula to form a potato cake. Cook the cake for 8 minutes, or until the bottom is browned and crisp, and invert the cake onto a plate. Add to the pan the remaining butter and oil and heat until hot. Slide the cake, uncooked side down, into the pan, and cook for 8 minutes more, or until the bottom is browned and crisp. Slide the cake onto a heated platter and cut it into wedges.

Orange and Olive Salad

Serves 6

2 tablespoons fresh lemon juice
1 tablespoon Dijon-style mustard
1 garlic clove, mashed
salt and pepper
½ cup olive oil
¼ cup thinly sliced scallion
1 large head of Boston lettuce,
   separated into leaves

1 bunch of watercress, well washed
   and tough stems removed
2 navel oranges, peeled, pith removed,
   halved, and cut crosswise into
   ½-inch slices
½ cup Kalamata olives or other brine-
   cured olives, halved and pitted

In a salad bowl combine the lemon juice, mustard, garlic, and salt and pepper to taste, add the oil in a stream, whisking, and whisk the dressing until emulsified. Stir in the scallion, then add the remaining ingredients, and toss the salad well.

Chocolate Raisin Cake

¾ stick (6 tablespoons) unsalted butter, melted
½ cup raisins
1½ cups all-purpose flour
1 cup sugar
3 tablespoons unsweetened cocoa powder
1 teaspoon baking soda
½ teaspoon salt
1 cup cold water
1 teaspoon cider vinegar
1 teaspoon vanilla

For the icing
3 tablespoons unsalted butter, softened
1½ cups sifted confectioners' sugar
2 to 3 tablespoons milk or heavy cream
¾ teaspoon vanilla
unsweetened cocoa powder for dusting the cake

In a small bowl combine the melted butter and raisins and let the mixture stand for 20 minutes.

Into a 9-inch round cake pan, 1½ inches deep, sift together the flour, sugar, cocoa, baking soda, and salt, add the raisin mixture, water, cider vinegar, and vanilla, and stir the mixture well with a fork. Scrape the bottom and sides of the pan with a rubber spatula, combining the batter well, and bake the cake in a preheated 350° F. oven for 30 to 35 minutes, or until a cake tester comes out clean. Let the cake cook in the pan on a rack.

Make the icing: In a bowl with an electric mixer cream the butter and confectioners' sugar. Beat in enough of the milk or cream to make the icing of a spreading consistency, then beat the icing until it is light and fluffy. Stir in the vanilla. Spread the icing over the top of the cake and sift the cocoa over the top decoratively. Cut the cake into wedges and remove the wedges with a spatula to a rack or a cake plate.

ONE DISH DOES IT

Tamale Pie
Sliced Avocados with Onion Vinaigrette
Mango Cream

ↄ

Lirac or other full, soft Southern Rhône

SUGGESTIONS

It goes without saying: if you are lucky enough to have a source of fresh mangoes, use fresh mangoes to make Mango Cream. Selecting a ripe mango is not easy, however, because, contrary to what is generally thought, the color of the mango skin—very rosy in some cases, very green in others—indicates *not* ripeness but variety. We've found that the most trustworthy way of judging the readiness of a mango is to feel it. If the flesh gives slightly to the touch, buy it, whether it is red or green. You will need enough fresh mango to make ¾ cup purée; in short, 1 medium mango.

ↄ

You can easily prepare the beef mixture for Tamale Pie in advance. Let it come to room temperature while you prepare the topping, which should not be prepared ahead of time.

Prepare Mango Cream no more than about 2 hours in advance of serving. Whipped cream, as a general rule, is best prepared at the last minute.

Tamale Pie

Serves 6

For the beef mixture

1 cup chopped onion
1 cup chopped green bell pepper
2 tablespoons vegetable oil
1 pound lean ground beef
an 8-ounce can tomato sauce
2 tablespoons tomato paste
a 10-ounce package frozen corn, thawed
1 cup sliced Spanish olives
1 tablespoon ground cumin
2 teaspoons unsweetened cocoa powder
½ teaspoon ground allspice
2 teaspoons chili powder
1 tablespoon Worcestershire sauce
1 teaspoon Tabasco
1 tablespoon yellow cornmeal
salt and pepper

For the topping

1 cup all-purpose flour
1 cup yellow cornmeal
3 tablespoons sugar
2 teaspoons double-acting baking powder
3 tablespoons unsalted butter, melted
   and cooled
¾ cup milk
1 large egg, beaten lightly
½ cup grated sharp Cheddar
a 4-ounce can green chili peppers,
   chopped

Tamale Pie

Make the beef mixture: In a large skillet cook the onion and green pepper in the oil over moderately low heat, stirring, until the vegetables are softened. Add the beef, and cook the mixture over moderate heat, stirring, until the beef is no longer pink. Stir in the remaining ingredients for the beef mixture with salt and pepper to taste, simmer the mixture, stirring occasionally, for 30 minutes, and add additional Worcestershire sauce and Tabasco if desired. Spoon the mixture into a shallow 2½-quart casserole.

Make the topping: Into a bowl sift together the flour, cornmeal, sugar, and baking powder. Add the butter, milk, and egg, and stir until the batter is just combined. Stir in the Cheddar and chili peppers. Drop the batter by large spoonfuls around the edge of the casserole. Bake the pie in a preheated 400° F. oven for 10 minutes, reduce the heat to 350° F., and bake the pie for 30 minutes more.

Sliced Avocados with Onion Vinaigrette

Serves 6

3 tablespoons red-wine vinegar
1½ teaspoons Dijon-style mustard
salt and pepper

½ cup olive oil
3 tablespoons minced red onion
2 avocados

In a small bowl whisk the vinegar and the mustard with salt and pepper to taste. Add the oil in a stream, whisking, whisk the dressing until emulsified, and stir in the onion.
    Peel and slice the avocados, arrange them on a platter, and drizzle them with the dressing.

Mango Cream

Serves 6

a 14-ounce can mangoes, drained and cut
    into pieces (see Suggestions)
2 tablespoons fresh lime juice

1 teaspoon grated lime rind
1 cup well-chilled heavy cream

In a food processor fitted with the metal blade or in a blender purée the mangoes with the lime juice and the lime rind. In a chilled bowl beat the cream until it holds stiff peaks, and fold in the purée.

MEAT AND POTATOES FOR DINNER

Broiled Sirloin Steak
O'Brien Potatoes
Beer-Batter Onion Rings
Caesar Salad
Chilled Zabaglione

Chianti Classico 1979

SUGGESTIONS

If you prefer steak without garlic flavoring, broil it with lots of freshly ground pepper and/or serve it with a compound butter such as green peppercorn (page 103) or horseradish.

Caesar Salad is most frequently served with croutons added. See page 31 for making your own. Another variation—crumbled blue or Roquefort cheese.

An appealing alteration to this menu would be to serve the salad as a first course. In that case, you would want to complete the steak, potatoes, and onions, and keep them warm, covered and/or in a slow oven (200° F.). If you elect to stick to the original menu, you will want to dress the salad at the last moment, not before.

Reminder: For Beer-Batter Onion Rings you will need to prepare the batter as well as the onions 2 hours in advance.

Given that you can prepare the greens for the salad and the vegetable mixture for the potatoes ahead of time, allow about 30 minutes total time for final assembly for this dinner—meaning, broiling the steak, finishing the potatoes, and deep-frying the onions.

Broiled Sirloin Steak with O'Brien Potatoes

Broiled Sirloin Steak

Serves 4 to 6

a 3-pound sirloin steak, about
   1½ inches thick
1 garlic clove, mashed to a paste
   with 1 teaspoon salt

freshly ground pepper

Rub the steak with the garlic paste and season it with the pepper.

Broil the steak under a preheated broiler about 5 inches from the heat for 8 minutes on each side for medium-rare meat, then let it stand for 5 minutes before slicing.

O'Brien Potatoes

Serves 4 to 6

⅔ cup chopped onion
¼ cup minced green bell pepper
⅓ cup drained and chopped bottled
   pimiento

⅓ cup vegetable oil
4 large Idaho potatoes, peeled and
   cut into ½-inch dice
salt and pepper

In a large heavy skillet cook the onion, green pepper, and pimiento in 1 tablespoon of the oil over moderately low heat, stirring, until the vegetables are softened, and transfer the vegetables to a bowl.

In the skillet heat the remaining oil over moderately high heat until hot but not smoking, and in it sauté the potatoes, stirring, for 15 to 20 minutes, or until tender and crisp. Stir in the vegetable mixture with salt and pepper and heat the mixture over moderately low heat until heated through.

Beer-Batter Onion Rings

Serves 6

For the batter
1½ cups all-purpose flour
1½ teaspoons salt
1½ cups beer
2 teaspoons vegetable oil
½ cup minced fresh parsley leaves

2 pounds yellow onions,
   cut into ¼-inch slices and
   separated into rings
vegetable oil for deep-frying
salt

Make the batter: In a bowl combine the flour and salt, add the beer and the 2 teaspoons vegetable oil, and stir until smooth. Pour the batter through a sieve into another bowl. Let the batter stand, covered, at room temperature for 2 hours, and stir in the parsley.

Meanwhile, let the onions soak in a bowl of ice water for 2 hours. Drain and pat dry.

In a deep fryer heat 2 inches vegetable oil to 375° F. Dip the onion rings in batches into the batter, coating them well, and fry them in batches, turning them, for 3 minutes, or until golden brown. As the onions are fried transfer them to paper towels to drain, then sprinkle them with salt. Serve the onions rings immediately.

Beer-Batter Onion Rings

Caesar Salad

1 large egg in the shell
2 garlic cloves, mashed to a paste
10 anchovy fillets, chopped fine
3 tablespoons fresh lemon juice
salt and pepper

2 small heads of romaine, torn into pieces
⅓ cup olive oil
⅔ cup freshly grated Parmesan
1 cup croutons (optional)

Serves 4 to 6

In a saucepan of boiling water simmer the egg in the shell for 1 minute and drain it.

In a small bowl whisk together the egg, garlic, anchovies, lemon juice, and salt and pepper to taste. In a salad bowl toss the romaine with the oil, add the egg mixture, Parmesan, and croutons, if desired, and toss.

Chilled Zabaglione

Chilled Zabaglione

Serves 4

4 large egg yolks
¼ cup sugar
a pinch of salt

½ cup sweet Marsala
⅓ cup heavy cream

In a metal bowl set over simmering water combine the egg yolks, sugar, and salt. With an electric mixer or rotary beater beat the mixture at high speed for 5 minutes, or until thick and fluffy. Add the Marsala in a thin stream, beating constantly, and continue to beat the mixture for 5 to 8 minutes, or until the mixture is triple in volume, holds soft peaks, and feels warm to the touch, indicating that the eggs have been cooked. Transfer the mixture to a bowl set in a bowl of cracked ice and stir until cold.

In a chilled small bowl beat the cream until it holds stiff peaks, and fold it into the chilled mixture. Spoon the *zabaglione* into individual dessert glasses and chill for 1 hour.

INVITATIONS TO DINE . . .
IN SEASON

We've grouped the five menus that follow according to season, with several suggested for summertime serving, to emphasize two salient features among all of them: namely, the reliance upon flavorful fresh ingredients and simple preparation, a combination that has yet to be beaten and keeps gaining in reputation for health and nutrition reasons. Note, for instance, on page 239, the unsullied pure flavors and basic cooking directions of the fish and vegetable courses in a trout dinner for when the leaves fall. Very few fats have been added. Instead, wonderful ingredients have been simply combined to allow the original good flavors to shine through.

So whether you are actually preparing these dinners according to the calendar we've called for is not that important. Broil the hens on page 226 in your oven, instead of on an outdoor grill, in the winter, if you like. It's the spirit of the season that matters. Take the time to find the best ingredients available. Raid your greengrocer. Plunder your own garden. These dinners, each one of them, can only be enhanced by that.

AN ITALIAN SUMMER MENU
FOR EIGHT

Souffléed Spinach Gnocchi
Tuna-Stuffed Peppers
Oranges in Marsala

Rivera Rosato, Castel del Monte

SUGGESTIONS

Gnocchi, Italian dumplings, can be made in several varieties: with all-purpose flour, with riced potatoes, or with semolina flour, as they are here. Like all good dumplings, they are meant to be light and airy and, as such, make a very fine first course. An Italian winter menu, for example, might start with Souffléed Spinach *Gnocchi* and be followed by roast Rock Cornish Game Hens with Rosemary (page 226) and a green salad.

A nice addition to the tuna filling for the Italian peppers would be cooked macaroni, *orzo*, or Arborio rice. Some toasted pine nuts would be good, too.

The combination of orange and chocolate is a splendid one. If time allows, accompany the Oranges in Marsala with a plate of Florentines (page 249).

∾

Even though we wish we could say this entire summer menu can be made in advance, we can't. The *gnocchi* batter, because of its beaten egg whites, must be prepared at the last minute. Assuming you have all the ingredients chopped and ready to go, allow about 30 minutes for the preparation of the batter and another 30 minutes for baking the *gnocchi*. As soon as they are puffed and golden brown, serve immediately. Once the *gnocchi* are in the oven, relax and enjoy yourself. We're trusting you've realized that the peppers and oranges can both be made *well* in advance.

Souffléed Spinach Gnocchi

Serves 8

2 cups milk
1¾ sticks (14 tablespoons) unsalted butter, cut into bits
1½ teaspoons salt
1 teaspoon coarsely ground pepper
¼ teaspoon freshly grated nutmeg
1 cup fine semolina flour*
5 large egg yolks

¼ pound mozzarella, cut into ¼-inch pieces
¼ cup thawed and well-squeezed chopped frozen spinach
5 large egg whites at room temperature
a pinch of cream of tartar
a pinch of salt
½ cup freshly grated Parmesan

*Available at specialty-foods markets.

In a large, heavy saucepan combine the milk, 10 tablespoons of the butter, the salt, pepper, and nutmeg, and bring the milk to a boil, stirring. Reduce the heat to low, stir in the semolina flour all at once, and cook the mixture, stirring, for 2 minutes, or until it leaves the sides of the pan. Remove the pan from the heat and beat in the egg yolks, 1 at a time, beating well after each addition. Add the mozzarella and spinach, stir the mixture until the cheese is just melted, and transfer it to a large bowl.

In a clean, non-plastic bowl beat the egg whites with the cream of tartar and salt until they hold stiff peaks, stir one-fourth of them into the semolina mixture, and fold in the remaining whites gently but thoroughly.

Form rounded tablespoons of the mixture into ovals using 2 tablespoons dipped in hot water, and arrange the ovals in one layer in a buttered shallow 2-quart baking dish. Dot the ovals with the remaining 4 tablespoons butter, sprinkle them with the Parmesan, and bake them in a preheated 400° F. oven for 30 minutes, or until they are puffed and golden brown.

Tuna-Stuffed Peppers

Tuna-Stuffed Peppers

eight 5-inch Italian green peppers
½ cup chopped celery
½ chopped onion
½ cup chopped red bell pepper
1 tablespoon unsalted butter
two 7-ounce cans light tuna packed in olive oil, drained, 3 tablespoons of the oil reserved

½ cup peeled, seeded, and chopped tomato
⅓ cup chopped black olives
3 tablespoons minced fresh parsley leaves
2 tablespoons drained capers
1 to 2 tablespoons fresh lemon juice
salt and pepper

Serves 8

Cut off the top of each pepper on the diagonal, discard the stems, and mince the tops. Scrape out the seeds and the ribs from the peppers, and in a kettle blanch the peppers in boiling salted water to cover for 5 minutes. Drain, refresh under cold water, and pat the peppers dry.

In a skillet cook the minced pepper tops, celery, onion, and red bell pepper in the butter and 1 tablespoon of the reserved tuna oil over moderate heat, stirring, for 4 minutes, add the tomato, and cook the mixture, stirring, for 2 minutes. Transfer the mixture to a bowl and combine it with the remaining ingredients and salt and pepper to taste.

Stuff the peppers with the tuna filling and arrange them in one layer in a buttered shallow baking dish. Drizzle the remaining reserved tuna oil over the peppers, and bake the dish, covered, in a preheated 350° F. oven for 10 minutes, or until heated through. Serve the peppers warm or at room temperature.

Oranges in Marsala

Serves 8

6 large navel oranges
1 tablespoon sugar, or to taste

¼ cup sweet Marsala, or to taste

Working over a shallow glass dish, with a sharp knife remove and discard the rind and pith from the oranges. (For further tips on peeling, see Suggestions, page 161.) Slice the oranges thin horizontally, arrange the slices in the dish, and sprinkle them with the sugar. Drizzle the Marsala over the oranges and chill them, covered, overnight.

A SUMMER WEEKEND DINNER

Rock Cornish Game Hens with Rosemary
Herb-Roasted Corn on the Cob
Tomato and Hearts of Palm Salad
with Basil Vinaigrette
Nectarine Fool

∽

Rosso di Montalcino

SUGGESTIONS

You can make the grilling of the hens easier for yourself and at the same time anticipate a small eater's special order by splitting the birds in half before grilling.

For a light, citrusy aroma, slip a few very thin slices of lemon between the skin and flesh of each hen.

Very similar in nature to Nectarine Fool but even simpler to do would be lush sliced peaches in cream. Decorate with a few pieces of candied ginger sprinkled over the fruit or grated chocolate.

∽

This menu was conceived with the weekend traveler in mind so that dinner happens easily once you arrive at your destination. Therefore, start the birds marinating well in advance, then pack them in a cold case for the journey. Prepare the nectarine purée in advance as well. The vegetables can be bought along the way, at a local stand. When you arrive, you only have to start the fire, organize the salad, and finish the dessert—a simple matter of whipping cream to soft peaks.

Rock Cornish Game Hens with Rosemary

Serves 4

four 1- to 1½-pound fresh Rock Cornish
  game hens

For the marinade
¼ cup fresh lemon juice
¼ cup olive oil
2 garlic cloves, minced
1½ teaspoons minced fresh thyme or
  ½ teaspoon dried
½ bay leaf, crumbled
½ teaspoon salt
4 large sprigs of rosemary or
  1 teaspoon crumbled dried

melted unsalted butter for brushing
  the hens
salt and pepper
sprigs of watercress for garnish

With a sharp knife cut along one side of the backbone of each hen from neck to tail. Spread the hens open, cut along the other side of the backbone from neck to tail, and remove the backbone. Put the hens skin side down on a cutting board, pull out the breastbone, and flatten the hens slightly with the flat side of a cleaver or a large knife. Turn the hens over, cut a horizontal slit through the skin between the lower breast and each thigh of each hen, and tuck the tips of the legs through the slits. Tuck the wing tips behind the shoulders and remove and discard the fat.

Make the marinade: In a bowl combine well all the marinade ingredients.

Arrange the hens in 2 dishes, divide the marinade between the dishes, and brush the hens with the marinade. Tuck a rosemary sprig under each hen or sprinkle the undersides of the hens with the crumbled rosemary. Let the hens marinate, covered and chilled, turning them occasionally, for at least 2 hours or overnight. Transfer the hens to a plate, reserving the rosemary sprigs if used, and pat them dry.

Brush the hens on all sides with the melted butter and season them with salt and pepper. Top each hen with a reserved rosemary sprig and grill the hens, skin side up, over glowing coals. Or broil them, skin side down, under a preheated broiler about 4 inches from the heat, turning them once and brushing them with the butter, for 20 to 25 minutes, or until the juices run clear when a thigh is pricked with a skewer. Transfer the hens to a heated platter and garnish the platter with the watercress.

Rock Cornish Game Hens with Rosemary, Herb-Roasted Corn on the Cob,
and Tomato and Hearts of Palm Salad

Herb-Roasted Corn on the Cob

Serves 4

For the herb butter
1½ sticks (¾ cup) unsalted butter,
    softened
1½ tablespoons minced fresh parsley
    leaves
1½ tablespoons snipped fresh chives

1½ tablespoons minced scallion
1½ teaspoons fresh lemon juice
¾ teaspoon salt
Tabasco and Worcestershire sauce to taste

8 ears of corn

Make the herb butter: In a bowl combine well all the herb-butter ingredients and chill, covered, for at least 1 hour. You will need to remove the butter from the refrigerator well in advance of using. It should be of spreading consistency, well softened.

Peel back but do not detach the husks from the ears of corn and discard the silk. Spread each ear of corn with 1 tablespoon of the butter, wrap the husks carefully around the corn, and wrap each ear in foil.

Roast the corn on a grill over glowing coals or broil it under a preheated broiler about 4 inches from the heat, turning it, for 30 minutes, or until the kernels are tender. Unwrap the corn, detach the husks, and brush the corn with more of the herb butter.

Tomato and Hearts of Palm Salad
with Basil Vinaigrette

Serves 4

For the basil vinaigrette
    (makes about 1 cup)
3 tablespoons white-wine vinegar
2 teaspoons Dijon-style mustard
1 garlic clove, minced (optional)
salt and pepper
½ to ¾ cup olive oil, or to taste
2 tablespoons minced fresh basil leaves

½ pound spinach, trimmed, washed,
    and dried
1 large head of Bibb lettuce, separated
    into leaves
4 tomatoes, cored and cut into wedges
a 14-ounce can hearts of palm, drained
    and cut into 1-inch pieces
1 cup Kalamata olives, or to taste

Make the basil vinaigrette: In a bowl combine the vinegar, mustard, garlic, and salt and pepper to taste, add the oil in a stream, beating, and beat the dressing until emulsified. Or in a food processor fitted with the metal blade or in a blender combine all the ingredients, except the oil. With the motor running add the oil and blend until emulsified. Stir in the basil.

Line a platter with the greens, arrange the tomatoes and hearts of palm in the center, and sprinkle the salad with the olives. Drizzle some of the vinaigrette over the salad and serve the remaining vinaigrette separately.

Nectarine Fool

4 very ripe large nectarines, peeled, pitted, and quartered
1 tablespoon fresh lemon juice
¼ teaspoon cinnamon, or to taste

1 cup well-chilled heavy cream
2 tablespoons confectioners' sugar
blanched, skinned, and chopped pistachio nuts for garnish

Serves 4

In a food processor fitted with the metal blade purée the nectarines with the lemon juice and cinnamon until smooth. Transfer the purée to a glass bowl and chill it, covered, for at least 2 hours.

In a chilled bowl beat the cream with the sugar until it holds soft peaks, fold it into the purée, and divide the dessert among bowls. Garnish each serving with some of the pistachios.

A GRILLED DINNER IN AUGUST

Marinated Pork Kebabs
Grilled Peppers and Onions
Vegetable Rice Salad with Yogurt Dressing
Summer Pudding with Raspberries

∽

Napa Valley Sauvignon Blanc

Marinated Pork Kebabs

Serves 6

For the marinade
½ cup vegetable oil
⅓ cup medium-dry Sherry
2 tablespoons soy sauce
2 tablespoons honey
2 tablespoons fresh lemon juice
2 garlic cloves, minced
1 tablespoon minced fresh sage leaves or
   1 teaspoon dried
1½ teaspoons fresh thyme or
   ½ teaspoon dried
1 bay leaf, crumbled

3 pounds boneless pork shoulder,
   cut into 2-inch cubes
additional sage leaves for threading
   on the skewers
additional bay leaves for threading
   on the skewers
Grilled Peppers and Onions
   (recipe follows)

In a shallow dish let six 10-inch wooden skewers soak in water to cover for 2 hours and let them drain on paper towels.

Make the marinade: While the skewers are soaking, in a glass bowl combine well all the marinade ingredients.

Add the pork to the marinade, tossing it, and let it marinate, covered and chilled, for 2 hours. Drain the pork and reserve the marinade.

Thread the pork and additional sage and bay leaves, halved, on the skewers, alternating the meat and herbs. Brush the kebabs with the reserved marinade, then grill them over glowing coals or broil them about 4 inches from the heat, turning them frequently, for 20 to 25 minutes, or until the juices run clear when the meat is pierced with a fork. Serve each kebab on a bed of the Grilled Peppers and Onions.

Grilled Peppers and Onions

4 large red bell peppers
4 large green bell peppers
1 tablespoon fresh lemon juice,
  or to taste

2 tablespoons olive oil, or to taste, plus
  additional oil for brushing the onions
salt and pepper
two ¾-pound onions, quartered

Serves 6

Grill the red and green bell peppers over glowing coals or broil them under a preheated broiler about 4 inches from the heat, turning them frequently, for 12 to 20 minutes, or until they are blistered and charred. Enclose the peppers in a paper bag and let them steam until cool enough to handle. Peel the peppers, slice in halves, and discard the ribs and seeds. Cut the peppers lengthwise into strips.

In a bowl combine the peppers with the lemon juice, 2 tablespoons oil, and salt and pepper to taste and let them stand for at least 15 minutes.

Thread the onions on two 10-inch metal skewers, brush them with the additional oil, and sprinkle them with salt and pepper to taste. Grill the onions over glowing coals or broil them under a preheated broiler about 4 inches from the heat, turning them frequently, for 20 to 25 minutes, or until tender. Remove the onions from the skewers and toss them with the peppers.

SUGGESTIONS

Rice salad is one of those wonderful combinations that allows for any number of additions or subtractions. For example, dress it with an herb French dressing (page 185 or 186). Or add what is best in your garden—beans, peas, or corn. Or replace this recipe with another rice salad, the one that is made with curry powder, Curried Rice Salad (page 114). You might also use the salad, dressed with oil and vinegar, as a filling for hollowed-out tomato shells.

You will need wooden and metal skewers for this dinner.

∽

With the rice salad fully prepared, the pork marinating, and the peppers for the vegetable course cooked, it is just a matter of grilling the meat and onions. We maintain that a summer dinner should be easy. This one is just that.

Vegetable Rice Salad with Yogurt Dressing, Marinated Pork Kebabs, and Grilled Peppers and Onions

Vegetable Rice Salad with Yogurt Dressing

Serves 6

10 cups water
1 tablespoon salt
1 cup long-grain rice
¼ pound wax beans, trimmed and halved
¼ pound snow peas, strings removed,
    blanched in boiling water to cover for
    5 seconds, drained, and refreshed
    under cold water
1½ cups sliced seedless cucumber
1 cup sliced radish
1 cup minced scallion
salt and pepper

For the yogurt dressing
    (makes about 1½ cups)
1 cup plain yogurt
1 tablespoon white-wine vinegar
1 teaspoon Dijon-style mustard
1 garlic clove, minced
½ teaspoon ground cumin
¼ cup olive oil

snipped fresh chives for garnish

In a large saucepan bring the water to a boil with the salt. Stir in the rice and boil for 15 minutes. Drain the rice in a colander and rinse under running cold water. Then put the colander over another saucepan of boiling water and steam the rice, covered with a dish towel and the lid, for 15 to 20 minutes, or until fluffy and dry. Transfer the rice to a large bowl.

In a large saucepan of boiling salted water cook the wax beans for 5 minutes, or until just tender, drain, and refresh under cold water.

Pat the beans and snow peas dry, then add them and the remaining ingredients to the bowl of rice. Toss, add salt and pepper to taste, and chill, covered, for at least 1 hour.

Make the yogurt dressing: While the salad is chilling, in a bowl combine all the dressing ingredients, except the oil, salt, and pepper. Add the oil in a stream, beating, and beat the dressing until combined. Add the salt and pepper to taste and transfer the dressing to a serving bowl.

To serve: Divide the salad among chilled plates, garnish with the chives, and serve with the dressing.

Summer Pudding with Raspberries

14 slices of very thin homemade-type white broad, crusts removed, with 8 of the slices halved crosswise
4 cups raspberries with additional raspberries for garnish

½ cup sugar
2 tablespoons *eau-de-vie de framboise* or dry white wine
lightly sweetened whipped cream as an accompaniment

Serves 4 to 6

Using a 1-quart charlotte mold as a guide, trim 1 whole bread slice to fit the bottom of the mold. Arrange the halved slices overlapping slightly around the sides of the mold, and press the round into the bottom.

In a 6-quart saucepan combine the 4 cups raspberries, sugar, and *framboise*, bring to a simmer over moderate heat, stirring, and simmer, stirring, for 2 to 3 minutes, or until the berries are just slightly crushed and the sugar is dissolved. Remove the pan from the heat and let cool.

Spoon one-third of the raspberry mixture into the mold and top with 1 whole slice of bread. Spoon half the remaining raspberry mixture into the mold and top with 1 more slice of bread. Spoon the remaining raspberry mixture over the bread and cover it with enough of the remaining bread, cut into pieces, to cover the top completely. Cover the mold with a round of wax paper cut to fit the inside of the mold and a saucer. Weight the pudding with a 2-pound weight, and chill overnight.

Remove the weight, saucer, and wax paper, run a thin knife around the edge of the mold to loosen it, and invert a large round serving plate over the mold. Invert the pudding onto the plate, garnish it with the remaining raspberries, and serve it with the whipped cream.

SWORDFISH FOR DINNER

Grilled Swordfish Steaks
Broiled Tomatoes Provençale
Steamed Wax Beans
Sesame Toasts
Angel Food Cake with Bitter
Chocolate Sauce

Savigny-les-Beaune Blanc '84

SUGGESTIONS

The menu of swordfish for dinner is very obviously a summer one, when you have the grill fired up and hot to go. A total variation on the theme—one that does not necessitate the grill or a marinade—would be to poach the swordfish in a *court bouillon* (page 68) at a very low simmer for 6 to 8 minutes, or until it feels tender when tested with a knife. Chill, with a little of the poaching liquid sprinkled over the top, then pat dry, and serve on a bed of leafy lettuce with a flavored mayonnaise on the side.

Assuming that the Sesame Toasts and Angel Food Cake and sauce are made well in advance and that you've started the fish marinating, all that remains will be to finish the tomatoes and steam the beans while the fish grills. This amounts to a very simple swordfish dinner.

Grilled Swordfish Steaks, Broiled Tomatoes Provençale,
and Steamed Wax Beans

Grilled Swordfish Steaks

Serves 4

four 6-ounce swordfish steaks, each
   about ¾ inch thick
½ cup vegetable oil
3 tablespoons soy sauce
2 tablespoons medium-dry Sherry
1½ teaspoons peeled and grated
   gingerroot

1 teaspoon grated orange rind
freshly ground pepper
additional vegetable oil for brushing
   the grill pan
parsley sprigs for garnish

Arrange the swordfish in a dish just large enough to hold it in one layer. In a bowl combine the oil, soy sauce, Sherry, gingerroot, orange rind, and pepper to taste, add the marinade to the dish, and turn the fish to coat it with the mixture. Let the fish marinate, covered and chilled, turning it occasionally, for at least 2 hours or overnight.

Heat a heavy ridged grill pan over high heat until hot, brush it with the additional oil, and heat the oil until hot. Grill the fish in the pan in batches for 4 minutes on each side, or until firm to the touch, transferring it as it is done to a heated platter. Or grill the fish over glowing coals, basting it with some of the marinade, for 4 to 5 minutes on each side, or until firm to the touch. Arrange Broiled Tomatoes *Provençale* and Steamed Wax Beans (recipes follow) on the platter and garnish the dish with the parsley.

Broiled Tomatoes Provençale

Serves 4

4 large plum tomatoes
olive oil for brushing the tomatoes
¼ cup fresh bread crumbs
3 tablespoons freshly grated Parmesan

2 tablespoons minced fresh parsley leaves
1 small garlic clove, minced
salt and pepper

Halve the tomatoes horizontally and trim the ends so that they will stand level, cut side up. Brush them all over with the oil and bake them, cut side up, on a baking sheet in the middle of a preheated 325° F. oven for 20 minutes.

In a small bowl combine the remaining ingredients with salt and pepper to taste and divide the mixture among the tomatoes. Drizzle oil over the tomatoes and broil them under a preheated broiler about 4 inches from the heat for 2 to 3 minutes, or until the topping is golden brown.

Steamed Wax Beans

¾ pound wax beans, washed and
   trimmed

2 tablespoons unsalted butter
salt and pepper

Serves 4

In a steamer set over boiling water steam the beans, covered, for 5 to 7 minutes, or until they are just tender, and refresh them under running cold water. In a skillet heat the beans in the butter over moderate heat, tossing them, for 1 minute, or until they are well coated, and season them with salt and pepper.

Sesame Toasts

1½ sticks (¾ cup) unsalted butter
2 teaspoons Oriental sesame oil*
   (optional)
1 loaf of Italian or French bread,
   cut crosswise at a slight angle into
   ½-inch slices

1 large egg, beaten slightly with
   ½ teaspoon salt
½ cup sesame seeds

*Available at Oriental markets and some
   supermarkets.

Serves 6 to 8

In a small saucepan melt the butter with the sesame oil, if using, over moderately low heat and keep the mixture warm. Brush both sides of each slice with some of the butter mixture, brush 1 side of each slice with the egg mixture, and dip that side immediately into the sesame seeds. Bake the slices, sesame-seed sides up, on baking sheets in the middle of a preheated 375° F. oven for 20 minutes, or until golden and crisp. Serve the toasts warm. The toasts may be stored in an airtight container for 1 week and reheated.

Angel Food Cake with Bitter Chocolate Sauce

Makes one 10-inch tube cake

1 cup sifted cake flour (not self-rising flour)
1¼ cups sugar
9 large egg whites at room temperature
1 tablespoon fresh lemon juice
½ teaspoon salt
1 teaspoon cream of tartar
1 tablespoon vanilla
1 cup Bitter Chocolate Sauce (recipe follows)

Into a bowl sift together the flour and ¼ cup of the sugar. In a large bowl with an electric mixer beat the egg whites with the lemon juice and the salt until they are foamy, add the cream of tartar, and beat the whites until they begin to hold soft peaks. Beat in the remaining sugar, 1 tablespoon at a time, add the vanilla, and beat the whites until they hold stiff peaks. Sift one-fourth of the flour mixture over the whites, fold it in gently but thoroughly, and sift and fold in the remaining flour mixture, one-fourth at a time, in the same manner.

Spoon the batter into an ungreased angel-food-cake pan or 10-inch tube pan fitted with a removable bottom, and bake the cake in the middle of a preheated 350° F. oven for 40 to 45 minutes, or until a cake tester inserted halfway between the center and the outside edge comes out clean. Invert the pan onto a rack or prop it, inverted, on the neck of a long-neck bottle and let the cake cool completely in the pan. Run a thin knife around the edge of the pan and the center tube and invert the cake onto a plate. Loosen the removable bottom from the cake and cut the cake into slices. Arrange the slices on dessert plates, spoon a pool of sauce around each slice, and serve the remaining sauce separately.

Bitter Chocolate Sauce

Makes about 1 cup

3 ounces dark sweet chocolate, chopped
1½ ounces unsweetened chocolate, chopped
2 tablespoons water
⅔ cup heavy cream, scalded

In a small heavy saucepan melt the sweet and unsweetened chocolate with the water over moderately low heat, stirring, until smooth. Add the hot cream and cook, stirring, until heated through and smooth. Serve warm or at room temperature.

A TROUT DINNER FOR FALL

Herbed Biscuits with Creamed Leeks
Trout Baked on Orange Wild Rice
Braised Celery Hearts
Purée of Acorn Squash with Mushrooms
Chocolate Cranberry Roll

∽

One of the 1982 Chardonnays of Napa Valley;
they have generally low-key flavor

SUGGESTIONS

Herbed Biscuits are delicious with or without creamed leeks as a filling. If you're making them as a bread, simply use the 3-inch cutter throughout. Addendum: Biscuits are best served hot from the oven. In general, reheating makes them lose their lightness and dries out the crumb. And if time is a factor, substitute frozen *vol-au-vent* puff pastry shells or toast as a vehicle for the creamed leeks.

Wild rice is an indisputable luxury. If you'd like to cut down on the amount called for in the baked trout recipe, substitute 1 cup raw white rice. Prepare it in a separate saucepan and undercook slightly. Add it when you combine the cooked wild rice, butter, and scallions.

∽

Components of the courses in this menu can be prepared 1 day ahead. These include the leek filling, wild rice, squash purée with mushrooms added, chocolate cake, and cranberry filling. If you're lucky enough to have two ovens, final assembly of this dinner will be a snap. If you're like most of the world, with one oven available, you will have to juggle space and time. Here's how we'd go about it.

Bring the squash purée to room temperature, fill the squash shells, then bake them for the last 15 minutes of the trout's cooking time.

Simultaneously, but on the top of the stove, warm the leek filling and the celery.

Remove the trout from the oven and keep warm with the squash shells. Fill the biscuits and serve.

Herbed Biscuits with Creamed Leeks

*Makes
12 biscuits,
serving 6*

For the creamed leeks

1¼ cups heavy cream
¼ cup water
salt and pepper
the white part of 4 leeks,
    halved lengthwise, washed well,
    and chopped
2 teaspoons fresh lemon juice

For the biscuits

½ cup minced onions
3 tablespoons cold unsalted butter
1 teaspoon crumbled dried thyme
1 teaspoon crumbled dried rosemary
½ teaspoon crumbled dried sage
2 cups all-purpose flour
1 tablespoon double-acting baking
    powder
½ teaspoon salt
½ teaspoon sugar
2 tablespoons cold vegetable shortening
¾ to 1 cup buttermilk

Make the creamed leeks: In a heavy saucepan combine the cream with the water and salt and pepper to taste and bring the mixture to a boil. Add the leeks and simmer the mixture for 30 to 40 minutes, or until it has thickened. Add the lemon juice and keep the leeks warm.

Make the biscuits: In a skillet cook the onions in 1 tablespoon of the butter over moderately low heat until they are softened. Add the herbs, cook the mixture, stirring, for 2 minutes, and let it cool.

Into a bowl sift together the flour, baking powder, salt, and sugar. Add the shortening and the remaining 2 tablespoons butter, and blend the mixture until it resembles meal. Make a well in the center, add ¾ cup of the buttermilk and the onion mixture, and stir the mixture, adding more buttermilk if necessary, until it just forms a dough.

On a floured surface roll the dough ¼ inch thick, and using a 3-inch cutter cut out 24 rounds (it will be necessary to reroll the scraps several times). Using a 2-inch cutter cut holes in the center of half the rounds to form rings and small rounds.

Arrange the 12 small rounds and the 12 large rounds on an ungreased baking sheet and top the large rounds with the rings, brushing the underside of the rings with water so that they adhere to the rounds. Bake the biscuits and the small rounds in a preheated 450° F. oven for 15 minutes, or until golden.

Arrange 2 of the biscuits on each of 6 heated plates, divide the leek mixture among the biscuits, and top the biscuits with the small rounds.

Trout Baked on Orange Wild Rice

Serves 6

2 cups wild rice, rinsed well and drained
1½ teaspoons salt
6 cups cold water
¾ stick (6 tablespoons) unsalted butter
1 large bunch of scallions, chopped,
   ¼ cup of the green part reserved
   for garnish

six ¾-pound brook trout, cleaned and
   boned, the heads and the tails intact
pepper
½ lemon, cut into 6 wedges
1 cup fresh orange juice
2 teaspoons grated orange rind
6 thin slices of orange and 6 parsley sprigs
   for garnish

In a saucepan combine the wild rice with the salt and the water, bring the water to a boil, and simmer the mixture for 35 to 45 minutes, or until the wild rice is just tender. Drain the wild rice if all the water has not been absorbed and toss it with 3 tablespoons of the butter, softened, and the scallions. Spread the wild rice evenly in a buttered large shallow baking dish.

Cut the remaining 3 tablespoons butter into 6 slices. Season the cavities of the trout with salt and pepper and stuff each cavity with a wedge of the lemon and 1 slice of butter. Arrange the trout on top of the rice, pour the orange juice over them, and bake the mixture, covered with buttered wax paper and foil, in a preheated 400° F. oven for 30 minutes, or until the trout just flakes. Sprinkle the wild rice with the reserved ¼ cup scallions and the orange rind, and garnish each trout with a twist of the sliced orange and a parsley sprig.

Braised Celery Hearts

Serves 6

½ onion, minced
¼ pound plum tomatoes, peeled, seeded,
   and chopped
1 tablespoon minced peeled gingerroot
5 celery hearts, trimmed to 5 inches in
   length, peeled and quartered

salt and pepper
3 tablespoons unsalted butter
1 cup dry white wine, heated
1 cup hot water

In a buttered shallow flameproof baking dish sprinkle the onion, tomatoes, and gingerroot, arrange the celery in one layer over the mixture, and season the mixture with salt and pepper. Dot the celery with the butter and pour the heated wine and the water over it. Bake the dish, covered with buttered wax paper and foil, in a preheated 350° F. oven for 1 to 1¼ hours, or until the celery is tender. Transfer the celery with a slotted spoon to a platter and keep it warm, covered loosely.

Reduce the braising liquid over high heat to about 1 cup, add salt and pepper to taste, and pour the liquid over the celery hearts.

Purée of Acorn Squash with Mushrooms

2 acorn squash	½ pound mushrooms, halved and sliced	*Serves 6 to 8*
½ stick (¼ cup) unsalted butter	toasted acorn squash seeds	
1 tablespoon brown sugar	(optional; recipe follows)	
salt and pepper		

Halve the squash crosswise, scoop out the seeds, reserving them if desired for toasted acorn squash seeds. Bake the squash halves, cut sides down, on a buttered baking sheet in a preheated 400° F. oven for 20 minutes. Turn the squash, cut sides up, and bake them for 20 minutes more, or until tender. Scoop out the pulp, leaving about ¼ inch in the shells, cut the shells in half, and reserve them.

In a food processor or blender purée the pulp with 2 tablespoons of the butter, the sugar, and salt and pepper to taste.

In a saucepan cook the mushrooms in the remaining 2 tablespoons butter over low heat, stirring, for 5 to 8 minutes, or until almost all the juice has evaporated. Season them with salt and pepper, and in a bowl combine them with the purée.

Mound the purée in the reserved squash shells, and on a baking sheet heat the purée-filled shells in a preheated 350° F. oven for 15 minutes, or until hot. Sprinkle the squash with the toasted acorn seeds, if desired.

Toasted Acorn Squash Seeds

the seeds of 2 acorn squash	salt to taste
1 tablespoon unsalted butter, melted	

Rub off any stringy membranes clinging to the seeds. In a bowl toss the seeds with the butter, and in a small baking dish toast them in a preheated 350° F. oven for 15 minutes, or until golden brown. Transfer the seeds to paper towels to drain and sprinkle them with salt.

Chocolate Cranberry Roll

*Makes one
16-inch roll*

For the cake
½ pound semisweet chocolate, chopped
¼ cup water
7 large egg yolks at room temperature
⅔ cup sugar
7 large egg whites at room temperature
a pinch of salt
a pinch of cream of tartar

For the filling
3 cups cranberries, picked over
1 cup sugar
1 cup water

For the icing
1 cup well-chilled heavy cream
3 tablespoons confectioners' sugar
1 tablespoon brandy (optional)

½ cup chocolate shavings for garnish
  (optional)

Make the cake: Butter a 15½-by-10½-by-1-inch jelly-roll pan, line it with wax paper, and butter the paper. In the top of a double boiler set over barely simmering water melt the chocolate with the water, stirring until the mixture is smooth, and let it cool slightly. In a bowl with an electric mixer beat the egg yolks with ⅓ cup of the sugar until the mixture is thick and pale. Add the chocolate mixture, stirring.

In a large bowl beat the egg whites with the salt until they are frothy, add the cream of tartar, and beat the whites until they hold soft peaks. Add the remaining ⅓ cup sugar gradually and beat the whites until they hold stiff peaks. Stir one-fourth of the whites into the chocolate mixture and fold in the remaining whites. Pour the batter into the prepared pan and spread it evenly with a metal spatula. Bake the cake in the middle of a preheated 350° F. oven for 15 minutes. Turn off the oven, open the oven door, and let the cake stand for 5 minutes. Transfer the pan to a rack and let the cake cool completely.

Make the filling: In a saucepan combine all the filling ingredients, bring the liquid to a boil, stirring, and simmer the mixture, stirring occasionally, for 15 minutes. Let the filling cool to lukewarm.

Make the icing: In a chilled bowl with an electric mixer beat the cream until it holds soft peaks, add the sugar and, if desired, the brandy, and beat the cream until it holds stiff peaks.

Cover the top of the cake with a dish towel and a baking sheet, invert the cake onto the baking sheet, and peel off the wax paper. Spread the cranberry mixture (warmed, if necessary, to make it easier to spread) over the cake, leaving a 1-inch border, and roll the cake up tightly lengthwise, lifting it with the towel and finishing with the seam side down. Transfer the roll to a platter, cover it with the icing, and sprinkle it with the shaved chocolate if desired.

INVITATIONS TO DINE . . .
WITH DASH

The word *dash* implies energy, style, and spirit. It also conveys speed. What you have in this small final grouping of menus in Chapter Four is just that: dinners with that little bit of something extra added, that something that sets them apart as special and exceptionally fine, but not burdensome to do. For example, a dinner for family and friends stars stuffed cabbage. You will need leftovers on hand to assemble it and a certain amount of time for it to cook, but once it and its gorgeous tomato sauce are made, dinner is on the table.

You will note that each of the menus that follow has its own very distinct persona. The cabbage dinner is homey. You imagine a cold winter night, a great wooden table, and lots of shining faces, all ages, sitting round. An anniversary dinner, on the other hand, is intimate: fresh flowers, *filets mignons*, an Apple Tart as a sweet. A scintillating dinner, our last one in the chapter, pulls out all the stops. *You* decide upon the occasion. A birthday? A promotion? Maybe both, maybe neither. One thing we're sure—a wonderful event is in store.

A DINNER FOR FAMILY AND FRIENDS

Eggs with Roquefort Cream
Lamb-Stuffed Cabbage
Florentines
Baked Pears

෨

White Zinfandel

SUGGESTIONS

The superb thing about a dish like stuffed cabbage is that it uses up leftovers in a wonderful way—one, without even seeming to, and, two, with all the verve of an original dish. The onus is really on the cook to figure out how to have all those leftovers on hand—a complete turnabout when you think back on the number of times you've tried to dream up ways to disguise the remains! So, simply anticipate when you want to serve stuffed cabbage, then arrange your week's menu, knowing that you'll need cooked lamb and rice as ingredients.

Substitute ground cooked beef for the lamb if you have it on hand.

For a very subtle flavoring, one that is far less pronounced than Roquefort but equally interesting, use fresh goat cheese in the filling for the eggs.

⌒

Do all you can in advance, including hard-boiling the eggs and preparing winter tomato sauce; the leftovers, of course; the pears and cookies. Then assemble the cabbage. During its last half hour of cooking, fill the eggs.

Eggs with Roquefort Cream

Serves 8

8 hard-boiled large eggs, halved
　　lengthwise (See Suggestions, page 4.)
shredded lettuce for lining the platter

For the filling
6 tablespoons sour cream
¼ pound cream cheese, cut into bits
　　and softened
2 ounces Roquefort cheese, crumbled

2 scallions, including the green tops,
　　chopped
1 tablespoon Dijon-style mustard,
　　or to taste
cayenne to taste
fresh lemon juice to taste
salt and pepper
ground walnuts for garnish

Transfer the yolks to the bowl of a food processor fitted with the metal blade. Arrange the whites on a platter lined with the lettuce and chill them, covered.

Make the filling: Add the sour cream, cream cheese, and Roquefort to the processor and blend until smooth. Add the remaining ingredients, except the walnuts, season the mixture with salt and pepper, and blend until combined well. Transfer the filling to a pastry bag, pipe it into the whites, and garnish the filling with the walnuts.

Serve any remaining filling separately with crackers.

Lamb-Stuffed Cabbage

Serves 8

For the stuffing
3 cups ground cooked lamb
½ cup cooked rice
½ cup raisins
¼ cup snipped fresh dill
¼ cup pine nuts, toasted lightly
2 large eggs, beaten lightly
1 tablespoon minced garlic
2 teaspoons ground cumin
½ teaspoon cinnamon
⅛ teaspoon ground cloves
salt and pepper
2 cups minced onions
½ stick (¼ cup) unsalted butter

a 2½- to 3-pound savoy cabbage, trimmed
3 cups chicken stock (page 154) or canned chicken broth
1 onion, chopped
½ carrot, chopped
½ stalk of celery, chopped
8 dill stems or 8 parsley stems
½ bay leaf
½ teaspoon dried thyme
1½ cups winter tomato sauce (page 185)

Make the stuffing: In a large bowl combine all the stuffing ingredients, except the onions and butter, and add salt and pepper to taste. In a skillet cook the onions in the butter over moderate heat, stirring, for 3 minutes. Add the onion mixture to the bowl to mix thoroughly with other stuffing ingredients.

Prepare the cabbage: In a kettle of boiling salted water blanch the cabbage for 10 minutes, drain it, and refresh it under cold water. Put the cabbage stem end down in the center of a large piece of doubled cheesecloth. Separate the leaves carefully until the core is visible. Cut out the core, mince it, and combine it with the stuffing. Mound half the stuffing in the center of the cabbage, distribute the remaining stuffing between the leaves, and reshape the cabbage. Bring the cheesecloth up around the cabbage to enclose it, and twist and tie the cloth on top so that the cabbage maintains its shape.

In a casserole just large enough to hold the cabbage combine 2 cups of the stock or broth, the onion, carrot, celery, dill stems, bay leaf, and thyme. Add the cabbage, pour the remaining 1 cup stock over it, and bring the liquid to a boil. Braise the cabbage, covered with a buttered piece of foil and the lid, in a preheated 375° F. oven, basting it occasionally, for 1½ hours, or until it is tender at the base. Transfer the cabbage to a colander and let it stand for 10 minutes. The cooking liquid may be strained into a small saucepan, reduced over moderately high heat to about 1 cup, and substituted for 1 cup of the canned beef broth in the winter tomato sauce. Remove the cheesecloth, transfer the cabbage to a heated platter, and spoon some of the sauce around. Serve the rest in a warm sauceboat.

Florentines and Baked Pears

Florentines

*Makes about
20 cookies*

¼ cup red glacéed cherries

¼ cup green glacéed cherries

½ cup plus 2 tablespoons heavy cream

½ cup sugar

5 tablespoons butter

1 cup blanched almonds, chopped fine

½ cup sliced blanched almonds

¼ cup all-purpose flour

¼ teaspoon almond extract

2 ounces semisweet chocolate

2 tablespoons strong brewed coffee

In a small heatproof bowl soak the cherries in boiling water to cover for 20 minutes, drain them well, and chop them.

In a heavy saucepan combine the cream, sugar, and 4 tablespoons of the butter, and bring the liquid to a boil over moderate heat, stirring until the sugar is dissolved. Remove the pan from the heat, stir in the chopped and sliced almonds, the cherries, flour, and almond extract, and blend the mixture well. Drop rounded tablespoons of the mixture 2 inches apart on well-buttered baking sheets, and flatten the mounds with a fork dipped in hot water. Bake the cookies in the upper third of a preheated 350° F. oven for 8 to 10 minutes, or until golden. Let the cookies cool on the baking sheet for 5 minutes and transfer them carefully with a spatula to a flat surface.

In the top of a double boiler set over simmering water melt the chocolate with the coffee and the remaining tablespoon of butter, and let the mixture cool until lukewarm. Form a cone from a doubled sheet of wax paper and fill it with the chocolate mixture. Snip the tip from the cone to form a $\frac{1}{16}$-inch opening, and pipe the chocolate in zigzag lines (see photograph) over the cookies. Let the cookies cool until the chocolate is set and arrange them on a serving plate.

Baked Pears

Serves 8

8 pears
8 whole cloves
1 lemon

For the syrup
3 cups dry white wine
2½ cups sugar
2 cups water
2 tablespoons fresh lemon juice
2 tablespoons orange-flavored liqueur
2 tablespoons grated orange rind
a 3-inch cinnamon stick

Peel the pears, leaving the stems intact, stud each pear with a clove near the stem, and drop the pears as they are peeled into a bowl of cold water acidulated with the juice of the lemon.

Make the syrup: In a flameproof casserole just large enough to hold the pears in one layer combine all the syrup ingredients, and bring the liquid to a boil over moderate heat, stirring to dissolve the sugar.

Add the pears to the casserole and bake them, covered with a round of wax paper and the lid, in a preheated 375° F. oven, turning them once, for 25 minutes, or until just tender. (Cooking time will vary according to the type and firmness of the pears used.)

Let the pears cool in the syrup. They can be served at room temperature or chilled overnight and served cold. Transfer with a slotted spoon to a serving bowl and spoon some of the syrup over them.

AN ANNIVERSARY DINNER

Smoked Salmon with Capers
Filets Mignons au Poivre with Peppers
Roasted Potato Sticks
Apple Tarts

∽

Santenay Rouge of 1981 or 1982 vintages

SUGGESTIONS

If you are really celebrating and the sky's the limit, opt for Norwegian smoked salmon, sliced very thin. It is a definite cut above the Nova Scotia variety and differs from it not only in flavor and texture but in price as well. Its buttery smoothness alone makes it well worth the additional investment.

Depending upon when your anniversary is, alter the fruit in the tarts to suit your tastes and the season.

∽

This anniversary menu is intentionally an easy one to prepare. Begin by making the Apple Tarts early in the day and keep them at room temperature. Then ready the bell peppers. The potatoes will require 1 hour's cooking time, during the last minutes of which you can cook the *filets mignons*. Keep them warm in the oven while you start celebrating with the salmon.

Smoked Salmon with Capers

¼ pound Nova Scotia smoked salmon, sliced very thin
2 teaspoons drained capers

freshly ground pepper
buttered toast points
lemon wedges

Serves 2

Divide the salmon between salad plates, sprinkle each serving with 1 teaspoon of the capers, and season with freshly ground pepper to taste. Serve the salmon with the toast points and the lemon wedges.

Filets Mignons au Poivre with Peppers

Serves 2

two 1½-inch-thick *filets mignons*
(each weighing about 6 ounces),
barded or wrapped with strips of
bacon and tied with kitchen string
salt
2 tablespoons white peppercorns, cracked
2 tablespoons black peppercorns, cracked
1 red bell pepper, cut into julienne strips

1 green bell pepper, cut into julienne
strips
3 tablespoons unsalted butter
freshly ground pepper
1 tablespoon vegetable oil
2 tablespoons brown stock (page 155) or
canned beef broth
2 tablespoons Tawny Port
⅓ cup heavy cream

Pat the steaks dry and sprinkle them with salt. In a bowl combine the peppercorns and with the heel of the hand press them firmly into the steaks, covering both sides evenly.

In a skillet sweat the red and green bell peppers in 1 tablespoon of the butter, covered with a buttered round of wax paper and the lid, over low heat, stirring occasionally, for 15 minutes, or until softened. Season with salt and sparingly with pepper, and keep warm.

In a heavy skillet heat 1 tablespoon of the butter and the oil over moderately high heat until the fat is hot, and in it sauté the steaks for 3 to 4 minutes on each side for rare meat. Transfer the steaks to a heated platter and remove and discard the barding and string.

Pour off the fat in the skillet, add the stock or broth and the Port, and deglaze the skillet over high heat, scraping up the brown bits clinging to the bottom and sides. Reduce the liquid until it is syrupy, stir in the cream, and reduce the liquid, stirring, until thickened slightly. Stir in the remaining tablespoon of butter, cut into bits, and salt and pepper to taste and nap the steaks with the sauce. Top the steaks with the peppers.

Roasted Potato Sticks

Serves 2

1½ pounds large boiling potatoes
salt and pepper

1 tablespoon unsalted butter

Cut the potatoes into sticks, 3 by 1 by ¾ inches, and arrange them in a well-buttered shallow flameproof baking pan just large enough to hold them in one layer. Add enough water to half cover, sprinkle them with salt and pepper, and dot with butter. Bring the water to a boil over high heat, transfer the pan to the lower third of a preheated 425° F. oven, and bake the potatoes for 30 minutes, or until the water is evaporated and the undersides are golden. Turn the potatoes carefully with a spatula and bake 30 minutes more, or until browned.

Marbled Mousses and Apple Tart

Apple Tarts

Basic Pastry Dough (page 202)
2 Golden Delicious apples, peeled, cored,
   and sliced crosswise very thin
2 tablespoons sugar, or to taste
2 tablespoons unsalted butter

For the glaze (makes about ½ cup)
½ cup apricot preserves, strained
1 tablespoon Cognac

Serves 2

Halve the pastry dough and reserve one-half of it, covered and chilled or frozen, for another use. Halve the remaining dough and roll each half on a lightly floured surface into a 7-inch round. Chill the rounds on a heavy baking sheet for 30 minutes.

Arrange the apple slices decoratively on the pastry rounds. Then sprinkle each round with about 1 tablespoon of the sugar and dot each with 1 tablespoon of the butter. Bake the tarts in the lower third of a preheated 425° F. oven for 30 minutes, or until the apples are browned and the pastry is golden brown. Transfer to a rack.

Make the glaze: While the tarts are baking, in a small saucepan bring the ingredients to a boil and simmer, stirring, for 1 minute.

While the tarts are still warm, brush lightly with the heated glaze. Serve warm or at room temperature with slightly sweetened whipped cream or vanilla ice cream, if desired.

A SCINTILLATING DINNER

Shrimp and Celery Rémoulade
Rack of Lamb Persillé
Green Bean Timbales
Orange Buttered Carrots
Marbled Mousses

Fine Bordeaux of 1966 or 1970 vintages

SUGGESTIONS

As superb as Shrimp and Celery *Rémoulade* is, *céleri rémoulade*, made with celery root—also known as celeriac and very different in texture—that is peeled and sliced thin, is also a winner.

If you have the good luck to have fresh herbs on hand for the rack of lamb, remember that the ratio of dried to fresh is 1 to 3. In short, ¼ teaspoon dried will amount to ¾ teaspoon fresh.

Unlike many recipes, the ones in this menu can be doubled with no untoward results, including the mousse recipe. A particularly nice note to remember when you are planning your next *dîner à quatre*.

This dazzling dinner is also an easy one to prepare. Begin the day before by making the mousses and marinating the lamb. Early on the day of the dinner ready the celery, shrimp, and *rémoulade* sauce and cook the beans for the timbales. About an hour before you intend to sit down for dinner, combine the first course. Then prepare the timbales and bake them. Remove from the oven and let stand as directed in the recipe. Immediately begin the rack and while it is roasting cook the carrots. You will need to remove the timbales from the water bath but keep them warm, covered. An hour, more or less, is a short time when you think of the lasting rewards you'll have with this dinner.

Rack of Lamb Persillé, Green Bean Timbales, and Orange Buttered Carrots (top)
Filets Mignons au Poivre with Peppers and Roasted Potato Sticks (bottom)

Shrimp and Celery Rémoulade

Serves 2

about 2 stalks of celery, strings removed,
    cut into 2-inch-long julienne strips
    (enough to measure ¾ cup)
½ pound shrimp
1 small bay leaf
a 1-inch piece of lemon rind
¼ teaspoon dried thyme

soft-leafed lettuce for lining the
    salad plates

For the rémoulade sauce
¼ cup Quick Mayonnaise (page 20)
1 tablespoon minced scallion
2 teaspoons Dijon-style mustard
2 teaspoons red-wine vinegar
1 teaspoon minced fresh parsley leaves
1 teaspoon fresh lemon juice
cayenne to taste
salt and pepper

Let the celery strips stand in a bowl of ice water for at least 30 minutes, or until very crisp.

Plunge the shrimp into a saucepan of boiling salted water with the bay leaf, lemon rind, and thyme, bring the water back to a boil, and immediately drain the shrimp in a colander. Rinse the shrimp under cold water, shell, and devein them.

Make the rémoulade sauce: In a bowl combine the sauce ingredients with cayenne, salt, and pepper to taste.

Fold the shrimp and celery, patted dry, into the sauce, and divide the mixture among salad plates lined with the lettuce.

Rack of Lamb Persillé

Serves 2

For the marinade
2 teaspoons Dijon-style mustard
1 teaspoon olive oil
1 garlic clove, crushed to a paste
a pinch of dried thyme
a pinch of dried rosemary, crumbled
salt and pepper

a 6-rib rack of lamb (about 1¼ pounds),
    trimmed of all but a thin layer of fat
    and with the bones trimmed and
    partially cracked for easy carving

1 tablespoon minced shallot
1 garlic clove, minced
3 tablespoons unsalted butter
½ cup stale bread crumbs
1 tablespoon minced fresh parsley leaves
¼ teaspoon dried thyme
¼ teaspoon dried rosemary
sprigs of watercress for garnish

Prepare the lamb: In a small bowl combine well all the marinade ingredients with salt and pepper to taste. Rub the lamb with the marinade, then let it marinate, covered and chilled, overnight.

In a skillet cook the shallot and garlic in the butter over moderate heat, stirring, until softened. Add the bread crumbs, parsley, thyme, rosemary, and salt and pepper to taste, heat the mixture, stirring, for 2 minutes, and remove the skillet from the heat.

Arrange the lamb, fat side up, in a heavy baking pan and roast it in a preheated 500° F. oven for 10 minutes. Pat the crumb mixture firmly onto the browned lamb fat, reduce the heat to 400° F., and roast the lamb for 10 to 12 minutes more for medium-rare meat. Arrange the lamb on a serving platter with Green Bean Timbales and Orange Buttered Carrots (both recipes follow) and garnish with the watercress.

Green Bean Timbales

½ pound green beans, trimmed
2 tablespoons minced shallot
1 tablespoon unsalted butter
3 tablespoons heavy cream

freshly grated nutmeg to taste
salt and pepper
1 large egg

Serves 2

In a saucepan of boiling salted water cook the beans for 6 minutes, drain, and chop the beans coarse. In a small skillet cook the shallot in the butter over moderately low heat, stirring, until softened, add the beans, and sweat the mixture, covered with a buttered round of wax paper and the lid, for 2 minutes.

In a food processor fitted with the metal blade purée the bean mixture with the cream, nutmeg, and salt and pepper to taste. With the motor running, add the egg and blend the mixture for just 3 seconds.

Divide the mixture between 2 well-buttered ¾-cup timbale molds, and cover the molds with buttered pieces of foil. Put the molds in a small baking pan, add enough boiling water to the pan to reach halfway up the sides of the molds, and bake the timbales in a preheated 350° F. oven for 25 to 30 minutes, or until a small knife inserted in the centers comes out clean. Remove the timbales from the water and let them stand for 5 minutes. Invert the molds onto the serving platter to unmold them.

Orange Buttered Carrots

Serves 2

½ pound carrots, cut into 2-by-½-inch
   strips
1½ tablespoons unsalted butter
¼ cup fresh orange juice

a pinch of sugar
salt and pepper
fresh lemon juice to taste (optional)

In a saucepan of boiling salted water cook the carrots for 3 to 4 minutes, or until just tender, and drain them.

In a small saucepan melt the butter over moderately high heat, add the carrots, orange juice, sugar, and salt and pepper to taste, and cook, stirring, until the liquid is evaporated and the carrots are glazed. Sprinkle them with the lemon juice, if desired.

Marbled Mousses

Serves 2

2 ounces bittersweet chocolate,
   cut into pieces
1 tablespoon strong freshly brewed coffee
2 large egg whites at room temperature
a pinch of cream of tartar

a pinch of salt
2 tablespoons sugar
½ cup well-chilled heavy cream
½ teaspoon vanilla

Fit two ⅓-cup ramekins with a 6-inch-wide band of wax paper, doubled and oiled with flavorless vegetable oil, to form a standing collar extending 1 inch above the rims of the molds.

In a heatproof bowl set over simmering water melt the chocolate with the coffee, stirring. Remove the bowl from the pan and let the chocolate cool.

In a small bowl beat the egg whites with the cream of tartar and salt until they hold soft peaks, add 1 tablespoon of the sugar, and beat the whites until they just hold stiff peaks. In another small bowl beat the cream with the remaining 1 tablespoon sugar and the vanilla until it holds stiff peaks.

Fold half the whites into the chocolate mixture, then fold in half the whipped cream. Fold the remaining whites and remaining cream together gently but thoroughly. Swirl the chocolate mixture into the egg white–cream mixture, leaving decorative traces of the chocolate. Scoop the mousse into the prepared ramekins and chill the dishes, covered loosely, for at least 1 hour or overnight. Remove the wax-paper collars before serving.

Chapter Five

Special Occasions

ဢ

Many of the occasions that we are calling special in Chapter Five happen to be much-loved holidays: Saint Valentine's Day, Thanksgiving, Christmas, and New Year's. Certain expectations imbue these days and the menus that accompany them. You can stray only so far from the traditional Thanksgiving turkey, and we did! In general, though, and as a guiding rule, tamper with tradition and that wonderful thing called nostalgia only up to a certain point.

All of which is to say that there is a slew of occasions, not holidays per se, that remain to be made special. These will be those days that are penciled in boldly on your own calendar—birthdays, anniversaries, engagements, christenings. If appropriate, use some of the menus in this chapter for such events. That's what we would call an *extra-special* personal remembrance.

A VALENTINE DINNER

Hearts of Palm and Beet Salad with Horseradish Cream
Herbed Lamb Chops
Buttered Wild Rice   Parsleyed Baby Carrots
Baked Custard Meringue Desserts
or Chocolate Fondue with Strawberries

A Saint-Emilion or Pomerol of 1979 vintage

The fourteenth of February presupposes something special. After all, it's Valentine's Day: a wonderful reason to add a little extra to the everyday routine. Roses. A card. A cozy candlelight dinner with a menu like the one that follows, suited to the occasion. It's elegant, effortless, and, if you prepare both desserts, guaranteed to end sweet.

SUGGESTIONS

Green Bean Salad with Horseradish Dressing (page 191) is a very suitable replacement for the salad of hearts of palm and beets.

A rack of lamb is a section of the ribs that are still attached to one another. As a consequence, a certain amount of trimming is required and can probably be most expeditiously done by your butcher.

Sautéed mushrooms and/or chopped toasted nuts—almonds or pine nuts—would be delicious additions to the wild rice.

Accompany the strawberries with ripe, sweet pineapple spears or clementine or mandarin-orange sections.

Prepare the custards in advance up to the point of browning the tops.

The lettuce and beets for the salad can also be readied well ahead of serving.

Cook the rice ahead, if you like, but toss it with the butter at the last minute.

Then allow about 30 minutes for the final assembly of dinner, which means roasting the rack, heating the rice, cooking the carrots, and dressing the salad.

While you brew up a pot of espresso, combine the fondue and finish the custards.

Chocolate Fondue with Strawberries and
Baked Custard Meringue Desserts

Herbed Lamb Chops with Buttered Wild Rice and Parsleyed Baby Carrots

Hearts of Palm and Beet Salad with Horseradish Cream

Serves 2

soft-leafed lettuce for lining the
    salad plates
4 canned hearts of palm, halved
    lengthwise
2 small cooked beets (page 272), patted
    dry, quartered, and sliced ¼ inch thick

For the dressing
3 tablespoons heavy cream
1 tablespoon fresh lemon juice
1 teaspoon bottled horseradish, or to taste
salt and pepper
1 tablespoon olive oil

Line 2 salad plates with the lettuce and arrange the hearts of palm and beet slices decoratively on the greens.

Make the dressing: In a small bowl whisk together the cream, lemon juice, horseradish, and salt and pepper to taste for 10 seconds, or until frothy, add the oil, drop by drop, whisking, and whisk until combined well. Spoon the dressing over the salads.

Herbed Lamb Chops

a 1- to 1¼-pound 4-rib rack of lamb,
  trimmed of all but a thin layer of fat,
  prepared for easy cutting, and the
  bones shortened

2 teaspoons olive oil
¼ teaspoon dried rosemary, crumbled
salt and pepper

Serves 2

Rub the lamb with the oil and rosemary, sprinkle it with salt and pepper, and let it stand at room temperature for 1 hour.

Roast the lamb, fat side up, in a small roasting pan in a preheated 500° F. oven for 10 minutes, and reduce the heat to 400° F. Roast for 8 minutes more for medium-rare meat. Let the lamb stand for 10 minutes, transfer it to a cutting board, and cut it into chops.

Buttered Wild Rice

⅓ cup wild rice
2 tablespoons unsalted butter

salt and pepper

Serves 2

Rinse the rice in a sieve under running cold water for 2 minutes, drain it well, and in a small saucepan combine it with enough water to cover it by 3 inches. Bring the water to a boil, simmer the rice for 30 to 45 minutes, or until fluffy, and drain it in a colander.

In the saucepan melt the butter over moderate heat, add the rice, and heat it, stirring, for 2 to 3 minutes, or until heated through. Season the rice with salt and pepper.

Parsleyed Baby Carrots

½ pound baby carrots, peeled and
  trimmed to the same size
1 tablespoon unsalted butter

1 teaspoon minced fresh parsley leaves
salt and pepper

Serves 2

In a saucepan of boiling salted water boil the carrots 4 to 6 minutes, until tender; drain.

In the saucepan melt the butter with the parsley over moderate heat, add the carrots, and heat them, swirling the pan, for 1 to 2 minutes, or until coated well with the butter. Season the carrots with salt and pepper.

Baked Custard Meringue Desserts

Serves 2

For the custard
1 large whole egg
1 large egg yolk
1½ tablespoons sugar
¼ teaspoon grated lemon rind
1 cup milk, scalded
3 tablespoons seedless raspberry jam

For the meringue
1 large egg white
a pinch of cream of tartar
a pinch of salt
2 tablespoons granulated sugar
confectioners' sugar for sifting over
  the meringue

Make the custard: In a heatproof bowl beat together the whole egg, egg yolk, sugar, and lemon rind, add the hot milk, in a stream, whisking, and strain the mixture through a fine sieve into 2 round 1-cup ovenproof dishes. Cover each dish with foil and put the dishes in a baking pan just large enough to hold them. Add enough hot water to the pan to reach 1 inch up the sides of the dishes, and bake the custards in the middle of a preheated 325° F. oven for 25 minutes, or until a knife inserted in the center comes out clean. Transfer the dishes to a rack, remove the foil covers, and let the custards cool to room temperature.

In a small pan melt the raspberry jam over moderately low heat, spread it evenly over the custards, and chill the custards, covered, for at least 2 hours, or overnight.

Make the meringue: In a bowl beat the egg white with the cream of tartar and salt until it holds soft peaks, add 1 tablespoon of the granulated sugar, and beat the meringue until it holds stiff peaks. Fold in the remaining tablespoon granulated sugar.

Spread the meringue over the custards, leaving a ⅓-inch edge, and sift the confectioners' sugar lightly over it. Bake the custards in the middle of a preheated 425° F. oven for 5 minutes, or until the meringue is golden.

Chocolate Fondue with Strawberries

Serves 2

6 ounces Toblerone milk chocolate,
  broken into pieces, or another good-
  quality milk chocolate

¼ cup heavy cream
1 pint strawberries, unstemmed,
  rinsed and patted dry

In the top of a double boiler set over simmering water melt the chocolate with the cream, stirring occasionally, until the mixture is smooth and heated through. Pour the chocolate into a heated fondue pot or 2 heated individual serving bowls. Arrange the berries on a platter and serve them with the fondue.

Any remaining chocolate fondue may be kept, covered and chilled, and served, reheated, as a sauce over ice cream.

PASSOVER SEDER

Haroseth
Chicken Soup with Knaidlach
Gefilte Fish
Chopped Liver
Brisket of Beef
Potato Kugel
Matzo-Meal Pancakes
Tzimmes
Beet Salad
Passover Nut Cakes
Passover Spongecake

§

Passover, one of the most momentous events in Jewish history, commemorates the flight of the children of Israel from Egyptian bondage. It is an eight-day religious remembrance begun by a Seder, the festive ceremony symbolic of the last meal Jews ate before beginning their exodus. The Seder starts at sundown on the first night of the holiday in the Jewish home with the reading of the *Haggadah*, the narrative of the exodus, at the Seder table. Then the Seder dinner begins, filled with traditional dishes and enlivened by the laughter of children and grown-ups playing Passover games. It is a time specific to sharing with family and friends and a unique reminder of a journey, both literally and figuratively, from darkness into light.

SUGGESTIONS

The much-loved recipes of a Seder are traditionally handed down from grand-mother to mother to daughter, from family to family, and from friend to friend. Individual interpretation of these recipes is, of course, part of the delight of the celebration. For example, some prefer to make matzo balls that are large and fluffy; others, those that are small and hard. Some make chicken stock with the skins left on the onions, rendering it rich and coppery in color; others prefer a clear soup made with onions that have been peeled and quartered. In general, the food at a Seder is home cooking at its very best.

A strick observance of the eight days of Passover means that no leavening agents are eaten or used in the preparation of the holiday food. Matzo meal, potato flour, or eggs are used instead. There should also be no legumes or grains.

And just as certain foods are proscribed, so others are required as part of the tradition and the Seder service. They include: three whole matzos, wrapped in a special cloth set out on a plate, two of these representing the loaves set out in the Temple, the third, the Passover; a roasted lamb shank, symbolizing the Passover sacrifice; parsley or another green herb, signifying the hope of renewal; the top part of a horseradish root, symbolizing the bitterness of past experience; and a roasted egg, the symbol of life.

At each table setting, moreover, there should be a wine glass and a plate of haroseth, which represents the mortar for the bricks the Israelites had to make as slaves. On the table a plate of matzos, a bowl of salt water, and some prepared horseradish should be arrayed.

The service will be read from *Haggadahs*, which in many families have been collected, like the Passover recipes, lovingly, over time.

ᕽ

There is such joyous anticipation in the approach of a Seder that the preparation of the food for it starts early. Stock is made and frozen. Matzo balls are tested—and sometimes remade. Extras, like little macaroons, start being baked; fruit is stewed, then left to mellow in its own sweet syrups.

The closer the Seder comes, the more intense the preparations. By this time the shopping is complete, and the serious cooking can get underway. You might start with the Gefilte Fish; it takes time and might best be done with a friend. Then the other courses will fall into place. With the exceptions of the Tzimmes and pan-cakes, all can be made in advance. The dilemma is not really how to schedule them but how to store them until the celebration.

Passover Spongecake and Passover Nut Cakes

Haroseth (Apple and Nut Spread)

Makes about 4 cups

2 large McIntosh apples
½ cup raisins, chopped coarse
½ cup walnuts, chopped coarse
½ cup almonds, chopped coarse
½ cup pitted dates

1 teaspoon cinnamon
1 teaspoon ground ginger
¼ to ⅓ cup sweet red wine, such as
    Concord grape wine

Quarter, peel, and core the apples, then chop them coarse.

In a bowl combine the apples, raisins, nuts, dates, and spices, then stir in the wine.

To serve, spread on pieces of matzo and eat with the pieces of bitter herb, which represent the bitterness of slavery.

Chicken Soup with Knaidlach (Matzo Balls)

Makes about 8 cups, serving 8

For the matzo balls (makes about six to
    eight 1½-inch matzo balls)
2 large eggs, beaten lightly
2 tablespoons rendered chicken fat,
    melted and cooled
½ cup matzo meal

1 teaspoon salt
2 tablespoons seltzer or chicken stock
1 teaspoon minced fresh parsley

8 cups chicken stock (page 154) or
    canned chicken broth

Make the matzo balls: In a bowl combine eggs and chicken fat. Stir in the matzo meal and salt. Add the seltzer and parsley and stir just to combine. Chill, covered, for 30 minutes.

In a large saucepan bring the stock or broth to a gentle boil. Then dip your hands in cold water and start forming rounded tablespoons of the matzo mixture into balls. Add the balls to the stock and simmer them, covered, for 20 to 30 minutes, or until tender when pierced with a wooden toothpick.

Divide the matzo balls among heated bowls and ladle the stock over them.

Gefilte Fish

Serves 8 to 10

For the stock
2 pounds bones and trimmings of
    whitefish, pike, and carp
8 cups water
4 onions, sliced
2 large carrots, sliced
1 stalk of celery
1 teaspoon salt

2 pounds pike fillets, skinned
2 pounds whitefish fillets, skinned
1 pound carp fillets, skinned
1 onion, sliced
3 large egg yolks
2 tablespoons matzo meal
salt and pepper
3 large egg whites
matzos and bottled horseradish
    as accompaniments

Make the stock: In a large saucepan combine all the stock ingredients and bring to a boil over moderately high heat. Reduce the heat to moderate, skimming off the froth that rises to the surface, and simmer for 25 minutes. Strain the stock through a fine sieve into another saucepan, pressing hard on the solids. Discard the solids and reserve the stock.

Grind the three types of fish fillets through the fine disk of a food grinder into a large bowl. In a food processor fitted with the metal blade purée the onion with the egg yolks and beat the purée into the fish mixture until combined. Sprinkle the matzo meal over the top with 1½ teaspoons salt and pepper to taste, combine well, and transfer to a bowl.

In another bowl beat the egg whites with a pinch of salt until they just hold stiff peaks but are not dry, and fold one-fourth of them into the fish mixture. Fold in the remaining whites gently but thoroughly.

Bring the reserved stock to a vigorous simmer. Then dip your hands in cold water and start forming the fish mixture into ovals about 2 inches long. Add the dumplings, 1 at a time, to the stock and cook at a bare simmer, covered partially, for 2 hours. Remove the lid, let the dumplings cool in the stock, and transfer them to a platter. Chill, covered. Pour the stock into a shallow dish and chill it for 1 hour, or until set.

To serve, chop the jellied stock and arrange it around the fish dumplings on the platter. Serve accompanied by the horseradish and matzos.

Chopped Liver

*Serves 4 to 6
as an hors
d'oeuvre*

1 pound chicken livers, trimmed
3 onions, chopped
¼ cup rendered chicken fat
3 hard-boiled eggs, quartered
1 teaspoon salt

½ teaspoon pepper
¼ teaspoon allspice
matzos as an accompaniment
additional hard-boiled egg, sieved,
   and/or minced onion for garnishes

Pat the chicken livers dry. On the rack of a broiler pan broil the livers under a preheated broiler about 3 inches from the heat, turning them, for 5 to 6 minutes in all, or until golden. Let cool.

In a large, heavy skillet cook the onions in the chicken fat over moderately low heat, stirring, for 5 minutes, or until softened, and transfer to a bowl. Add the livers and the eggs, salt, pepper, and allspice. Combine, then grind the mixture through the fine disk of a food grinder into another bowl. Add more allspice and salt and pepper to taste and grind the mixture again through the fine disk of the food grinder into a serving bowl.

To serve, spread the chopped liver on pieces of matzo and garnish each with the sieved egg and/or minced onion.

Brisket of Beef

Serves 6

a 3-pound first-cut brisket of beef
salt and pepper
5 onions, sliced

1 teaspoon minced garlic
2 teaspoons potato starch

Rub the brisket with salt and pepper.

Into a heavy casserole just large enough to hold the brisket arrange the onions, top them with the beef, and sprinkle the garlic over the top. Cover the brisket with foil and the lid and bake it in a preheated 325° F. oven for 2½ to 3 hours, or until tender. Let the meat stand in the pan for 20 minutes, then transfer it to a cutting board.

Skim the fat from the pan juices, sprinkle the potato starch over the onions, and simmer the mixture, stirring, for 2 minutes, or until just thickened. Remove the casserole from the heat immediately and pour the sauce into a heated sauceboat. Slice the brisket thin, arrange it on a heated platter, and nap it with some of the sauce.

Potato Kugel (Potato Pudding)

Serves 6 to 8

1 cup minced onion
⅓ cup peanut oil
3 pounds potatoes, grated coarse
2 large eggs, beaten lightly

¼ cup potato starch
1 teaspoon salt
¼ teaspoon cinnamon
¼ teaspoon pepper

In a heavy skillet cook the onion in the peanut oil over moderately low heat, stirring, for 3 to 5 minutes, or until softened. Remove the skillet from the heat and let cool.

In a large bowl combine the onion mixture with the remaining ingredients. Transfer the mixture to a well-oiled 1½-quart baking dish and bake in a preheated 400° F. oven for 1 hour, or until crusty and golden.

Matzo-Meal Pancakes

Serves 4

½ cup matzo meal
½ cup water
3 large egg yolks

½ teaspoon salt
3 large egg whites
3 tablespoons unsalted butter

In a small bowl combine the matzo meal and water. In another bowl beat the egg yolks until pale and thick, and beat in the matzo-meal mixture with the salt.

In a bowl beat the egg whites with a pinch of salt until they just hold stiff peaks but are not dry. Stir one-fourth of them into the meal mixture, then fold in the remaining whites.

In a heavy skillet heat the butter until it is foamy, drop in the batter by heaping tablespoons, and cook the pancakes over moderate heat for 1 minute on each side, or until golden. Serve with jam.

Tzimmes (Candied Carrots)

Serves 6

8 large carrots, cut into ¼-inch slices
⅔ cup honey
2 tablespoons unsalted butter

1 tablespoon fresh lemon juice
salt

In a saucepan combine the carrots with enough cold water to cover them by 1 inch, and bring the water to a boil over moderately high heat. Simmer the carrots for 5 minutes, or until barely tender. Pour off the water, and add the remaining ingredients with salt to taste. Simmer the carrots for 10 to 15 minutes, or until they are tender and coated well with the honey mixture. Transfer the carrots to a heated serving dish.

Beet Salad

Serves 6

1½ pounds small beets
1 onion, chopped
2 tablespoons red-wine vinegar

1 small garlic clove, mashed to a paste
salt and pepper

Scrub and trim the beets, leaving the roots and 2 inches of the stems attached. Reserve the beet greens for another use.

Put the beets in a large saucepan, add enough cold water to the pan to cover the beets by 2 inches, and bring the water to a boil. Simmer the beets, covered, for 35 to 45 minutes, or until tender. Drain, peel the beets, and cut them into bite-size pieces.

In a bowl combine the beets with the remaining ingredients and salt and pepper to taste, toss well, and let stand, covered, at room temperature for 6 hours. Chill the salad, covered, stirring occasionally, overnight.

Passover Nut Cakes

*Makes four
8-inch loaves*

12 large egg yolks
2 cups sugar
3 tablespoons water
3 tablespoons fresh lemon juice
1 tablespoon vegetable oil

1½ cups matzo cake meal
1 cup finely chopped walnuts
½ cup potato starch
12 large egg whites
a pinch of salt

In a large bowl with an electric mixer beat the egg yolks and the sugar until light and lemon-colored, then beat in the water, lemon juice, and oil. Stir in the cake meal, nuts, and potato starch.

In another large bowl with the electric mixer beat the egg whites with the salt until they hold stiff peaks. Stir one-fourth of them into the batter, then fold in the remaining whites gently but thoroughly. Spoon the batter into 4 well-oiled 8½-by-4½-by-2⅝ loaf pans and bake in a preheated 325° F. oven for 50 minutes, or until a cake tester comes out clean. Invert a rack over the cakes and invert the cakes onto it. Let cool for 15 minutes.

Passover Spongecake

9 large egg yolks
1 cup sugar
¾ cup matzo cake meal
¼ cup potato starch
2 tablespoons fresh lemon juice

1 tablespoon grated lemon rind
9 large egg whites at room temperature
a pinch of salt
3 tablespoons club soda or water

*Makes one
9-inch
tube cake*

In a bowl with an electric mixer beat the egg yolks with ½ cup of the sugar until light and lemon-colored. Stir in the cake meal, potato starch, lemon juice, and rind.

In a large bowl with the electric mixer beat the egg whites with the salt until they hold soft peaks. Add the remaining ½ cup sugar, 1 tablespoon at a time, beating, and beat the meringue until it holds stiff peaks.

Add the soda water or plain water to the cake batter, then stir in one-fourth of the meringue. Fold in the remaining meringue gently but thoroughly. Spoon the batter into a well-oiled 9-inch tube pan, and bake in a preheated 325° F. oven for 1 hour, or until a cake tester comes out clean. Invert a rack over the cake and invert the cake onto it. Let cool for 20 minutes.

COCKTAILS AFTER THE DERBY

Horse's Necks
Mint Juleps
Benne Wafers
Cheddar Bites
Open-Faced Ham Biscuits
Grits and Sausage Croquettes
Kentucky Hot Browns

Not even world wars were able to bring about a cancellation of the running of the Kentucky Derby. It happens on the first Saturday in May at Churchill Downs and has been doing so since 1875. The traditions surrounding it, as you may imagine, are equally long-standing, like the famous Mint Julep and the Kentucky Hot Brown. So is the tradition of having a darn good time. If you're planning your own celebration of yet another Run for the Roses, do avail yourself of the Suggestions.

Horse's Necks
(Rye and Ginger Ale)

1 lemon
1 jigger (1½ ounces) straight rye
or blended whiskey

chilled ginger ale

Makes 1 drink

With a lemon zester remove the rind from the lemon in a long spiral, beginning at one end and working around the lemon.

Arrange the spiral in a highball glass, hooking one end of it over the edge of the glass, and fill the glass with ice. Add the rye and 1 teaspoon juice from the lemon, or to taste, and fill the glass with the ginger ale.

From the top: Benne Wafers, Cheddar Bites,
and Open-Faced Ham Biscuits

SUGGESTIONS

For the Mint Juleps you will need a supply of fresh mint on hand. To store, rinse and pat the sprigs gently dry; put in a plastic bag, add a dampened paper towel, then seal airtight. If you try to store mint like fresh parsley or dill, with only its stems submerged in water, its leaves will dry out.

Benne, in the South, is another word for sesame. Benne wafers hail from Charleston, South Carolina, and are a great favorite as a cocktail cracker. See below for how long to store the wafers.

Hominy—another Southern favorite—is the kernels of dried corn with the hull and germ removed. The grits are the ground kernels. Look for the quick-cooking variety of grits, called for in the recipe, in the cereal section of the supermarket. They will take roughly 5 minutes to prepare as opposed to the 30 minutes or so for the regular-cooking variety.

You will see that the cream sauce called for in the recipe for Kentucky Hot Browns—open-faced turkey, tomato, and cheese toasts—is made with unheated liquid being added to the *roux*. For information on making white sauces in general, see page 132.

∽

Make the sugar syrup for the Mint Juleps well in advance and chill.

Benne wafers can be made 5 days in advance if stored in an airtight container.

Cheddar Bites can be made 3 days ahead and sealed airtight. If you are serving them warm, reheat on baking sheets in a 300° F. oven for 5 minutes.

The biscuits for Open-Faced Ham Biscuits can be baked and frozen for up to 1 month. Thaw at room temperature before putting the topping on them.

The croquettes can be made up to 2 days ahead and kept covered and chilled. Reheat on a jelly-roll pan in a preheated 375° F. oven, shaking the pan occasionally, for 5 to 8 minutes, or until heated through.

As for the Kentucky Hot Browns, make the toasts 1 day ahead and store in an airtight container. Make the sauce the same day, but keep chilled.

Mint Juleps

Mint Julep

For the sugar syrup
1 cup granulated sugar
2 cups water

3 fresh mint leaves
crushed ice

1½ jiggers (2¼ ounces) bourbon
a sprig of fresh mint dusted with
    confectioners' sugar for garnish

Makes 1 drink

Make the sugar syrup: In a saucepan combine the sugar and water, bring the mixture to a boil, stirring and washing down any sugar crystals clinging to the sides with a brush dipped in cold water, until the sugar is dissolved, and cook the syrup over moderate heat, undisturbed, for 5 minutes. Let cool. The syrup will keep indefinitely, chilled, in a sealed jar.

In a silver julep cup or in a highball glass combine the mint leaves and 1 tablespoon of the sugar syrup. Bruise the mint leaves with a spoon, and mound the ice in the cup or glass. Pour in the bourbon, stir, and add enough more ice to mound it slightly above the rim. Freeze the drink for 30 minutes and garnish it before serving with the remaining mint.

Benne Wafers

*Makes about
75 wafers*

½ cup plus 2 tablespoons (about 3
    ounces) sesame seeds
2 cups all-purpose flour
1½ teaspoons salt
1 teaspoon double-acting baking powder
3 tablespoons cold unsalted butter,
    cut into bits

3 tablespoons cold lard or vegetable
    shortening, cut into bits
⅓ to ½ cup ice water
3 tablespoons melted unsalted butter

Spread ½ cup of the sesame seeds on a jelly-roll pan and toast them in a preheated 300° F. oven, shaking the pan once or twice, for 10 minutes, or until golden. Transfer the seeds to a bowl and chill, covered, until cold.

Into a bowl sift together the flour, salt, and baking powder. Add the cold butter and cold lard, and blend the mixture until it resembles coarse meal. Stir in the toasted sesame seeds and toss the mixture with enough of the cold water to just form the dough into a ball. Halve the dough, wrap each half in wax paper, and chill the dough for 1 hour.

Working with one-half of the dough at a time, roll it out ¹⁄₁₆ inch thick on a floured surface, prick it all over with a fork, and with a 2½-inch cutter cut out as many rounds as possible. Arrange the rounds 1 inch apart on ungreased baking sheets. Form the scraps into a ball and roll, prick, and cut the dough in the same manner. Brush the rounds with the melted butter, sprinkle a pinch of the remaining 2 tablespoons sesame seeds in the center of each round, and press them in gently. Bake the rounds in the middle of a preheated 425° F. oven for 6 to 7 minutes, or until they are slightly puffed and barely golden around the edges. With a metal spatula transfer the wafers to a rack and let them cool.

Cheddar Bites

*Makes about
90 hors
d'oeuvres*

2 sticks (1 cup) unsalted butter, softened
1 pound sharp Cheddar, grated
1 large egg yolk
½ teaspoon cayenne

2 teaspoons salt
2 cups all-purpose flour
1 large egg white, beaten lightly with a
    pinch of salt

In a food processor fitted with the metal blade or in a bowl with an electric mixer cream together the butter and Cheddar until smooth, then add the egg yolk, cayenne, and salt, and blend well. Add the flour and blend the mixture until it just forms a dough.

Working in batches, pack the dough into a cookie press fitted with a decorative tip and press it into mounds 2 inches apart on lightly buttered baking sheets. Brush the tops of the mounds with the egg white, bake the mounds in the middle of a preheated 375° F. oven for 10 minutes, or until puffed and lightly golden, and transfer them with a spatula to racks. The bites may be served warm or at room temperature.

Open-Faced Ham Biscuits

For the biscuits
2 cups all-purpose flour
1 tablespoon double-acting baking
   powder
1 teaspoon salt
2 tablespoons cold unsalted butter,
   cut into bits
1 cup heavy cream
about 2 tablespoons milk

For the topping
1 pound cooked smoked ham
1 cup Quick Mayonnaise (page 20) or
   commercial mayonnaise
¼ cup minced scallion
¼ cup minced fresh parsley leaves
1½ tablespoons Dijon-style mustard
1 tablespoon tomato paste
pepper to taste

*Makes about
70 hors
d'oeuvres*

Make the biscuits: Into a bowl sift together the flour, baking powder, and salt and blend in the butter until the mixture resembles coarse meal. Add the cream and, if necessary, enough cold water, 1 tablespoon at a time, to form a soft dough. Form the dough into a ball, flatten it slightly, and roll it out ½ inch thick on a floured surface. Prick the dough all over with a fork, cut out rounds with a 1½-inch cutter dipped in flour, and arrange them 1 inch apart on lightly buttered baking sheets. Form the scraps gently into a ball, roll, prick, and cut the dough in the same manner, and arrange the rounds on the baking sheets. Brush the tops of the rounds lightly with the milk and bake the rounds in the middle of a preheated 425° F. oven for 12 to 15 minutes, or until they are puffed and golden. Transfer the biscuits to racks and let them cool.

Make the topping: In a food processor fitted with the metal blade grind the ham fine. In a bowl combine the ham and the remaining topping ingredients with pepper to taste.

Halve the biscuits and arrange them, cut side up, on baking sheets. Transfer the ham topping to a pastry bag fitted with a large fluted tip and pipe it onto the biscuits. Or spread the biscuits with the topping, then heat them in the middle of a preheated 400° F. oven for 4 to 5 minutes, or until heated through.

Grits and Sausage Croquettes

Makes about 100 hors d'oeuvres

1¾ cups water
½ cup quick-cooking hominy grits (see Suggestions)
¼ teaspoon salt
1 pound pork sausage meat
1 large egg yolk, beaten lightly

2 ounces Gruyère, grated
salt and pepper
1 cup fine stale bread crumbs
vegetable shortening for deep-frying

In a small heavy saucepan bring the water to a boil, stir in gradually the grits and salt, and cook the mixture, covered, over moderately low heat, stirring once or twice, for 5 minutes, or until thick. Remove the pan from the heat and let the mixture stand, covered, for 5 minutes. Transfer the grits to a bowl and let cool.

In a heavy skillet cook the sausage meat over moderate heat, stirring and breaking up the clumps, for 10 to 15 minutes, or until the liquid has evaporated and the sausage is golden. Drain the sausage in a fine sieve set over a bowl, pressing hard on the meat and discarding the fat. Add the sausage and the egg yolk to the grits, and combine well. Stir in the Gruyère and salt and pepper to taste and chill the mixture, covered, for at least 2 hours or overnight.

Form teaspoons of the mixture into balls, dredge the balls in the bread crumbs, coating them well, and in a deep fryer fry them in batches in 2 inches hot vegetable shortening (375° F.) for 1 minute, or until golden, transferring them as they are fried to paper towels to drain.

Kentucky Hot Browns

Makes about 44 hors d'oeuvres

For the toasts
44 slices of Italian or French bread, each cut ⅓ inch thick
1 stick (½ cup) unsalted butter, melted and cooled

For the sauce
3 tablespoons unsalted butter
¼ cup all-purpose flour
1¼ cups milk
1 tablespoon medium-dry Sherry
2 ounces Gruyère, grated
½ cup freshly grated Parmesan
1 large egg, beaten lightly

½ pound lean sliced bacon, cooked until crisp, drained well, and crumbled
1½ tablespoons Dijon-style mustard
1½ teaspoons Worcestershire sauce
salt and pepper

a combination of Quick Mayonnaise (page 20) and Dijon-style mustard for spreading on the toasts
1 pound thinly sliced cooked turkey breast
11 cherry tomatoes, each cut lengthwise into 4 slices

Make the toasts: Brush one side of each bread slice with the butter and bake the slices, buttered sides up, in one layer on baking sheets in the middle of a preheated 350° F. oven for 10 minutes, or until the undersides are golden and the toasts are crisp.

Make the sauce: In a heavy saucepan melt the butter over low heat, add the flour, and cook the *roux*, stirring, for 3 minutes. Remove the pan from the heat, add the milk in a stream, stirring, and bring the mixture to a boil over moderate heat, stirring constantly. Add the Sherry and simmer the sauce, stirring, for 2 minutes. Remove the pan from the heat, stir in both cheeses, and, if necessary, heat the mixture over low heat, stirring, until the cheeses are just melted. Remove the pan from the heat, beat in the egg, and stir in the bacon, mustard, Worcestershire, and salt and pepper to taste.

Spread a thin layer of the mustard mayonnaise on the buttered sides of the toasts and divide the turkey among the toasts. Top each toast with 1 slice of tomato and spread about 1 tablespoon of the sauce over each toast, covering the turkey and tomato. Broil the toasts on baking sheets under a preheated broiler about 2 to 3 inches from the heat for 1 to 2 minutes, or until the sauce is puffed and browned lightly.

A FATHER'S DAY LUNCH

Chilled Pea Soup
Duck, Papaya, and Walnut Salad
Corn Muffins with Cracklings
Ginger Rum Ice Cream

Napa Valley Johannisberg Riesling

It doesn't seem quite cricket that fathers and mothers only get one day a year, respectively, for their near and dear to say, We think you're great. But, since one day is all that has been officially designated, we say, Do that day up proud. Let Dad plan his own special event, or no event at all, but build into the agenda this special lunch for him. It's doable, relaxed, and easy. It can be prepared entirely in advance, can be had inside or out, and better still, ends with sensational homemade ice cream. We can't think of one father who wouldn't get the drift.

Chilled Pea Soup

3 scallions, including the green tops, chopped
2 tablespoons unsalted butter
2 tablespoons flour
2½ cups chicken stock (page 154) or canned chicken broth
4 cups shelled peas (about 4 pounds unshelled) or two 10-ounce packages frozen peas, thawed

the leaves from 2 sprigs of mint plus additional mint leaves for garnish
1 teaspoon sugar
½ teaspoon white pepper
1½ cups half-and-half
additional white pepper to taste
salt

Makes about 6 cups, serving 4

In a large saucepan cook the scallions in the butter over moderately low heat, stirring occasionally, for 10 minutes, or until softened, add the flour, and cook the *roux*, stirring,

Duck, Papaya, and Walnut Salad and
Corn Muffins with Cracklings

for 3 minutes. Add the stock in a stream, whisking, and stir in the peas, mint, sugar, and white pepper. Bring the mixture to a boil and simmer it, stirring occasionally, for 30 minutes.

Purée the mixture through the fine disk of a food mill into a large bowl, let it cool, and chill it, covered, for 3 hours. Stir in the half-and-half, additional pepper, and salt to taste and combine well. Ladle the soup into chilled bowls and garnish each with the remaining mint leaves.

SUGGESTIONS

If you don't have a food mill, purée the soup base in a food processor or a blender. It will be somewhat less smooth in texture but will taste every bit as good.

Sour cream is also a very acceptable garnish for the soup—for almost any cream- or milk-based soup for that matter.

Be sure to cut off and remove as much fat as possible from the ducks, and freeze the duck liver for making *pâté*. Also, if you have in mind cleaning your oven, do so *after* this meal. There is no help for it: duck fat splatters terribly.

Walnut oil, a luxury and lovely on almost any plain green salad or on endive, is best kept in the refrigerator. It has the tendency to go rancid if stored at room temperature.

If a ripe papaya is not available, substitute sliced peaches brushed with fresh lemon juice in the salad.

Do not overstir the muffin batter or the muffins will lose their light crumb.

For the ice cream, you will need to scald the sugar, milk, and cream mixture. Scald does not mean boil, but rather heat to the point where bubbles form around the edges of the pan.

Cookies with a little chocolate, such as the ones on pages 24, 116, or 249—how can you deny Dad?—would be a most appropriate accompaniment to that grand ice cream.

ဢ

Prepare the soup in advance up to the point of adding the half-and-half and chill. Swirl in the cream at the last minute.

All components of the salad—the duck, greens, papaya, and walnuts—can be readied in advance. Arrange the ingredients on the platter according to your own schedule but dress the salad just before serving.

Make the muffins in advance, too. Reheat quickly, uncovered, in a hot oven.

Prepare the ice cream at your leisure. If you have difficulty finding preserved gingerroot, look for it at Oriental markets.

Duck, Papaya, and Walnut Salad

Serves 4

two 4¼-pound ducks, thawed if frozen
1 lime, halved
½ teaspoon dried rosemary, crumbled
salt and pepper
1 papaya
¼ cup fresh lime juice

½ cup walnuts
1 head of curly endive or chicory
¼ teaspoon white pepper
2 tablespoons walnut oil
½ cup vegetable oil
2 tablespoons snipped fresh chives

Pat the ducks dry and put 1 of the lime halves, half the rosemary, and salt and pepper to taste into each cavity. Salt and pepper the outsides of the ducks, prick them all over with a skewer, and put them, breast side up, on a rack in a large roasting pan. Roast the ducks in a preheated 450° F. oven for 10 minutes, reduce the heat to 350° F., and roast the ducks for 20 minutes more. Prick the ducks all over with the skewer and roast them, breast side down, for 30 minutes. Prick the ducks all over again with the skewer and roast them, breast side up, for 20 minutes, or until the juices run pink when a thigh is pricked with the skewer. Let the ducks cool for 30 minutes.

Remove and reserve the duck skin for making Corn Muffins with Cracklings (recipe follows) and carve the ducks. Put the duck meat on a plate, moisten it with some of the juices that accumulate on the plate, and cover it.

Peel and seed the papaya, slice it thin lengthwise, and in a shallow bowl let it macerate in the lime juice for 30 minutes. Drain the papaya, reserving 3 tablespoons of the juice.

Put the walnuts in one layer on a jelly-roll pan and toast them in a preheated 350° F. oven, shaking the pan occasionally, for 10 minutes. Chop the walnuts coarse.

Line a platter with the endive and arrange the duck meat and the papaya slices decoratively on it. In a small bowl combine the reserved lime juice with ¼ teaspoon salt and the pepper, add the oils in a stream, whisking, and whisk the dressing until emulsified. Spoon the dressing over the salad and sprinkle the papaya with the walnuts and the duck with the chives.

Corn Muffins with Cracklings

*Makes about
12 muffins*

the skin from the 2 roasted ducks
    (see the preceding recipe) or 8 slices
    of lean bacon, chopped fine
1 large egg, beaten lightly
1 cup milk
3 tablespoons sugar
½ stick (¼ cup) unsalted butter, melted
    and cooled

¾ cup yellow cornmeal
    (preferably stone-ground)
1¼ cups all-purpose flour
1 tablespoon double-acting baking
    powder
1½ teaspoons salt

In a heavy skillet cook the duck skin or the bacon over low heat, stirring occasionally, until brown and crisp, and let it drain on paper towels.

In a large bowl combine the egg, milk, sugar, and butter. Into a bowl or onto a piece of wax paper sift together the cornmeal, flour, baking powder, and salt. Add the flour mixture and two-thirds of the cracklings to the egg mixture and stir the batter until just combined. (The batter will be lumpy.) Divide the batter among buttered ½-cup muffin tins, filling them two-thirds full, sprinkle the muffins with the remaining cracklings, and bake them in a preheated 425° F. oven for 15 minutes, or until golden.

Ginger Rum Ice Cream

Makes about 1 quart

1 cup sugar
2 cups milk
2 cups heavy cream
8 large egg yolks

½ cup dark rum
½ cup drained and minced preserved gingerroot*

*Available at specialty-foods stores.

In a saucepan combine the sugar, milk, and cream and scald the mixture over moderate heat, stirring. In a large bowl beat the egg yolks until they are light and thick and pour in the milk mixture through a sieve in a stream, stirring. Pour the mixture into a saucepan and cook the custard over moderate heat, stirring constantly, until it coats the spoon, *but do not let it boil*. Transfer the custard to a metal bowl set in a bowl of ice and stir it until cool.

In a small saucepan over moderately high heat reduce the rum by half and let it cool.

Stir the rum and the gingerroot into the custard and chill the mixture, covered, for 2 hours in the refrigerator. Then freeze the custard in an ice-cream freezer according to the manufacturer's instructions.

A BACHELOR DINNER

Steak Tartare
Spareribs with Chinese-Style Barbecue Sauce
Confetti Rice Casserole
Wilted Lettuce Salad
Chocolate Coconut Cream Pie

Beer

Assuming this dinner will be made by a man for men to celebrate one of the final evenings of his bachelorhood—a significant event as life goes—the menu for it is a particularly good one. To begin with, it is festive from start to finish. And cooking it will be fun, too. And simple. The starter takes mere assembling, with some inventive seasoning before serving. The barbecue sauce, best made ahead, bubbles down in one pan; the ribs need only baking and basting. The rice casserole, once assembled, also needs only baking. That leaves the pie, and it has a crumb crust and a two-step custard filling. In short, the kind of food that's perfectly suited to a happy evening.

Steak Tartare

Serves 8 as an hors d'oeuvre

2 pounds top round of beef, cut into
    1-inch pieces
8 anchovy fillets, minced
4 teaspoons stone-ground mustard or
    Dijon-style mustard
2 large egg yolks

1 tablespoon capers
2 teaspoons salt, or to taste
1½ teaspoons Worcestershire sauce
freshly ground pepper
1 cup minced scallion
sour cream (optional)

In a food processor fitted with the metal blade grind the beef medium in texture in batches. Transfer the beef to a bowl and stir in the remaining ingredients, not including the scallion, and pepper to taste. Transfer the mixture to a serving bowl and with a long-tined fork mix in the scallion. Serve the steak tartare immediately, with rolls or toast points, and, if desired, sour cream.

SUGGESTIONS

You do not want to grind the beef for steak tartare in advance as it will darken in color—an untoward state of events given what a good starter it is. Either grind it yourself as directed in the recipe or have the butcher do it, but then serve it *at once*.

Country-style ribs are pork ribs, as any good Southerner will tell you. Country-style also means meatier, these ribs being cut from the shoulder end of the loin.

Softened vanilla ice cream would be good with the pie. In that case, you will not need the whipped-cream topping—unless, of course, you are throwing caution, calorie-watching, and common sense to the wind—not a bad thing to do every once in a while!

∽

Spareribs with Chinese-Style Barbecue Sauce

Serves 8

For Chinese-style barbecue sauce
   (makes about 9 cups)
4½ cups chopped onions
6 garlic cloves, minced
2 sticks (1 cup) unsalted butter
3 cups canned tomato purée
2 cups firmly packed light brown sugar
¾ cup soy sauce

¾ cup rice vinegar
6 tablespoons chili paste with garlic*

12 pounds country-style spareribs,
   trimmed of excess fat and with the
   ribs still attached (see Suggestions)

*Available at Oriental markets.

Make the barbecue sauce: In a large, heavy saucepan cook the onion and garlic in the butter over low heat, stirring, for 15 minutes, or until softened. Add the remaining sauce ingredients, bring the sauce just to the boil, and simmer, stirring occasionally, for 30 minutes.

While the sauce is simmering, blanch the spareribs in batches in a large kettle of simmering water for 30 minutes and drain them. Arrange the ribs, meaty side up, in 2 baking pans large enough to hold them in one layer, and bake them in a preheated 375° F. oven for 20 minutes. Brush the ribs lightly on both sides with some of the barbecue sauce and bake, meaty side down, in a preheated 350° F. oven for 20 minutes. Turn the ribs meaty side up, baste them generously with the sauce, and bake them for 20 minutes.

Transfer the ribs to a cutting board and cut between the bones to separate them. Return them, meaty side up, to the pans, baste them generously with the sauce, and bake them 20 minutes more. Serve the ribs on a slightly heated large platter with plenty of napkins.

Grind the beef for steak tartare just before the guests arrive, and chill it, well sealed, in the refrigerator. Stir in the remaining ingredients just before serving.

Chinese-style barbecue sauce can only improve in flavor if made in advance. Store in a jar in the refrigerator.

Finish the sparcribs entirely in advance. Reheat in a preheated 350° F. oven, turning and basting them, for 30 minutes.

Have the rice casserole fully assembled. Then bake it as you either finish baking the ribs or reheating them. The oven temperature for both dishes, as luck would have it, is the same.

Have the ingredients for the salad all ready, but dress it only at the last minute. Otherwise you will get a very slippery mess.

By all means prepare the pie the day before up to the point of garnishing it with the topping. It takes no time to ready the cream.

Confetti Rice Casserole

Serves 8

8 cups water
3 cups unconverted brown rice
1 teaspoon salt
¾ cup sliced scallion
¾ cup sour cream
½ cup chopped pimiento

½ cup sliced pitted black olives
two 4-ounce cans green chili peppers,
    drained, seeded if desired, and chopped
5 tablespoons unsalted butter,
    cut into bits
1¾ cups grated jack cheese

In a large saucepan bring the water to a boil, sprinkle in the rice and salt, and return the water to a boil over high heat, stirring. Boil the rice, stirring occasionally, for 20 minutes, drain it in a colander, and rinse it under cold water. Set the colander over a pan of boiling water and steam the rice, covered with a dish towel and the lid, for 15 to 20 minutes, or until fluffy and dry.

In a buttered 2-quart casserole combine the rice with the remaining ingredients, reserving 3 tablespoons of the butter and ¼ cup of the cheese. Dot the top of the casserole with the remaining butter, sprinkle it with the remaining jack, and bake the casserole in a preheated 350° F. oven for 30 minutes.

Wilted Lettuce Salad

Serves 8

2 small onions, cut into slices
⅛ inch thick
1 large head of leafy lettuce, rinsed,
patted completely dry, and torn
into pieces
1 large head of curly endive, rinsed,
patted completely dry, and torn
into pieces

⅔ cup olive oil
⅓ cup cider vinegar
2 tablespoons sugar
2 hard-boiled eggs, sliced
¼ cup crumbled blue cheese
salt and pepper

Let the onions stand in a bowl of ice water for 15 minutes.

Arrange the greens in a large heatproof salad bowl.

In a small saucepan heat the olive oil over moderate heat until hot but not smoking, and drizzle it in a stream over the greens. (The lettuce must be completely dry or the oil will splatter.) Add the vinegar and sugar and toss well. Drain the onions, pat dry, and toss them with the greens. Garnish the salad with the eggs and blue cheese and add salt and pepper to taste.

Chocolate Coconut Cream Pie

*Makes one
10-inch pie*

For the shell
2 cups chocolate wafer crumbs
⅓ cup sugar
¾ stick (6 tablespoons) unsalted butter,
cut into bits and softened
2 large egg whites
a pinch of salt

For the filling
2 cups milk
1 cup heavy cream
2 large whole eggs
2 large egg yolks
¾ cup granulated sugar
a 4-ounce can shredded sweetened
coconut
¾ teaspoon vanilla

For the topping
1¼ cups well-chilled heavy cream
¼ cup confectioners' sugar
1 teaspoon vanilla

¼ cup shredded sweetened coconut,
toasted lightly on a baking sheet in
a preheated 350° F. oven, stirring
occasionally, until amber-colored

*Spareribs with Chinese-Style Barbecue Sauce
and Wilted Lettuce Salad*

Make the shell: In a bowl combine the crumbs, sugar, and butter, and press the mixture onto the bottom and sides of a lightly buttered 10-inch glass pie plate. Bake the shell in a preheated 300° F. oven for 15 minutes, and let it cool on a rack. In a small bowl beat the egg whites with the salt until frothy and spoon them into the shell, spreading them with the back of a spoon to cover the bottom completely. Bake the shell in the 300° F. oven for 5 minutes and let it cool on the rack.

Make the filling: In a saucepan scald the milk and the cream. In a bowl beat the whole eggs, egg yolks, and sugar together until just combined. Add the scalded milk mixture in a stream, beating, and stir in the coconut and vanilla. Spoon the filling into the shell and bake the pie in the lower third of a preheated 350° F. oven for 30 minutes, or until a knife inserted in the center comes out relatively clean. (The pie filling will not be set.) Let the pie cool on a rack. (The pie may be made ahead up to this point and chilled overnight.)

Make the topping: In a chilled bowl beat the topping ingredients together until the cream holds soft peaks.

Spoon mounds of the whipped cream over the filling in concentric circles to cover the pie completely and sprinkle the pie with the toasted shredded coconut.

Chocolate Coconut Cream Pie

A BRIDESMAIDS' LUNCHEON

Chilled Avocado and Cucumber Soup
Curled Melba Toasts
Shrimp and Straw Mushroom Salad with Ginger Dressing
Meringue Tartlets with Hazelnut Ice Cream and Fruit
Raspberry Sauce

Collio Pinot Grigio

A bridesmaids' luncheon acknowledges the nearness of a splendid event—a wedding. It's a time for a singular show of friendship and conviviality and an occasion around which lovely memories will hinge. It's part of the pageant of being married. The food that accompanies such a time deserves to be exceptional, too. Shrimp and Straw Mushroom Salad with Ginger Dressing is that, as are Meringue Tartlets with Hazelnut Ice Cream and Raspberry Sauce. Moreover, all of this menu can be prepared in advance.

Chilled Avocado and Cucumber Soup

Makes about 9 cups, serving 8

3 cups chicken stock (page 154) or
  canned chicken broth
2 scallions, chopped
3 very ripe avocados, peeled, pitted, and
  mashed with a fork
1 cucumber, peeled, seeded, and chopped
3 cups half-and-half
1 cup sour cream
2 tablespoons fresh lemon juice,
  or to taste
salt and white pepper
snipped fresh dill for garnish

In a saucepan heat the stock or broth with the scallions until hot, remove the pan from the heat, and stir in the avocados and cucumber.

In a blender purée the mixture in batches and transfer the purée to a large bowl. Stir in the remaining ingredients except the dill, with salt and white pepper to taste, and chill the soup, covered, for at least 1 hour. Ladle the soup into chilled bowls and garnish each serving with some of the dill.

Curled Melba Toasts

Makes about 40 toasts

1 loaf of day-old unsliced homemade-
  type white bread

Put the loaf in the freezing compartment of the refrigerator for 2 hours, or until firm but not frozen. Then, with a very sharp knife, cut the loaf into paper-thin slices.

Arrange the slices on baking sheets, making sure they do not touch, and bake in a preheated 250° F. oven, turning them occasionally, for 1½ hours, or until they curl and are golden brown. Store the toasts in an airtight container.

SUGGESTIONS

As a starter for this luncheon, consider something as simple as salted nuts or a platter of magnificent assorted blanched vegetables—broccoli and cauliflower flowerets, miniature carrots, asparagus spears, radishes, and snow peas—with a tangy mustard mayonnaise.

Dandelion greens have a slightly bitter, very refreshing flavor. For almost the same effect you can substitute *rugola*. Buy it the day before serving and keep it in the refrigerator, its roots in water.

As we all know, homemade ice cream is incomparable. If time and logistics do not allow, a rich brand of store-bought butter pecan would be perfectly acceptable. Be sure to make the hazelnut ice cream on some occasion, though. It is especially good, luxurious in texture.

෨

This luncheon is as simple to prepare as it is elegant to serve. Starting in reverse order of the courses, you can make and store the meringue tartlets up to 1 week in advance. Keep airtight.

The 1½-hour cooking time needed for the Curled Melba Toast might not fit easily into your schedule. If so, replace with Herb Biscuits (page 240) without the leeks.

Prepare the ice cream a day or two in advance as well, and the sauce. Remember to let the ice cream soften before serving. The fruit, on the other hand, should stand no more than 1 hour.

Make the *court bouillon* and cook the shrimp in it the day before the luncheon. Drain and shell. Then make the dressing and marinate the shrimp in it overnight. That same day ready the other salad ingredients and make the soup base.

The day of the luncheon—finish the soup and arrange the salad.

Shrimp and Straw Mushroom Salad with Ginger Dressing

Shrimp and Straw Mushroom Salad with Ginger Dressing

Serves 8

For the court bouillon
5 cups water
1 cup dry white wine
1 onion, sliced
a 2-inch piece of gingerroot, sliced
2 teaspoons salt

Tie together in a cheesecloth bag
1 bay leaf
6 peppercorns
6 coriander seeds
6 parsley stems

2 pounds shrimp

For the ginger dressing
   (makes about 1 cup)
3 tablespoons rice vinegar* or
   white-wine vinegar
2 tablespoons peeled and minced
   gingerroot
2 tablespoons fresh lemon juice

2 tablespoons light soy sauce
2 teaspoons Dijon-style mustard
salt and pepper
6 tablespoons vegetable oil
¼ cup Oriental sesame oil*
1 garlic clove, minced (optional)
2 tablespoons snipped fresh chives
   (optional)

2 cups cooked peas
an 8-ounce can straw mushrooms,*
   drained and blanched in boiling water
   for 1 minute
a 9-ounce can hearts of palm, drained
   and sliced

For the garnish
endive and dandelion greens
3 carrots, sliced into thin shavings
   with a vegetable peeler and chilled
   in ice water for at least 30 minutes

*Available at Oriental markets.

Make the court bouillon: In a saucepan combine all the ingredients, bring the liquid to a boil, and simmer for 20 minutes.

Prepare the shrimp while the court bouillon cooks: Without shelling the shrimp, make a lengthwise slit along the back of each and remove the dark intestinal vein with the point of a sharp small knife. Rinse the shrimp under cold water.

Make the ginger dressing: In a bowl combine the vinegar, gingerroot, lemon juice, soy sauce, mustard, and salt and pepper to taste. Add the oils in a stream, whisking, and whisk the dressing until emulsified. Whisk in the garlic and chives, if desired.

   Bring the *court bouillon* to a boil, add the deveined shrimp, and simmer, stirring, for 1 to 2 minutes, or until they curl and are just opaque. Pour the mixture into a large heatproof bowl and let cool.

To assemble the salad: Drain and shell the shrimp. In a large bowl combine the shrimp, peas, mushrooms, hearts of palm, and the dressing and let stand for 30 minutes.

Line a platter with the endive and dandelion greens, arrange the salad in the center, and garnish with the carrot shavings patted dry.

Meringue Tartlets with Hazelnut Ice Cream and Fruit

For the tartlets

6 large egg whites at room temperature

¼ teaspoon cream of tartar

1½ cups granulated sugar, ground to a powder in a food processor fitted with the metal blade or in a blender

1 tablespoon Frangelico (hazelnut-flavored liqueur; optional)

confectioners' sugar to taste

For the hazelnut ice cream

(makes about 1½ quarts)

6 ounces shelled hazelnuts

¾ cup sugar

¼ cup water

½ cup boiling water

6 large egg yolks

2 cups well-chilled heavy cream

2 teaspoons vanilla

For the fruit

seasonal fruit such as plums, raspberries, nectarines, or strawberries, prepared as necessary

sugar to taste

fresh lemon juice to taste

Frangelico to taste (optional)

Raspberry Sauce (recipe follows)

Serves 8

Make the tartlets: In a bowl with an electric mixer beat the egg whites at moderate speed until foamy, add the cream of tartar, and beat the whites until they hold soft peaks. Add the granulated sugar, 1 tablespoon at a time, beating, and beat the meringue until it holds very stiff peaks. Beat in the Frangelico, if desired, and transfer the meringue to a pastry bag fitted with the decorative tip.

Cover 2 baking sheets with parchment paper, and using a 4-inch ring (a biscuit or cookie cutter, or small plate) as a guide draw 4 circles onto each piece of paper. Invert the paper onto the baking sheets and attach it by putting a dab of the meringue on the underside of each corner. Pipe the meringue inside the circles to form bases ½ inch thick, and pipe a ring of the meringue around the edge of each base to form sides 1½ inches high. Sift the confectioners' sugar lightly over the tartlets, then bake them in a preheated 200° F. oven for 1½ to 2 hours, or until they are firm and dry. Loosen the meringues from the paper carefully with the tip of a small knife. Store the tartlets, if necessary, in airtight containers.

Meringue Tartlets with Hazelnut Ice Cream and Fruit

Make the hazelnut ice cream: Spread the hazelnuts in one layer on a baking pan and toast them in a preheated 350° F. oven for 10 to 15 minutes, or until they are colored lightly and the skins blister. Then wrap the nuts in a dish towel and let them steam for 1 minute. Rub the nuts in a towel to remove the skins and let them cool. In a food processor fitted with the metal blade grind the hazelnuts to a paste.

In a small, heavy saucepan combine the sugar with the ¼ cup water, and cook the mixture over moderate heat, stirring and washing down any sugar crystals clinging to the sides with a brush dipped in cold water, until it begins to color slightly. Continue to cook it, swirling the pan and being careful not to let it burn, until it is amber-colored. Add the ½ cup boiling water immediately in a slow stream, bring the mixture to a boil, stirring, and cook it, stirring, until the caramel is dissolved completely.

In a bowl with an electric mixer beat the egg yolks until they are lemon-colored. With the mixer running, add the caramel in a stream and beat until cool. Transfer the mixture to a large bowl and stir in the hazelnut paste.

In a chilled bowl beat the cream until it holds stiff peaks, then beat in the vanilla.

Stir one-fourth of the whipped cream into the caramel mixture and fold in the remaining whipped cream gently but thoroughly. Spoon the mixture into a bowl and freeze it, covered, in the freezing compartment of the refrigerator until firm.

Prepare the fruit: In a bowl combine the fruit with the sugar, lemon juice, and Frangelico, if used, to taste and chill, covered, for 30 minutes.

To serve: Fill the tartlets with hazelnut ice cream, arrange the macerated fruit over it, and transfer the desserts to serving plates. Serve the tartlets with Raspberry Sauce.

Raspberry Sauce

two 10-ounce packages frozen
   raspberries, thawed, the juice reserved

2 tablespoons fresh lemon juice or to taste
sugar to taste (optional)

*Makes about
2 cups*

In a food processor fitted with the metal blade or in a blender purée the raspberries with their juice, the lemon juice, and sugar, if desired. Strain the sauce through a fine sieve into a serving bowl, pressing hard on the solids.

A FLANK STEAK DINNER: PLAIN OR FANCY

Stuffed Flank Steak with Mellow Garlic Sauce
or Grilled Flank Steak
Mixed Potato Salad   Tossed Green Salad
Strawberry Chiffon Pie

California Petite Sirah '77 or Barbaresco '76

We feel you ought to be able to exercise your options when it comes to a special occasion; special occasions, by definition, being unique. What follows, therefore, is a very simple menu, but one with an elective—the main course. Flank steak. We've made it simple, meaning grilled, and we've also made it fancy, meaning stuffed and sauced. The choice is yours. So whether you're planning a quiet party for friends in celebration of nothing in particular but everything in general or a gala event, define it as you will. In either case, you'll eat well.

SUGGESTIONS

Make sandwiches with the grilled flank steak, sliced thin, and spread the bread—Italian or French—with a layer of mustard butter.

Stuffed Flank Steak makes a splendid party dish. For a crowd, simply double the recipe, but braise the steaks in the same amount of liquid called for on page 302. Reduce the braising liquid and glaze the steaks as described in the recipe.

Caesar Salad (page 219) or a platter of sliced summer tomatoes would both be fine accompaniments to either of the steak preparations.

Either of these menus recommends itself from a planning point of view because one (the stuffed flank steak) must be made entirely ahead in advance, and the other (the grilled flank steak) must be marinated in advance. With the latter, you have anywhere from 1 to 2 days for marination.

The potato salad can also be readied in stages. Cook the potatoes and dress them, but leave the final combining until just before serving.

While the chiffon pie needs a minimum of 3 hours to set, you should plan on making it the same day you intend to serve it. Because of its crumb crust, it will not weather the refrigerator well overnight.

Grilled Flank Steak and Stuffed Flank Steak

Stuffed Flank Steak

Serves 6

a 2¼-pound flank steak

For the stuffing
enough carrots cut into ½-inch cubes
    to measure ¾ cup
enough French or Italian bread, crusts
    removed, torn into small pieces, to
    measure 1 cup loosely packed
½ cup milk
a 6-ounce piece of prosciutto,
    cut into ½-inch cubes
6 ounces lean ground veal
6 ounces lean ground pork
½ cup freshly grated Parmesan
½ cup firmly packed trimmed, washed,
    and shredded spinach
½ cup minced fresh parsley leaves
2 large eggs, beaten lightly
1 tablespoon minced fresh rosemary or
    1 teaspoon dried
1 tablespoon minced fresh thyme or
    1 teaspoon dried

2¼ teaspoons minced fresh sage or
    ¾ teaspoon dried
½ teaspoon salt
pepper
½ cup chopped shallot
2 garlic cloves, minced
2 tablespoons unsalted butter

½ stick (¼ cup) unsalted butter
1 tablespoon oil
1 onion, chopped
1 carrot, chopped
1 stalk of celery, chopped
1 cup brown stock (page 155) or
    canned beef broth
½ cup dry red wine
2 tomatoes, chopped
1 bay leaf
Mellow Garlic Sauce (recipe follows)

Cut a pocket along the grain in the flank steak, leaving a 1-inch border on 3 sides.

Make the stuffing: In a saucepan of boiling salted water blanch the carrots for 2 minutes and drain them. In a small bowl let the bread soak in the milk for 15 minutes, squeeze out the milk, and in a large bowl combine it with the carrots and the remaining stuffing ingredients up to and including the salt. Add pepper to taste.

In a small skillet cook the shallot and garlic in the butter over moderate heat for 2 minutes, or until the shallot is softened, add the mixture to the stuffing, and combine well.

Sprinkle the pocket of the flank steak with salt and pepper and fill it with the stuffing. Sew the opening closed and tie the meat at 1-inch intervals with kitchen string. In a large flameproof casserole brown the stuffed flank steak in 2 tablespoons of the butter and the oil over moderately high heat and transfer it to a plate. Pour off the fat, add the remaining 2 tablespoons of butter, and in it cook the onion, carrot, and celery over moderate heat, stirring, for 5 minutes, or until softened. Add the stock or broth, wine, tomatoes, and bay leaf, return the flank steak to the casserole, and bring the liquid to a boil. Transfer the casserole to a preheated 350° F. oven and braise it, covered, for 1¼ hours.

Transfer the flank steak to a plate and let it cool. Skim the fat from the cooking liquid and strain the liquid through a fine sieve into a saucepan. Bring the liquid to a boil over moderately high heat and reduce it to ¼ cup, or until it is a thick glaze. Brush the flank steak with the glaze, let it cool completely, and chill it. Serve the steak, cut into ¼-inch slices, chilled or at room temperature, with Mellow Garlic Sauce.

Mellow Garlic Sauce

15 garlic cloves, unpeeled
½ cup sour cream

½ cup heavy cream plus additional
    cream as needed
salt and pepper

*Makes about
1 cup*

In a small saucepan of boiling water boil the garlic cloves for 20 minutes, or until softened. Drain and peel.

In a bowl mash the garlic cloves, stir in the sour cream, heavy cream, and salt and pepper to taste, then chill the sauce, covered, for at least 1 hour. If desired, thin the sauce with additional heavy cream.

Grilled Flank Steak

For the marinade
1½ cups beer
3 scallions, minced
⅓ cup olive oil
3 tablespoons soy sauce
2 tablespoons sugar

1 tablespoon peeled and grated
    gingerroot
2 large garlic cloves, minced
1 teaspoon salt
¼ teaspoon Tabasco

a 2½-pound flank steak

Serves 6

Make the marinade: In a shallow dish just large enough to hold the steak combine all the marinade ingredients.

Add the steak to the marinade and let it marinate, covered and chilled, turning it occasionally, for 1 to 2 days.

Drain the steak, pat it dry, and grill it over a bed of glowing coals for 3 to 4 minutes on each side for medium-rare meat. Or broil the steak on the rack of a broiler pan under a preheated broiler about 2 inches from the heat for 3 to 4 minutes on each side. Transfer the steak to a cutting board and cut it across the grain on the diagonal into very thin slices.

Mixed Potato Salad

Serves 6

For the dressing
2 tablespoons wine vinegar or fresh
   lemon juice
1 teaspoon Dijon-style mustard
salt and pepper
⅓ to ½ cup olive oil

¾ pound small red potatoes, scrubbed
1 large head of Boston lettuce, leaves
   separated, rinsed, dried, and torn
   into bite-size pieces

1 bunch of watercress, stems removed
1½ cups thinly sliced celery
2 large tomatoes, sliced
½ cup sliced pimiento-stuffed olives
¼ cup thinly sliced scallion
2 tablespoons minced fresh parsley leaves

Make the dressing: In a bowl combine the vinegar, mustard, and salt and pepper to taste. Add the oil in a stream, whisking, and whisk the dressing until emulsified.

   Arrange the potatoes in a vegetable steamer set over cold water, bring the water to a boil, and steam the potatoes, covered, adding more boiling water if necessary, for 20 minutes, or until just tender. Peel the potatoes while still warm, cut them into ½-inch pieces, and in a large bowl toss them gently with the dressing. Add the remaining ingredients, toss the salad, and season it with salt and pepper.

Strawberry Chiffon Pie

*Makes one
10-inch pie*

1½ cups chocolate wafer crumbs
¼ cup sifted confectioners' sugar
½ stick (¼ cup) unsalted butter, melted
2½ teaspoons unflavored gelatin
½ cup water
¼ cup fresh lemon juice
1 cup granulated sugar

1 pound strawberries plus 6 large
   strawberries for garnish
½ cup plain yogurt
⅛ teaspoon salt
2 large egg whites at room temperature
a pinch of cream of tartar
a pinch of salt

In a bowl combine well the wafer crumbs, confectioners' sugar, and butter, press the mixture into a deep 10-inch glass pie plate, and chill the shell for 30 minutes.

   In a bowl sprinkle the gelatin over ¼ cup of cold water and let it soften for 10 minutes. In a small saucepan combine the lemon juice with the remaining ¼ cup water, bring the liquid to a boil, and stir it into the gelatin mixture, stirring until the gelatin is dissolved.

While the mixture is still warm stir in ¾ cup of the granulated sugar, stirring until the mixture is dissolved.

In a food processor fitted with a metal blade or in a blender purée in batches 1 pound of the strawberries and stir the purée into the gelatin mixture with the yogurt and salt. Set the bowl in a bowl of ice and ice water and stir the mixture until it begins to thicken.

In another bowl beat the egg whites with the cream of tartar and salt until they hold soft peaks, beat in the remaining ¼ cup granulated sugar, 1 tablespoon at a time, and beat the meringue until it holds stiff peaks. Stir one-fourth of the meringue into the strawberry mixture and fold in the remaining meringue gently but thoroughly. Spoon the filling into the shell and chill the pie for 2 hours, or until it is nearly set.

Slice the remaining 6 strawberries lengthwise, arrange them on the pie, and chill the pie, covered loosely, for 1 hour, or until set.

Strawberry Chiffon Pie

A POST-GRADUATION DAY BUFFET

Shrimp with Mustard Sauce
Smoked Beef Tongue   Piquant Relish
Asparagus, Potato, and Beet Salad
White Chocolate "Brownies"
or Brownie Thins

Grignolino

Even though the recipes in this menu yield 4 servings each as written, we're calling it a buffet because they could just as easily accommodate 16 to 20. In short, it is a menu that can be doubled or tripled, then doubled again, without hesitation. Further, it is cold food and needs only to be set out to be successful.

Shrimp with Mustard Sauce

Serves 4

1½ cups beer
2 sprigs of dill
4 parsley stems
1 bay leaf
1 teaspoon red pepper flakes
¼ teaspoon ground allspice
2 garlic cloves, crushed
2 pounds unshelled shrimp

For the sauce
1 cup Quick Mayonnaise (page 20)
3 tablespoons sour cream
1 tablespoon Dijon-style mustard
1 tablespoon stone-ground mustard*
1 tablespoon white-wine vinegar
2 drops of Tabasco

*Available at specialty-foods stores.

In a kettle combine the beer, dill, parsley, bay leaf, red pepper flakes, allspice, and garlic and bring the beer to a boil over moderately high heat. Add the shrimp and cook them, covered, for 3 minutes. Drain, refresh under cold water, and drain the shrimp again.

Make the sauce: In a bowl combine well all the sauce ingredients.
    Arrange the shrimp decoratively on serving plates and serve them with the sauce.

SUGGESTIONS

This is a wonderful menu for a gathering—a graduation gala, a summer open house, or a late relaxed supper—because, with the exception of the brownies, every one of the recipes can be doubled or even tripled. (For best results, simply make multiple individual batches of the brownies.)

If you are expecting a group, shell the shrimp before serving them. It's awkward trying to peel them from a plate balanced on your knees.

Serve the tongue, very like corned beef in flavor, not only with the Piquant Relish that is called for but with several assorted mustards. Sliced rye bread or the Rye Rolls on page 22 would be good, too. If it fits into your plans and/or the weather is chilly, heat the tongue slightly. It will bring out still more of its flavor.

White chocolate is really not chocolate at all, but cocoa butter, milk solids, and sugar combined. It is sold in bars or in blocks and can be found at specialty-foods stores or candy stores. Store, well wrapped, at room temperature. A nice turn would be to serve chocolate brownies along with the white ones. See page 310 for a recipe for "thin" chocolate brownies, another interesting variation.

The shrimp and their sauce, the tongue and its relish, and the components for the salad, as well as the brownies, can be made at least 1 day in advance. Save dressing the salad until the last minute. An easy and most agreeable menu, all in all.

Smoked Beef Tongue

a 3- to 4-pound smoked beef tongue
1 carrot, quartered
1 onion stuck with 3 cloves
3 stalks of celery, quartered

3 sprigs of parsley
1 bay leaf
a pinch of dried thyme
Piquant Relish (recipe follows)

Serves 4

In a large bowl cover the tongue with cold water and chill it overnight.

Drain the tongue and put it in a kettle with cold water to cover. Bring the water to a simmer, skimming off the froth as it rises to the surface. Add the carrot, onion, celery, parsley, bay leaf, and thyme, and simmer the tongue, covered partially, for 3 to 3½ hours, or until tender. Let the tongue cool in the cooking liquid, uncovered, and drain it.

Slit the skin lengthwise on the underside of the tongue, peel it to the edges, and discard it. Make a crosswise slit at the base of the top side of the tongue, peel off the skin, and discard it. Cut away the fat, bone, and gristle, turn the tongue on its side, and slice the meat very thin, beginning with diagonal slices at the tip and gradually cutting vertically. Arrange the slices on a platter and serve with the relish.

Piquant Relish

Makes about 1 cup

1 tablespoon red-wine vinegar
salt and pepper
¼ cup vegetable oil
2 tablespoons capers
¼ cup minced sweet gherkins
¼ cup minced sour gherkins

2 teaspoons minced garlic
¼ cup minced pimiento-stuffed olives
2 tablespoons Dijon-style mustard
¼ cup minced fresh parsley leaves
¼ teaspoon sugar

In a bowl combine the vinegar and salt and pepper to taste, add the oil in a stream, whisking, and whisk until emulsified. Add the remaining ingredients, combine the relish well, and transfer it to a serving bowl.

Asparagus, Potato, and Beet Salad

Serves 4

¾ pound very thin asparagus, peeled
8 small new potatoes (about 1¼ pounds)
8 small beets (about 1¼ pounds),
   scrubbed and trimmed, leaving 1 inch
   of the stem attached
1 hard-boiled egg yolk, minced
1 hard-boiled egg white, minced

For the dressing
2 tablespoons white-wine vinegar
½ teaspoon Dijon-style mustard
¼ teaspoon salt
¼ teaspoon pepper
a dash of Worcestershire sauce
⅓ cup olive oil
2 tablespoons snipped fresh dill

In a large skillet bring 1 inch of water to a boil, add the asparagus, and simmer it for 4 minutes, or until just tender. Drain and refresh under cold water. Pat the spears dry and chill them, covered, for 2 hours.

In a kettle cover the potatoes with salted cold water, bring the water to a boil, and boil the potatoes for 10 minutes, or until just tender. Drain, refresh under cold water, and let cool. Chill the potatoes for 2 hours and slice them thin.

In the kettle cover the beets with salted cold water, bring the water to a boil, and boil for 20 minutes, or until the beets are just tender. Drain the beets and refresh under running cold water. Peel the beets and let cool. Chill the beets for 2 hours and slice thin.

Asparagus, Potato, and Beet Salad

Make the dressing: In a bowl combine the vinegar, mustard, salt, pepper, and Worcestershire, add the oil in a stream, whisking, and whisk the dressing until emulsified. Add the dill and combine.

Arrange the potatoes, beets, and asparagus decoratively on a platter, garnish the vegetables with the minced egg yolk and white, and spoon the dressing over the salad.

White Chocolate "Brownies"

Makes about 12 brownies

3 ounces white chocolate, chopped
1 stick (½ cup) unsalted butter
½ cup ground almonds
1¾ cups all-purpose flour
½ teaspoon double-acting baking powder

¼ teaspoon salt
3 large eggs
1½ cups sugar
1 teaspoon vanilla

In the top of a double boiler set over simmering water or in a small bowl in the oven melt the chocolate and the butter, stirring occasionally, and let cool.

Spread the almonds on a baking sheet and toast them in a preheated 350° F. oven for 15 minutes, or until golden.

Into a bowl sift together the flour, baking powder, and salt. In a large bowl beat the eggs lightly with the sugar and vanilla, stir in the chocolate mixture, the flour mixture, and the almonds, and pour the batter into a buttered and floured baking pan, 13 by 9 by 2 inches. Bake the brownies in a preheated 350° F. oven for 35 to 40 minutes, or until a cake tester inserted in the center comes out clean. Let cool in the pan on a rack and cut the brownies into 3-inch squares.

Brownie Thins

Makes about 27 brownies

5 tablespoons unsalted butter
¼ cup unsweetened cocoa powder
½ cup granulated sugar
1 large egg, beaten lightly
¼ cup all-purpose flour

½ teaspoon vanilla
a pinch of salt
¼ cup walnuts, chopped, or hazelnuts,
    toasted, skinned, and chopped
confectioners' sugar (optional)

Line the bottom of a buttered 9-inch square baking pan with wax paper and butter the paper.

In the top of a double boiler set over simmering water melt the butter with the cocoa, stirring until the mixture is smooth. Remove the top of the double boiler from the heat and stir in the sugar. Beat in the egg and stir in the flour, vanilla, salt, and the nuts. Spread the mixture evenly in the baking pan and bake it in the middle of a preheated 350° F. oven for 10 to 15 minutes, or until it is just firm to the touch and pulls away slightly from the sides of the pan. Let the dessert cool completely in the pan on a rack, then cut the brownies into 3-by-1-inch pieces. Peel off the wax paper and serve.

A THANKSGIVING DINNER— WITHOUT TURKEY

Corn Crêpes with Pumpkin Filling
Steamed Broccoli with Wheat Germ and Lemon
Baked Stuffed Cod with Leeks
Buttered Carrot and Turnip Dice
Baked Apples with Cranberries and Walnuts
Maple Custard Sauce

Sakonnet Vineyards Chardonnay

Cooking without meat, as its practitioners well know, does not necessarily have to mean lentils, brown rice, and more lentils. It can be as inventive and tasteful, as attractive and colorful, as the recipes for the Thanksgiving menu that follows. Interestingly, too, few of the traditional foods, with the exception of the turkey, of course, have been forsworn. Corn appears in crêpes with pumpkin filling. Carrots and turnips comprise a vegetable course. Stuffed cod, in certain parts, in fact, goes by the name of Cape Cod turkey. What is remarkable about this menu is not only its uniqueness, but its Americanness. It is a reminder of the abundance that is the American farmland.

Corn Crêpes with Pumpkin Filling

Serves 6 as a first course

For the corn crêpes (makes about 18 crêpes)
1 cup cooked corn
3 large eggs
¾ cup milk
½ cup all-purpose flour
⅓ cup yellow cornmeal (preferably stone-ground)
2 tablespoons unsalted butter, melted and cooled
1 teaspoon salt
Tabasco to taste
¼ cup minced scallion

additional melted unsalted butter for brushing the pan and crêpes
3 tablespoons freshly grated Parmesan

For the pumpkin filling
¼ cup minced shallot
1½ tablespoons unsalted butter
1⅓ cups canned pumpkin purée
⅔ cup cottage cheese
¼ cup minced scallion
3 tablespoons freshly grated Parmesan
salt and pepper

Make the corn crêpes: In a blender or food processor fitted with the metal blade blend the corn, eggs, milk, flour, cornmeal, butter, and salt for 30 seconds. Turn off the motor, scrape down the sides of the container with a rubber spatula, and blend the batter for 30 seconds more. Transfer the batter to a bowl, stir in the Tabasco and scallion, and let the batter stand, covered with plastic wrap, for 1 hour.

Corn Crêpes with Pumpkin Filling

To make crêpes: Heat a 6- or 7-inch crêpe pan (preferably iron) over moderate heat until hot, brush it lightly with melted butter, and heat the butter until hot but not smoking. Stir the batter well, fill a ¼-cup measure three-fourths full with it, and pour the batter into the hot pan. Tilt and rotate the pan quickly so that the batter covers the bottom in a thin layer, and return any excess batter to the bowl. Return the pan to the heat, loosen the edge of the crêpe from the pan with a metal spatula, and cook the crêpe until the underside is browned lightly. Turn and cook until the underside is similar in color. Transfer the crêpe to a plate or a sheet of wax paper.

Make crêpes with the remaining batter in the same manner, brushing the pan lightly with melted butter as necessary. Stack the crêpes and keep them covered.

Make pumpkin filling: In a heavy skillet cook the shallot in the butter over moderate heat, stirring, until softened. Add the purée and cook, stirring, for 1 minute. In a food processor fitted with the metal blade purée the mixture with the cottage cheese. Transfer the purée to a bowl and stir in the scallion, the 3 tablespoons Parmesan, and salt and pepper.

To serve, spread 1 rounded tablespoon of the filling on each crêpe and fold the crêpe in quarters to form a wedge. Arrange the crêpes, overlapping slightly, on a buttered ovenproof platter, brush them with melted butter, and sprinkle them with the remaining Parmesan. Bake in the middle of a preheated 425° F. oven for 8 to 10 minutes, or until the Parmesan is melted. Serve immediately.

SUGGESTIONS

If you want to make your own pumpkin purée, you can either steam, boil, or bake fresh pumpkin. To steam, cut the pumpkin into 1½- to 2-inch chunks. Steam, covered, over boiling water until tender, about 20 minutes, depending on the size and number of the chunks, and scrape the pulp from the peel. To boil, cut into chunks, and cook in boiling water about 15 minutes, or until tender, and peel. To bake, halve the pumpkin, remove the seeds and strings, and bake in a preheated 350° F. oven for about 1 to 1½ hours, or until tender. Let cool and remove the pulp from the rind.

Acorn-squash purée can be substituted for the pumpkin in the crêpe filling.

White rice is the polished kernels of the grain; brown rice, the unpolished kernels. Brown rice cooks in the same way as white—in boiling water—but for approximately *twice* the amount of time.

Rutabagas are also known as swedes or Swedish turnips in some markets. Technically they are not turnips, but can be cooked in very much the same way.

∽

Make the crêpes in advance and freeze in stacks wrapped in plastic wrap.

Steam both the carrots and turnips in advance as well. Reheat by tossing them in the butter.

Both the apples and sauce can be made the day before serving.

Steamed Broccoli with Wheat Germ and Lemon

2 pounds broccoli, separated into
   flowerets and stalks cut crosswise
   into ¼-inch slices
½ stick (¼ cup) unsalted butter,
   melted, cooled, and combined with
   1½ tablespoons fresh lemon juice

salt and pepper
3 tablespoons plain wheat germ

Serves 6

In a vegetable steamer set over boiling water steam the broccoli, covered, for 5 to 7 minutes, or until just tender but still crisp, transfer it to a heated bowl, and drizzle it with the lemon butter. Season the broccoli with salt and pepper and sprinkle it with the wheat germ.

Baked Stuffed Cod with Leeks

Serves 6

For the stuffing
the white part of 1 pound leeks,
    halved lengthwise, washed well,
    and sliced thin crosswise
½ stick (¼ cup) unsalted butter
2 cups cooked brown rice
12 oysters, shucked (page 324),
    drained, and chopped
1 large egg yolk, beaten lightly
2 tablespoons dry whole-grain
    bread crumbs
¼ cup minced fresh parsley leaves
1 teaspoon grated lemon rind
salt and pepper

2 large leeks, roots trimmed
a 6- to 7-pound cod, head and gills
    removed and the fish cleaned,
    split along the stomach to within
    2 inches of the tail, and the
    backbone removed
vegetable oil for brushing the fish

Make the stuffing: In a heavy skillet cook the white parts of leeks in the butter, covered, over moderately low heat, stirring occasionally, for 5 minutes, or until soft, and transfer them to a bowl. Add the remaining stuffing ingredients with salt and pepper to taste and combine the stuffing well.

In a large saucepan of boiling salted water boil the whole leeks for 5 minutes, transfer them carefully with a slotted spoon to a colander, and refresh them under cold water. Remove each leek leaf in one piece, one at a time, slitting the lower part lengthwise along the stalk, if necessary, to form a flat leaf. Rinse the leaves under cold water, lay them flat on paper towels, and pat them dry.

Fold and crimp together 2 large pieces of foil to form a piece large enough to enclose the cod, and brush the foil well with the oil. Put the cod in the center of the foil and brush the skin on both sides with the oil. Season the inside of the cod well with salt and pepper, spread the stuffing in it, and re-form the fish. Beginning at the large end of the cod lay the leek leaves, 1 at a time, overlapping slightly, over the fish and tuck the ends under. Crimp the edges of the foil together to enclose the cod completely, and with a ruler measure the thickness of the cod at its thickest point.

Slide the cod diagonally onto a large baking sheet and bake it in the middle of a preheated 425° F. oven for 10 minutes per inch of thickness. Open the foil carefully, cut the cod crosswise, following the lines of the leek leaves, into 1-inch slices, and transfer the slices with a spatula to a heated platter.

*Baked Stuffed Cod with Leeks and Buttered
Carrot and Turnip Dice*

Buttered Carrot and Turnip Dice

Serves 6

¾ pound rutabagas, peeled and cut into
⅓-inch dice
¾ pound carrots, cut into ⅓-inch dice
¾ pound turnips, peeled and cut into
⅓-inch dice

½ stick (¼ cup) unsalted butter
salt and pepper

In a kettle of boiling salted water boil the rutabagas for 2 minutes, add the carrots, and boil for 3 minutes. Add the turnips and boil the vegetables for 3 to 5 minutes, or until just tender. Drain.

In a large, heavy skillet heat the vegetables in the butter over moderately low heat, covered, stirring occasionally, for 3 to 5 minutes, or until heated through, and season well with salt and pepper.

Baked Apples with Cranberries and Walnuts

Serves 6

⅔ cup cranberries, picked over
and chopped
⅔ cup walnuts, toasted lightly
and chopped
¾ stick (6 tablespoons) unsalted butter,
softened
2 tablespoons maple syrup
2 tablespoons dark brown sugar

6 baking apples such as Rome Beauties,
halved lengthwise, cored with a
melon-ball cutter, leaving a 1½-inch
cavity, and the cavities rubbed
with ½ lemon
1 cup boiling water
1½ cups Maple Custard Sauce
(recipe follows)

In a small bowl combine well the cranberries, walnuts, 4 tablespoons of the butter, the maple syrup, and the sugar. Divide the mixture among the apple cavities and arrange the apples in a baking pan just large enough to hold them in one layer. Dot the apples with the remaining 2 tablespoons butter, add the water carefully to the pan, and bake the apples, covered with foil, in the middle of a preheated 375° F. oven for 35 to 40 minutes, or until they are just tender. Serve the apples warm or let them come to room temperature in the cooking liquid. Serve them with the Maple Custard Sauce.

Maple Custard Sauce

½ cup maple syrup
3 large egg yolks

1 cup half-and-half, scalded
1 teaspoon vanilla

*Makes about
1½ cups*

In a saucepan reduce the maple syrup over moderate heat to about ⅓ cup, and let it cool for 10 minutes.

In a bowl whisk the egg yolks, add the syrup in a stream, whisking, and whisk the mixture until combined well. Add the scalded half-and-half in a stream, stirring, and transfer the custard to a heavy saucepan. Cook the custard over moderately low heat, stirring, until it thickens slightly and a candy thermometer registers 175° F., *but do not let it boil*. Remove the pan from the heat and stir in the vanilla. Strain the sauce through a fine sieve into a metal bowl set in a bowl of ice, let it cool, stirring occasionally, and chill it, covered, for at least 1 hour.

A TREE-TRIMMING PARTY

Toasted Nut and Dried-Fruit Mix
Seafood Pie
Minted Vegetables
Gingerbread Triangles
Ambrosia

⌇

Forster Jesuitengarten Kabinett

A tree-trimming party presupposes a very congenial crowd—a group of friends—brought together to have fun making something unadorned sparkle and glitter aplenty. It is the season of light, after all. The menu on such an occasion should also be special, like Seafood Pie and Minted Vegetables. In keeping with the spirit, oranges, the aroma of which seems somehow specific to Christmas, and spicy dark gingerbread dusted with sugar serve as dessert.

Toasted Nut and Dried-Fruit Mix

1½ cups raw cashews*
1½ cups raw peanuts*
2 tablespoons unsalted butter, melted
salt

½ pound dried apricots, quartered
¼ pound raisins

*Both available at natural-foods stores.

Makes about 5 cups

In a bowl toss the nuts with the melted butter. Spread the nuts in a shallow baking pan and toast them in a preheated 350° F. oven, shaking the pan 2 or 3 times, for 15 to 20 minutes, or until golden. Sprinkle the nuts with salt, toss them to coat them well, and let them cool for 3 minutes.

   In a bowl combine the dried fruits, add the warm nuts, and toss. Cover the bowl with foil and let the mixture cool.

Seafood Pie

Serves 8

For the seafood filling
½ cup minced leek
½ cup minced celery
½ cup minced mushroom
1 shallot, minced
1 stick plus 1 tablespoon (9 tablespoons) unsalted butter
salt and pepper
1 cup bottled clam juice
½ cup dry white wine

Tie together in a cheesecloth bag
6 parsley stems
½ teaspoon fennel seeds, crushed
½ teaspoon dried thyme
1 small bay leaf

1 pound shrimp, shelled, deveined, and halved lengthwise
1 pound sea scallops
2 pounds halibut, cod, or other firm-fleshed white fish

2 cups milk
½ cup all-purpose flour
2 large egg yolks
¼ cup heavy cream
½ cup freshly grated Parmesan
½ cup grated Gruyère
1 tablespoon Dijon-style mustard
freshly grated nutmeg to taste
fresh lemon juice to taste
salt and pepper

For the topping
3 pounds baking potatoes, peeled and quartered
2 large leeks, well washed and sliced
7 tablespoons unsalted butter
¼ cup heavy cream
salt and pepper

1 tablespoon fresh bread crumbs
1 tablespoon freshly grated Parmesan
paprika

Make the seafood filling: In a saucepan sweat the leek, celery, mushroom, and shallot in 3 tablespoons of the butter with salt and pepper to taste, covered with a buttered round of wax paper and the lid, over low heat for 5 minutes. Add the clam juice, wine, and cheesecloth bag and arrange the shrimp and scallops in the pan. Cover the mixture with a buttered round of wax paper, bring the liquid to a boil, and remove the pan from the heat. Let the shellfish cool in the liquid, then transfer it with a slotted spoon to a large bowl, reserving the liquid, vegetables, and cheesecloth bag. Quarter the scallops, then cover the scallops and shrimp.

In a gratin dish poach the halibut in the milk over low heat for 5 minutes, or until it just flakes when tested with a fork. With a slotted spatula transfer the fish to a plate, reserving the milk, and flake it into the bowl containing the shellfish, discarding the skin and bones.

In a saucepan melt the remaining 6 tablespoons of butter over moderate heat, stir in the flour, and cook the *roux* over low heat, stirring, for 3 minutes. Remove the pan from the heat and add the reserved liquid, vegetables, cheesecloth bag, and milk, whisking. Simmer the mixture, stirring occasionally, for 20 minutes and strain the sauce into a large bowl.

In a small bowl combine the egg yolks with the cream and add the mixture to the sauce in a stream, whisking. Stir in the Parmesan and Gruyère, mustard, nutmeg, lemon juice, and salt and pepper to taste. Finally, fold in the scallops and shrimp and halibut.

Make the topping: In a kettle cook the potatoes and leeks in boiling salted water to cover for 20 to 25 minutes, or until tender, and drain. Rice the vegetables or force them through the medium disk of a food mill into a bowl, beat in 4 tablespoons of the butter, cut into pieces and softened, and stir in the cream and salt and pepper to taste.

To bake: Put the seafood filling in a buttered 2-quart baking dish and sprinkle it with the bread crumbs and Parmesan. Transfer the potato purée to a large pastry bag fitted with a fluted tip and pipe it around the edge of the dish. Sprinkle the potatoes with paprika and drizzle the remaining 3 tablespoons butter, melted, over the pie. Bake the pie in the middle of a preheated 400° F. oven for 25 to 30 minutes, or until golden and bubbling.

SUGGESTIONS

Another wonderful starter would be to serve Cheddar Bites (page 278) with the Nut and Dried-Fruit Mix. An added plus: the bites can be prepared 3 days in advance. Reheat in a 300° F. oven for 5 minutes.

Golden raisins, dried apples, pears, or pineapple, and some Brazil nuts would also be good in the starter. In short, invent your own combination.

While the recipe for Seafood Pie looks lengthy, it really involves only 3 steps: the preparation of the seafood, the *roux*, and the potato topping. See page 132 for tips on making a *roux* and below for do-ahead pointers.

The pie would also be particularly fine and have a lovely New England feel to it if accompanied by Herbed Biscuits (page 240) without leeks. In that case, you would probably want a simpler vegetable—steamed broccoli or green beans with lemon butter.

Gingerbread is also very good topped with applesauce.

Sliced bananas are also sometimes added to the oranges in ambrosia. You would do that just before serving, as a garnish around the rim of the dish.

∽

Given how simple the nut and fruit mix is to prepare, make it the day it is needed to ensure freshness.

The Seafood Pie, on the other hand, can be assembled through the step of piping the potatoes over the top 24 hours in advance. Chill, covered.

Minted vegetables can also be completely readied in advance. You might under-cook them slightly so as not to overcook them in the reheating.

Make ambrosia the day it is to be served. The gingerbread, though, can be baked at least 1 day in advance. If wrapped airtight, the buttermilk in it will keep it nice and moist.

Minted Vegetables

Serves 8

1 pound mushrooms, sliced thick
3 cups water
5 tablespoons unsalted butter
1 teaspoon fresh lemon juice
salt and pepper
¼ cup minced onion
4 cups sliced celery

½ cup chicken stock (page 154) or
    canned chicken broth
1 tablespoon minced fresh mint leaves
    or 1 teaspoon dried
a 10-ounce package frozen peas, thawed
½ cup sliced pimientos, drained well

In a saucepan combine the mushrooms, water, 2 tablespoons of the butter, the lemon juice, and salt and pepper to taste, bring the water to a boil, and simmer the mushrooms for 5 minutes.

In another saucepan cook the onion in the remaining 3 tablespoons of butter over moderate heat, stirring, until softened. Add the celery, stock or broth, mint, and salt and pepper to taste, and cook the mixture, covered, over low heat for 5 minutes. Stir in the peas and cook, covered, over moderate heat, stirring, for 5 minutes, or until the peas are tender.

Drain the mushrooms, add them to the pea mixture with salt and pepper to taste, and heat the vegetables, stirring, until heated through. Transfer the vegetables to a serving bowl and garnish them with the pimientos.

Gingerbread Triangles

Serves 8 to 10

1 stick (½ cup) unsalted butter,
    cut into bits
⅔ cup firmly packed light brown sugar
1 large whole egg
1 large egg yolk
½ cup unsulfured molasses
½ cup buttermilk
1 tablespoon minced lemon rind
2 cups all-purpose flour

1 tablespoon ground ginger
2 teaspoons cinnamon
1½ teaspoons baking soda
½ teaspoon freshly grated nutmeg
½ teaspoon salt
¼ teaspoon ground allspice
sifted confectioners' sugar for dusting
    the triangles

In a bowl with an electric mixer cream the butter until light and fluffy, add the brown sugar, and beat until light and fluffy. Add the whole egg and egg yolk and beat until the eggs are just incorporated. Stir in the molasses, buttermilk, and lemon rind.

Into a large bowl sift together the flour, ginger, cinnamon, baking soda, nutmeg, salt, and allspice. Add the molasses mixture and stir until the batter is just combined. Pour the batter into a buttered 9-inch square cake pan, and bake in a preheated 350° F. oven for 30 minutes, or until a cake tester inserted in the center comes out clean. Let the cake cool in the pan on a rack for 10 minutes. Turn it out onto a plate and let it cool 10 minutes more. Cut the gingerbread into triangles and dust the triangles with the confectioners' sugar.

Ambrosia and Gingerbread Triangles

Ambrosia

6 navel oranges, peeled, pith removed, and sliced crosswise

2 cups freshly grated coconut (see page 329) or canned sweetened grated coconut

⅓ cup sugar, or to taste

Serves 8

In a shallow dish arrange a layer of the orange slices, cover them with a layer of the coconut, and sprinkle the coconut with some of the sugar. Continue to layer the remaining ingredients in the same manner, ending with a layer of the oranges. Garnish the center of each orange slice with some of the coconut and chill the ambrosia, covered, for at least 2 hours.

HOW TO PREPARE CLAMS, MUSSELS, AND OYSTERS FOR COOKING

To Clean Hard-Shelled Clams

Scrub the clams thoroughly with a stiff brush under running cold water, discarding any that have cracked shells or that are not shut tightly.

Keep well chilled in the refrigerator until ready to use. To open clams, see page 100.

To Clean Mussels

Scrub the mussels well in several changes of water, scrape off the beards, and rinse the mussels. Let the mussels soak in salted cold water just to cover for several hours to disgorge any sand. Or let the mussels soak in salted cold water sprinkled with a handful of cornmeal for 1 hour. Drain the mussels and rinse them under running cold water.

Keep well chilled in the refrigerator until ready to use.

To Shuck Oysters

Scrub the oysters thoroughly with a stiff brush under running cold water. Break off the thin end of the shells. Hold each oyster in the palm of the hand with the hinged end facing you. Force an oyster knife between the shells at the broken end and twist it to force the shells apart, cutting the large muscle close to the flat upper shell. Break off and discard the flat shell and slide the knife under the oyster to release it.

Serve at once on a bed of crushed ice or store the oysters in a container, covered, until ready to use.

NOTE: As you can imagine, it is all too easy for the knife to slip just at the point of trying to force apart the shells, and even experienced oyster shuckers nick and cut themselves. If you are new to oyster shucking, proceed carefully the first few times.

DINNER ON CHRISTMAS EVE

Sautéed Scallops with Mushrooms and Tomatoes
Glazed Carrots   Buttered Zucchini
Escarole and Rugola Salad with Sherry Vinegar Dressing
Poached Pears in Orange Syrup

Vernaccia di San Gimignano

Christmas Eve has a character very much its own. It's a quiet time, a lovely lull between all the anticipation of Christmas and the excitement of the actual day. Dinner on this night should be easy. A simple sauté, with vegetables, a lovely green salad, and pears poached in syrup fit just fine. We have kept this menu intentionally light for several reasons—the festivities and feasting of the next day and the fact that Christmas, for many, has a way of starting well before dawn!

SUGGESTIONS

If you are truly in the spirit, have smoked salmon as a starter. Serve on thin-sliced dark bread with lemon wedges and capers as directed on page 251.

Rice would be a good addition to this menu. It would be a shame to let all that fragrant sauce on the scallops go begging.

Almond Crescent Cookies (page 135) would go very well with the Pears in Orange Syrup. Making them would also be a dandy way to have cookies on hand for the holidays.

Scallops are so splendid in flavor and texture and so delicate in nature that they should really only be prepared at the last minute. With that in mind, therefore, do all that you possibly can ahead:

The pears can be done, in entirety; the cutting of the vegetables; the washing of the salad greens; even the dressing.

Assuming that you have all the ingredients for the scallop sauté ready, allow 15 minutes, more or less, to cook the sauté and prepare both the vegetables. Not a long time as entrée preparations go.

Sautéed Scallops with Mushrooms and Tomatoes

Serves 4

1½ pounds bay scallops
¼ cup olive oil
½ stick (¼ cup) unsalted butter
flour for dusting the scallops
salt and pepper
3 tablespoons minced shallot
¼ pound mushrooms, sliced
1½ teaspoons minced fresh thyme or
   ½ teaspoon dried

1 tablespoon minced fresh basil or
   ½ teaspoon dried
½ cup dry white wine
1 cup peeled, seeded, and chopped
   tomato
1 garlic clove, minced, or to taste
2 tablespoons minced fresh parsley leaves
fresh lemon juice to taste.

In a skillet large enough to hold the scallops in one layer heat 3 tablespoons of the oil and 1 tablespoon of the butter over moderately high heat until hot. In a large colander dust the scallops with the flour, shaking off the excess, and season them with salt and pepper. Sauté the scallops in the skillet for 3 to 4 minutes, or until just firm to the touch, and transfer them to a bowl.

Add the remaining oil and butter to the skillet, heat the fat over moderately high heat until hot, and in it cook the shallot, stirring, for 1 minute. Add the mushrooms and herbs with salt and pepper to taste and cook, stirring, for 2 to 3 minutes, or until the mushrooms begin to give off their liquid. Add the wine and reduce it over high heat by half. Stir in the tomato and any accumulated juices from the bowl of scallops and reduce the sauce, stirring, until thick. Stir in the scallops, garlic, and salt and pepper to taste. Cook the mixture until the scallops are heated through, and add the parsley and the lemon juice. Serve on heated plates.

Glazed Carrots

Serves 4

1 pound carrots, cut diagonally on a
   sharp angle into ¼-inch slices
3 tablespoons unsalted butter

1 teaspoon sugar
salt and pepper

In a saucepan combine all the ingredients and salt and pepper to taste with enough water to just cover the carrots, bring the water to a boil over moderately high heat, and simmer the carrots for 6 to 8 minutes, or until just tender. Reduce the liquid over moderately high heat to about ¼ cup, and cook the carrots, shaking the pan, until the liquid is almost completely reduced and the carrots are evenly glazed.

Sautéed Scallops with Mushrooms and Tomatoes, Glazed Carrots, Buttered Zucchini,
and Escarole and Rugola Salad with Sherry Vinegar Dressing

Buttered Zucchini

Serves 4

1 pound zucchini, trimmed and cut
   diagonally on a sharp angle into
   ¼-inch slices

3 tablespoons unsalted butter
salt and pepper

In a saucepan of boiling salted water cook the zucchini over moderately high heat for 4 to 6 minutes, or until tender. Drain and in a bowl toss the zucchini with the butter and salt and pepper to taste.

Escarole and Rugola Salad with Sherry Vinegar Dressing

Serves 4

For the dressing (makes about ⅔ cup)
3 tablespoons Sherry vinegar*
½ teaspoon Dijon-style mustard
½ teaspoon minced fresh parsley leaves
salt and pepper
½ cup olive oil

*Available at specialty-foods stores.

the leaves from 1 small head of escarole,
   rinsed, dried, and torn into bite-size
   pieces
the leaves from 1 small head of Boston
   lettuce, rinsed, dried, and torn into
   bite-size pieces
¼ pound *rugola* or watercress leaves,
   rinsed and patted dry
1 cup thinly sliced radish
the white part of 1 leek, washed well and
   cut into julienne strips

Make the dressing: In a bowl combine the vinegar, mustard, parsley, and salt and pepper to taste, add the oil in a stream, whisking, and whisk the dressing until emulsified.

In a salad bowl combine the greens, radish, and leeks, then toss the salad with the dressing.

Poached Pears in Orange Syrup

1 cup sugar
a 2-inch cinnamon stick
4 cloves
1 tablespoon grated orange rind
2 cups water
4 Bartlett pears, peeled, quartered,
   and tossed with 3 tablespoons
   fresh lemon juice

2 teaspoons orange-flavored liqueur,
   or to taste
¼ cup sliced blanched almonds, toasted
1 cup sour cream

Serves 4

In a saucepan combine the sugar, cinnamon stick, cloves, orange rind, and the 2 cups water, bring the mixture to a boil, stirring, and cook the syrup over moderate heat for 10 minutes. Add the pears with the lemon juice and simmer, covered with wax paper, for 3 to 5 minutes, or until the pears are just tender. Transfer the mixture to a bowl, let cool, and chill, covered, for 1 to 2 hours, or until the pears are cold. Remove the pears with a slotted spoon to a serving dish and chill, covered, until ready to serve.

Strain the syrup into a saucepan, reduce it over moderately high heat, stirring, for 5 to 7 minutes, or until thickened, and stir in the liqueur. Let the syrup cool and add any accumulated juices from the pears.

To serve, nap the pears with the syrup, sprinkle them with the almonds, and serve them with the sour cream.

HOW TO GRATE FRESH COCONUT

Pierce the eyes of a coconut with an ice pick or a skewer, drain the liquid, and reserve it for another use.

Bake the coconut in a preheated 400° F. oven for 15 minutes, break it with a hammer, and remove the flesh from the shell, levering it out carefully with the point of a strong knife. Peel off the brown membrane with a vegetable peeler and cut the coconut meat into small pieces.

In a blender or food processor fitted with the metal blade grind the pieces, a few at a time. Or grate the meat on the fine side of a grater. Makes about 4 cups.

A NEW YEAR'S PARTY

Eggnog
Onion Toasts
Date Walnut Bread with Goat Cheese Spread
Apricot Nut Bread with Smoked Ham
Lemon Tartlets
Spice Cookie Hearts

∽

A good New Year's party usually means open house, with a stream of people, of all ages, coming and going all day long. And in the festive menu that follows you'll find we have thought of something for everyone. The children will love the breads and sweets; the adults the more savory, unusual combinations like Goat Cheese Spread on Date Walnut Bread. We've thought of the hosts, too. This is the kind of party fare that can sit out, looking particularly pretty, and, when the need arises, be replenished in a trice. Come to think of it, we have left one thing to you: the amount and kind of Champagne.

Eggnog

Makes about 16 cups, serving 12

12 large egg yolks
1½ cups superfine sugar
4 cups milk
6 cups well-chilled heavy cream
2 cups bourbon (see Suggestions)

1 cup dark rum (see Suggestions)
12 large egg whites at room temperature
a pinch of salt
a pinch of cream of tartar
freshly grated nutmeg to taste

In a large bowl with an electric mixer beat the yolks until they are pale. Beat in the sugar, a little at a time, and beat the mixture until it is thick and pale. Beat in the milk and 4 cups of the cream, and stir in the bourbon and rum.

Just before serving, in a bowl beat the egg whites with the salt until they are frothy, add the cream of tartar, and beat the whites until they hold soft peaks.

In a punch bowl fold the whites into the egg yolk mixture. In another bowl beat the remaining 2 cups cream until it holds soft peaks, and fold it into the eggnog. Sprinkle the eggnog with the nutmeg.

Eggnog, Date Walnut Bread with Goat Cheese Spread, and Apricot Nut Bread with Smoked Ham

SUGGESTIONS

For the eggnog, bourbon and rum are only suggestions, as are the amounts called for in the recipe. Experiment. Brandy, rye, and Madeira are good candidates.

Use dark bread as well as French bread as a base for the onion-cheese mixture in the canapés. You might want to add a little well-drained horseradish to give it some extra spice.

Goat cheese, called *chèvre* in France and in many specialty markets, is obviously made from goats' milk and comes in a dizzying number of varieties. There are California, French, and Italian goat cheeses. They are fresh or aged. The flavor is mild to slightly tangy. They come in logs, *pyramides*, and rounds. Some are covered with ash or with a rind. Some are marinated in oil and herbs. In sum, goat cheeses are wonderful varied stuff, very worth getting acquainted with if you haven't already done so. Serve them as an hors d'oeuvre, on crackers, or as a dessert cheese with fruit.

For a light, refreshing dessert in the summer remember the Lemon Tartlets. They are especially pretty garnished with fresh fruit: a ring of blueberries or tiny strawberries. Or serve the lemon custard as is, without the tart shell, but with some whipped cream.

∽

You can make the eggnog through stirring in the bourbon and rum in advance. Chill, covered.

Make the onion-cheese mixture ahead, too, but don't bake the toasts until the last minute.

Both the Date Walnut and Apricot Nut breads can be kept, wrapped in foil and chilled, for up to 5 days.

Make the lemon filling several days in advance and chill; the shells, 1 day ahead. Fill them at the last minute on the day you want to serve them.

Spice Cookie Hearts keep well. Make them at your leisure, and store them airtight.

Onion Toasts

2¼ cups minced onions
⅓ cup minced fresh parsley leaves
1 cup freshly grated Parmesan
1 tablespoon Worcestershire sauce

½ cup Quick Mayonnaise (page 20)
thirty-six ¼-inch-thick slices of French
   or Italian bread

*Makes about
36 hors
d'oeuvres*

In a bowl combine the onions, parsley, Parmesan, Worcestershire sauce, and mayonnaise. Spread about 1 teaspoon of the mixture on each slice of bread, covering the top of each slice completely. Then broil the slices on baking sheets under a preheated broiler about 6 inches from the heat for 3 to 5 minutes, or until the onion mixture is bubbling and golden.

Date Walnut Bread with Goat Cheese Spread

For the date walnut breads
   (makes 2 loaves)
3 cups chopped pitted dates
2 cups all bran cereal
2 cups boiling water
2 large eggs
½ cup dark unsulfured molasses
2 cups whole-grain pastry flour*
2 teaspoons double-acting baking powder
1 teaspoon baking soda
¼ teaspoon salt
1 cup coarsely ground walnuts

For the goat cheese spread
   (makes about 1 cup)
4 ounces cream cheese at room
   temperature
4 ounces goat cheese at room temperature
1 stick (½ cup) unsalted butter at room
   temperature

*Available at natural-foods stores and some
  supermarkets.

Makes 2 loaves

Make the date walnut breads: In a small heatproof bowl combine the dates and the cereal with the water and let stand for 30 minutes.

In a bowl with an electric mixer beat the eggs until pale, add the molasses in a stream, beating, and beat the mixture until thick.

In a small bowl combine the flour, baking powder, baking soda, and salt, and stir the mixture into the egg mixture alternately with the date mixture, including the water. Stir in the walnuts. Divide the batter between 2 well-buttered 8½-by-4½-inch loaf pans, and bake in a preheated 350° F. oven for 45 to 50 minutes, or until a wooden pick comes out clean.

Let the breads cool in the pans for 10 minutes, loosen the edges with a knife, and turn the loaves out onto a rack to cool completely.

Make the goat cheese spread: In a food processor fitted with the steel blade or a blender blend together all the spread ingredients until smooth. Transfer to a small serving bowl and chill, covered, for at least 1 hour or overnight. To serve, slice the bread thin and serve it with the spread brought to room temperature before serving.

Apricot Nut Bread with Smoked Ham

Makes 2 loaves

6 ounces dried apricots, chopped
½ cup dried currants
1 cup boiling water
2 tablespoons softened unsalted butter
1 cup firmly packed light brown sugar
1 large egg
¾ cup milk
¾ cup fresh orange juice
1 tablespoon grated orange rind

3 cups all-purpose flour
3½ teaspoons double-acting
   baking powder
¼ teaspoon baking soda
1 teaspoon salt
¾ cup chopped pecans

softened butter
sliced smoked ham or turkey

In a small heatproof bowl combine the apricots and currants with the water. Let stand for 20 minutes, and drain.

In a large bowl with an electric mixer cream together the butter and the brown sugar until light and fluffy. Beat in the egg, milk, orange juice, and orange rind, and beat until smooth.

Into a small bowl sift together the flour, baking powder, baking soda, and salt, and beat into the brown sugar mixture. Stir in the pecans and the apricots and currants. Divide the batter between 2 well-buttered 7¼-by 3½-inch loaf pans, and bake in a preheated 350° F. oven for 1 hour to 1 hour and 10 minutes, or until a wooden pick comes out clean. Let the bread cool in the pans for 10 minutes, loosen the edges with a knife, and turn the loaves out onto a rack to cool completely.

Serve the bread, sliced thin, with the butter and the ham.

Spice Cookie Hearts and Lemon Tartlets

Lemon Tartlets

Makes
12 tartlets

For the filling
1 stick (½ cup) unsalted butter
½ cup strained fresh lemon juice
1 tablespoon grated lemon rind
1½ cups sugar
5 large eggs, beaten lightly

For the shells
1¼ cups all-purpose flour
a pinch of salt

1 stick (½ cup) cold unsalted butter,
    cut into bits
2 tablespoons sugar
1 teaspoon grated lemon rind
1 large egg yolk
1 tablespoon fresh lemon juice

whipped cream and crystallized mimosa
    balls (available at specialty-foods shops)
    for decoration, if desired

Make the filling: In a heavy saucepan melt the butter over moderately low heat. Stir in the lemon juice, lemon rind, and sugar, and cook the mixture, stirring, until the sugar is dissolved. Whisk in the eggs and cook the mixture, whisking, for 15 to 20 minutes, or until smooth and thick. Let cool, covered with a buttered round of wax paper, and chill until just before serving.

Make the shells: In a bowl combine the flour and the salt, blend in the butter until the mixture resembles coarse meal, and toss the mixture with the sugar and the lemon rind. Add the egg yolk and lemon juice and combine the mixture well, kneading it against the side of the bowl.

Divide the dough into 12 pieces, press 1 piece into each of the twelve 3-inch fluted tartlet tins, pressing it into the bottom and halfway up the sides, and chill the shells for 30 minutes. Prick the shells all over with a fork and line each shell with foil. Bake the shells on baking sheets in a preheated 425° F. oven for 15 minutes, or until just cooked but not colored. Remove the foil, and bake in a 375° F. oven for 10 to 15 minutes more, or until pale golden. Let the shells cool completely in the tins, loosen them very carefully with the point of a knife, and remove them from the tins. Fill the shells with the lemon filling, smoothing the tops, and decorate the tartlets with the whipped cream and crystallized mimosa balls if desired.

Spice Cookie Hearts

Makes about 80 cookies, cut with a 2½-inch cutter

For the cookies
4½ cups all-purpose flour
¼ teaspoon salt
1 teaspoon cinnamon
½ teaspoon ground ginger
½ teaspoon ground allspice
1 cup dark corn syrup
¾ cup firmly packed dark brown sugar
1 stick (½ cup) plus 2 tablespoons
   unsalted butter, cut into bits

For the icing
1 large egg white at room temperature
1 teaspoon fresh lemon juice,
   or to taste
about 1 cup confectioners' sugar,
   sifted

Make the cookies: Into a large bowl sift together the flour, salt, cinnamon, ginger, and allspice. In a saucepan combine the corn syrup, brown sugar, and butter and cook over moderate heat, stirring, until the butter is melted. Stir into the flour mixture and combine the mixture well to form a soft dough. Halve the dough and on dampened baking sheets lined with foil roll out each half ⅛ inch thick. Chill the dough on the sheets for 30 minutes. With a floured heart-shaped cutter cut out cookies, leaving at least ½ inch between the cookies. Gather the scraps and reserve them. Bake in a preheated 350° F. oven for 10 to 12 minutes, or until colored lightly, and let cool completely on the baking sheets. Make more cookies in the same manner with the reserved dough scraps.

Make the icing: In a small bowl whisk the egg white with the lemon juice until it is frothy. Then whisk in the confectioners' sugar, a little at a time. If the icing seems too thick, thin it with a few drops of water, or, if too thin, whisk in some additional confectioners' sugar. Transfer the icing to a pastry bag fitted with a very small plain tip, and pipe it decoratively onto the cooled cookies. Let the icing harden and store the cookies in airtight containers.

Index

A NOTE ON THE TYPE

*The text of this book was set in a digitized version of Galliard, a type face
created by the English type designer Matthew Carter.
It was introduced by Mergenthaler Linotype Company in 1978.
The modern Galliard is an adaptation of the original type face of that name,
designed in 1570 by the distinguished French type cutter
and printer Robert Granjon (1523–1590).*

*Composed by Graphic Composition, Inc., Athens, Georgia.
New separations and film prepared by
Toppan Printing Co. (America), Inc., Mountainside, New Jersey.
Printed and bound by Usines Brepols, Turnhout, Belgium.*

*Typography and binding design
by Dorothy Schmiderer*